THE EUDORA USER'S GUIDE

THE
EUDORA
USER'S GUIDE

AP PROFESSIONAL
AP PROFESSIONAL IS A DIVISION OF ACADEMIC PRESS, INC.

BOSTON   SAN DIEGO   NEW YORK
LONDON   SYDNEY   TOKYO   TORONTO

AP PROFESSIONAL
An Imprint of ACADEMIC PRESS, INC.
A Division of HARCOURT BRACE & COMPANY

ORDERS (USA and Canada): 1-800-3131-APP or APP@ACAD.COM
AP Professional Orders: 6277 Sea Harbor Dr., Orlando, FL 32821-9816

Europe/Middle East/Africa: 0-11-44 (0) 181-300-3322
Orders: AP Professional 24–28 Oval Rd., London NW1 7DX

Japan/Korea: 03-3234-3911-5
Orders: Harcourt Brace Japan, Inc., Ichibancho Central Building 22-1, Ichibancho Chiyoda-Ku, Tokyo 102

Australia: 02-517-8999
Orders: Harcourt Brace & Co. Australia, Locked Bag 16, Marrickville, NSW 2204, Australia

Other International: (407) 345-3800
AP Professional Orders: 6277 Sea Harbor Dr., Orlando FL 32821-9816

Editorial: 1300 Boylston St., Chestnut Hill, MA 02167 (617) 232-0500

Web: http://www.apnet.com/approfessional

This book is printed on acid-free paper. ∞
Copyright © 1996 by Academic Press, Inc.
All rights reserved.
No part of this publication may be reproduced or transmitted in any form or by any means, electronic or mechanical, including photocopy, recording, or any information storage and retrieval system, without permission in writing from the publisher.

All brand names and product names mentioned in this book are trademarks or registered trademarks of their respective companies.

United Kingdom Edition published by
ACADEMIC PRESS LIMITED
24–28 Oval Road, London NW1 7DX

Library of Congress Cataloging-in-Publication Data
Reiss, Levi
    The Eudora user's guide / Levi Reiss
      p. cm.
    Includes index.
    ISBN 0-12-586355-1
    1. Electronic mail systems   2. Eudora (Computer file)
    3. Internet (Computer network)   I. Title
    TK5105.73.R46   1996
    005.7'13--dc20   96-27900
                                        CIP

Printed in the United States of America
96 97 98 99   IP   9 8 7 6 5 4 3 2 1

CONTENTS

CHAPTER 1: INTRODUCING THE INTERNET AND ELECTRONIC MAIL — 1
- ELECTRONIC MAIL — 2
- A BIT ABOUT EUDORA — 9
- E-MAIL PROGRAM FEATURES — 9

CHAPTER 2: GETTING STARTED WITH EUDORA — 17
- SYSTEM REQUIREMENTS — 18
- COMPOSING A MESSAGE — 19
- SENDING A MESSAGE — 22
- CHECKING FOR AND RECEIVING MAIL — 23
- REPLYING TO A MESSAGE — 27
- SAVING AN OUTGOING MESSAGE — 29
- MAIN WINDOW ICON — 31
- MAIN WINDOW TOOLBAR — 32
- CREATING AN OUTGOING MESSAGE — 34
- AUTOMATIC AND MANUAL MAIL CHECKING — 40
- QUITTING EUDORA — 42

CHAPTER 3: SENDING E-MAIL — 43
- SENDING A MESSAGE — 44
- SAVING OUTGOING MESSAGES — 51
- ATTACHMENTS — 52
- CREATING AND USING NICKNAMES — 54
- QUICK RECIPIENT LIST — 59
- SENDING REJECTED MESSAGES — 62

CONTENTS

MESSAGE PRIORITIES	63
CREATING A SIGNATURE FILE	64

CHAPTER 4: RECEIVING E-MAIL — 69

CHECKING FOR AND RECEIVING MAIL	70
MAILBOXES AND FOLDERS	75
CREATING A MAILBOX	76
OPENING A MAILBOX	78
INCOMING MESSAGE WINDOW	81
MESSAGE DELETION	83
FINDING TEXT WITHIN MESSAGES	85
SORTING MESSAGES WITHIN MAILBOXES	90
SAVING MESSAGES IN FILES	91

CHAPTER 5: ANSWERING E-MAIL — 99

TRANSFERRING A MESSAGE TO A DIFFERENT MAILBOX	100
MAILBOXES WINDOW	103
PROCESSING INCOMING MESSAGES	109
FORWARDING A MESSAGE	112
REDIRECTING A MESSAGE	114

CHAPTER 6: JOINING THE E-MAIL CULTURE — 119

THE SPECIAL NATURE OF ELECTRONIC MAIL	120
E-MAIL ETIQUETTE	125
SMILIES AND EMOTICONS	131

CHAPTER 7: ACCESSING INTERNET SERVICES — 137

MAILING LISTS	140

CHAPTER 8: BECOMING AN E-MAIL PRO — 153
- SYSTEM CONFIGURATION SETTINGS — 154
- MAIL STORAGE — 172
- SHARING A PC — 178
- MAIL TRANSPORT SERVERS — 178

CHAPTER 9: EUDORA PRO FOR WINDOWS — 183
- INSTALLING EUDORA PRO — 183
- DIFFERENCES RIGHT OFF THE BAT — 187
- MESSAGE FILTERING — 197
- CHECKING SPELLING — 206
- ADDITIONAL NEW FEATURES — 212
- OPTIONS — 219

APPENDIX A
Eudora Light Menu Commands and Installation Notes — 243

APPENDIX B
Installing Eudora Mac Versions — 257

APPENDIX C
Eudora and Eudora Pro for the Mac — 263

INDEX — 289

INTRODUCING THE INTERNET AND ELECTRONIC MAIL

Eudora is the most popular electronic mail application for the Internet. Anyone who reads newspapers and magazines or watches television has heard about the Internet and probably seen what it can do. Without a doubt, the Internet has been one of the favorite subjects of the rah-rah school of journalism in the last few years. Despite the hype, the Internet can do a lot for you, even if it won't change your life. Let's take a quick look at the Internet before focusing on one of its key aspects, electronic mail.

The Internet was created at the end of the 1960s by the world's most powerful computer user, the United

States Department of Defense. Military personnel wanted a network so decentralized that it would continue to function no matter how many bombs fell. While this aspect of the Internet was never tested in battle, the Internet did grow beyond anyone's wildest dreams. As you probably know, literally millions of people use (or misuse) the Internet every day, with the promise that dozens or hundreds of millions more will get connected very soon.

Recently, largely because of graphical, easy-to-use searching tools called browsers such as Netscape (Navigator), the Internet underwent a major change. No longer virtually restricted to researchers and computer types, the Internet has become accessible to the masses. It knows no bounds of geography and, arguably, few bounds of age, culture, and gender. Does the Internet foster peace among those of different backgrounds? Sometimes. Far too often it serves as a battleground, even for those of the same culture. Whether you use the Internet to foster peace, to fight battles, or like most people, for fun and profit, you should become familiar with electronic mail, and the most popular Internet electronic mail software package, **Eudora.**

ELECTRONIC MAIL

Electronic mail, commonly abbreviated **e-mail** (or **email**), is the ability to send and receive messages via networked computers. You can think of it as a high-tech, vastly improved post office. You don't have to be on the Internet to access e-mail. However, e-mail is a major, if not very sophisticated, Internet application. In fact, e-mail is one of the first Internet applications for Internet novices, affectionately (or not so affectionately) called "newbies." While we think electronic mail is great, we'll cut the hype by examining e-mail's advantages and disadvantages.

ADVANTAGES OF E-MAIL

You may ask yourself, "Advantages with respect to what?" E-mail is fast compared to the 19th- and 20th-century version of the Pony Express, the much-beloved Postal Service, known to the Internet crowd as "snail mail." However, e-mail can be slow compared to that relatively old-fashioned communication device, the telephone. The major e-mail advantages are the following:

- *Amiability.* Newcomers can be surprised by the amiability and genuine support in much of the cyberspace community. You won't get this sense of community from conference calls. E-mail users tend to feel that they are part of a special community.

- *Convenience.* For those millions of us with access to a computer, e-mail is usually available at a few mouse clicks. There is almost no excuse for not writing. It's so easy to reply to a friend's or relative's on-line letter that e-mail is helping to revive the lost art of letter writing.

- *Vast audience.* No sophisticated knowledge is required to e-mail a letter to hundreds of people in far-flung locations. Try doing so armed with a photocopier, envelopes, and a stamp machine, and you will immediately appreciate the power of e-mail.

- *Mailing lists.* E-mail makes it very easy to join Internet mailing lists. In addition to traditional mailing lists ("You-may-already-have-won-ten-million-dollars!"), there are thousands of specialized mailing lists destined for people such as Civil War buffs, chronic overeaters and their loved ones, skateboarders, and Java programmers. The anonymity alone can make it all worthwhile.

- *High speed.* It's a rare occasion when the Postal Service can deliver the mail as rapidly as the Internet does. Consider e-mail when overnight just isn't good enough.

- *Low cost.* Keep a close eye on this advantage—nobody knows what will happen to Internet fee schedules. E-mail is presently quite inexpensive once you're hooked up to the Internet.

E-mail Versus Telephone Cost

Many Internet providers offer unlimited e-mail services for about $5 a month—until you read the fine print. In my neighborhood, for that princely sum you can make fewer than one local telephone call per business day. And at those rates you'll have to forget about incoming calls—unless you have a friend willing to take them for you.

- *Elimination of telephone tag.* A major waste of time in this fin-de-siècle fun decade is the game of telephone tag. Aren't you surprised when you ask for Nancy Smith and actually reach her? The odds of playing telephone tag increase substantially when playing on the international level. The greater the time zone difference, the fewer the mutual working hours are. However, you need not be present to receive your e-mail. And the written communication is clearer and more permanent than the answering-machine playback. Gone are the days of hitting the rewind and pause buttons until your fingers ache just to get your party's phone number. (If only he stuttered.)

E-mail Versus Voice Mail

My voice mail system at work uses the digit "7" to replay a message and "3" to erase it. My home version uses "7" to erase a message and "5" to replay it. Both machines can be reached from external locations. If I forget which system I'm using and press the wrong key, that special message is lost and gone forever. In all fairness, e-mail systems have their share of incompatibilities, as anyone who has used multiple systems can testify. However, at least you get to see a menu of available options. And in many cases an Undo function is available.

- *Printouts.* E-mail lets you print what you want, when you want it. Far too often my office posts messages such as "Green Toyota Tercel with license plates ABX 997—you left your headlights on." No need to convert a twig to paper for that sort of thing. However, more important messages can be printed with a few mouse clicks or keystrokes.

Message Identification

As you will see shortly, e-mail messages come complete with the sender's address and the time the message was sent. Gone are the hours spent frantically rifling through wastebaskets, hoping against hope, looking for a scrap of paper with that special telephone number.

- *Anonymity.* Given the proper attention to security, your recipients need never know who you are. They won't be influenced by irrelevant factors such as age, gender, race, or physical appearance. You are what you write, independent of the recipient's prejudices. Anonymity has its drawbacks; we still have cautiously to approach letters signed "A Friend," especially if they allege a loved one's wrongdoing.

- *Attachments.* In its first incarnation, e-mail was virtually restricted to sending plain text: letters, numbers, punctuation marks, and a few additional characters such as $ and %. Present-day e-mail can transmit a wide variety of files, including programs, images, and sound. You'll find it easier (and cheaper) to send an associate a copy of your 250-page marketing proposal by e-mail than to send the proposal on diskette.

- *Electronic forms.* The lifeblood of business is forms. Many e-mail programs do electronic forms. When form-enabled, e-mail is an ideal tool for creating electronic forms, transmitting them to interested parties for completion, and retransmitting the completed forms.

DISADVANTAGES OF E-MAIL

Beware of the hype. Few things in life come without disadvantages; e-mail is clearly not one of them. Virtually every e-mail advantage has a corresponding disadvantage. E-mail is certainly worth doing, but don't go in blindfolded. Knowing and respecting its disadvantages will make you a more efficient and more effective e-mail user.

- *Likelihood of misinterpretation.* Arguably, the greatest disadvantage of electronic mail is the likelihood that the recipient will misinterpret the message. One of the reasons for this phenomenon is the absence of visual or verbal signals that tend to put the text in perspective. Chapter 6 offers valuable tips that may reduce misinterpretation.

- *Unwanted permanence.* Your electronic mail message may well outlive you. Your messages are probably saved in multiple archives, and as we will see in Chapter 2, the messages you send clearly identify you, the sender. These messages may be forwarded to multiple parties. Be careful about what you say—you may regret it later.

- *Cyberrodents.* While most people you meet in cyberspace are amiable, you are bound to cross paths with "cyberrodents", beings who consider netiquette (proper on-line behavior as discussed in Chapter 6) as annoying rules for others to follow. Perhaps these creatures are permanently compassion-challenged, or maybe they only woke up today on the wrong side of the information highway. You must learn how to deal with them, just as kids learn how to deal with schoolyard bullies and adults learn how to deal with the office idiot.

- *Occasional low speed.* One advantage of e-mail is its speed—usually. Most e-mail messages are delivered within minutes or hours after being sent, and the overwhelming majority reaches their destination before the end of the next business day. But sometimes that kind of speed just isn't good enough. You can't count on e-mail to arrive in two minutes, even if you mark it urgent. Don't expect telephone systems or fax machines to disappear from the planet.

- *Size limitation*. E-mail systems often limit the size of messages transmitted. They may not be able to transmit a 250 page report in one shot. Sometimes it is easier to use a courier service. Remember, even if your system can process them, long messages mean lengthy transmission time and can be expensive.

- *Distracting*. It is easier to ignore the e-mail bell than to lend a deaf ear to the ringing telephone. However, many individuals feel compelled to read each and every e-mail message as it comes in over the wire. A related but more insidious problem stems from the inveterate talker. Some people feel obliged to voice his or her opinion at every issue at every meeting. Such people are likely to flood the Internet with irrelevant missives.

Procrastinator's Delight

Another related problem is the just-can't-get-down-to-work syndrome. Instead of endlessly cleaning their desk or counting paper clips, wired procrastinators constantly open their e-mail mailbox, check for new mail, and reread messages that should have been trashed, if they were even worth sending in the first place. The solution: check your e-mail at coffee breaks.

A BIT ABOUT EUDORA

This book is devoted to one of the most popular e-mail programs, Eudora. Steve Dorner first wrote Eudora while working at the University of Illinois. Eudora was made freely available on the Internet. In 1992, Dorner joined the software company Qualcomm, where he continued to enhance Eudora. Eudora remains freeware; if you have an Internet connection, you can get Eudora absolutely free. Qualcomm distributes a commercial version of Eudora, known as Eudora Pro, described in detail in Chapter 9. How does Qualcomm make money if Eudora is free? First they get you hooked on the freeware version, sometimes known as Eudora Light. Then, if and when you need a more powerful e-mail program, you will probably find that Eudora Pro is your answer. Users familiar with Eudora won't have any trouble stepping up to Eudora Pro.

Both Eudora Light and Eudora Pro come in Macintosh versions. The Mac versions look and work quite a bit like their PC counterparts. Of course there are differences. Appendix A describes the options associated with the PC version of Eudora Light and how to install it. Appendix B describes what you need to know to install either version of Eudora on the Mac. Appendix C describes the changes between the Mac and PC versions of Eudora.

E-MAIL PROGRAM FEATURES

E-mail comes in a few dozen different varieties. Let's examine some of the features found in e-mail systems. Basic features are found in virtually all e-mail systems. They are pretty hard to live without. Intermediate features are found in most e-mail packages. Try them; you'll like them. Advanced features may be hard to find, but once you are used to them, you won't want to give them up. Eudora has most, but not all, of the following features, as well as many others that are not listed here.

BASIC FEATURES

These basic features are what you really need to get started with electronic mail. Eudora makes all of them easy to use.

- *Create*. This provides an editor to compose and modify messages. Eudora applies standard Windows editing keys for moving and or copying blocks of text and a search feature to locate specific characters or words.

- *Inbox*. This displays a list of messages and identifying material such as the date and subject in a window. You don't have to read your messages in the order they were sent.

- *Notify*. This emits an audible or visual signal that a message was just received. Of course, you don't have to stop everything and read the message as soon as it comes in.

- *Read*. This displays the message and usually the message header in a window.

- *Reply*. This prepares a response to the received message. Eudora automatically fills in the To: and Subject:

fields and reproduces the original message, prefixing each line in the original message by a >.

- *Save*. This allows you to save messages on the hard drive. If possible, save your message as you are composing it. You never know when the computer will cease functioning.

INTERMEDIATE FEATURES

Most experienced e-mail users will want these features. Consequently, Eudora includes most of these features.

- *Address book*. This maintains a list of correspondents. This can be a real time saver.

- *Attachments*. These include one or multiple files with a message. With Eudora you can send text files, animation, sound, and graphics. Eudora supports the industry standard **MIME**, Multipurpose Internet Mail Extensions, for sending and receiving attachments.

- *Carbon copies (CC)*. This sends a copy of the message to another party.

- *Blind carbon copies (BCC)*. This feature sends a copy of the message to another party without announcing so in the message. When it comes to personal correspondence, some feel that blind carbon copies are cheating a bit. If you're going to send someone else a copy, say so. However, blind carbon copies are often used in business correspondence.

- *Encryption.* This encodes stored and transmitted messages for privacy. Use encryption to protect sensitive messages.

- *Filing.* This feature saves messages in folders by subject. A good filing system can save hours. A poor one can waste days.

- *Forward.* This sends a message to a third party. Perhaps the message should have been directed to a friend or to your mother-in-law instead of to you. The system should allow you to add comments to the transmitted message.

- *Mailing lists.* These create lists of recipients who all receive a copy of the message whenever the destination is set to the list name.

- *Message priorities.* This feature specifies that some messages be considered more urgent than others. For example, Eudora defines five levels of priority: highest, high, normal, low, and lowest.

- *Message searching.* This sifts through saved messages to find those meeting one or more criteria such as subject and date.

- *Outbox.* This provides a list of messages that have been sent. Of course, once the message has reached the outbox, there is no way of stopping it.

ADVANCED FEATURES

The following features may not be necessary. However, once you are accustomed to them, you'll wonder how you ever lived without them.

- *Message management*. This helps organize and process messages.

- *Viewing attached files*. This feature displays graphics and other attached files in their correct form without accessing the associated application program.

SECURITY

There are a few things you should know about e-mail security. Don't think of e-mail as transmitting sealed letters. Rather, think of e-mail messages as postcards. If you don't take special action, interested parties can read your mail, and even modify it. There are two basic ways for individuals to protect their e-mail: encryption and digital signatures.

Encryption means coding your messages so that unauthorized individuals cannot read them. An excellent encryption program, Pretty Good Privacy (PGP) recently became available for both IBM-compatible and Macintosh computers.

A **digital signature** is a message that is automatically appended to someone's messages. It serves to authenticate the message. Some e-mail programs provide alternate signatures for personal and business use. Get in the habit of signing and then encrypting messages that you consider private.

MAKING ATTACHMENTS TO E-MAIL

Originally e-mail was fairly limited to sending text. However, snail mail users aren't limited to text. They can increase the impact of their letters by including family pictures, audio cassettes, and diskettes in the envelope. Why should e-mail users lag behind? With the right e-mail software, you can send computer programs, graphics, sound, and video files with two big IFs:

IF #1. The receiving party must have the right software to decode your attachments. (This does not mean that she or he must be using the same e-mail package that you're using.)

IF #2. You must respect the copyrights and other legal protection of the transmitted material. E-mail is not a license to steal.

Before seeing how you can send and receive attachments, let's see some of the standard formats for coding attachments. The generic term for an encoded file is a **binary file**, as opposed to a plain text or ASCII (American Standard Code for Information Interchange) file. ASCII files are easy to send and receive but are restricted to the English-language character set with a few additions such as punctuation. E-mail programs have trouble handling binary files such as graphics, sound, and video files in their native state. Such files must be processed (coded) prior to mailing and decoded upon reception. Three widely used coding standards are uuencoded files, BinHex files, and MIME extensions.

Uuencoded Files

Uuencoding is perhaps the most widely used file-encoding technique on the Internet. The uuencode program converts a binary file to ASCII format, after which it can be mailed. For those with the right e-mail software such as the commercial version of Eudora, encoding the file merely means clicking correctly. This isn't too hard because the Windows combo box is labeled Attachment Type and the proper selection is labeled Uuencode. Not-so-fortunate users of other e-mail programs may have to download the uuencode program and then convert the binary file before mailing. Upon receipt the coded file must be decoded into its original binary form using your e-mail program or the uudecode program.

Warning: Uuencoding a file may increase its size by about 35%.

BinHex Files

It is recommended that Macintosh users employ BinHex files, which are easily generated by Eudora and many other e-mail programs. If your e-mail program won't do BinHex, you may have to obtain a conversion program from the Internet.

MIME Files

MIME is short for Multipurpose Internet Mail Extensions. Can you guess where it's used and what it does? Unlike uuencoding and BinHex, MIME supports foreign-language character sets, so you can add snippets of French or

Spanish to your love letters without turning them into gibberish. Of course, your recipient's e-mail program must be able to process MIME files.

Tip: It is recommended that Macintosh users employ the compatible AppleDouble format.

FILE COMPRESSION

Many binary files are quite large and consequently take a long time to transmit. Some e-mail programs limit the size of files that they can receive. In many cases it is impractical to break up the file into smaller pieces. The solution is to compress the files, in essence squeezing the air out of them before transmission. In some cases the compression ratio can be 10 to 1, or even higher. Associated files can be compressed into a single file for easier handling. Commonly used file-compression utilities are PKZIP in the Windows environment and Stuffit in the Macintosh environment. Before sending a binary file, first compress and then encode. Upon reception, first decode. In many cases you won't even have to decompress the file; simply execute the compressed file and it will decompress itself automatically.

GETTING STARTED WITH EUDORA

Now that you have read about electronic mail and all the great things it can do for you, it's time to get started with the world's best electronic mail package, Eudora, specifically designed to run on the information highway. This chapter starts by listing Eudora's system requirements, which are basically the same as Internet system requirements. Then it takes you on a quick and easy path through the steps of composing and sending your first message. You'll learn how to check for mail and reply to messages that you receive. By this time, you'll be able to use Eudora.

The next step is to use Eudora efficiently. You'll start by learning Eudora's rich collection of icons and buttons. Then you'll return to the message creation and checking processes to examine them in greater detail. The last thing you'll learn in this chapter is how to exit Eudora.

SYSTEM REQUIREMENTS

Qualcomm Incorporated of San Diego offers several versions of their electronic mail program commonly called Eudora. The freeware versions, available without cost as explained in Appendix A, are officially called Eudora Light for Windows, or Eudora Light for Macintosh, depending on the computer platform. The commercial versions, available from Qualcomm or many software stores, are officially called Eudora Pro for Windows, or Eudora Pro for Macintosh, depending on the computer platform. These products are commonly known as Eudora and Eudora Pro.

Eudora Light for Windows and Eudora Pro for Windows have the same minimum system requirements:

- IBM PC or compatible (minimum 286 processor).

- Microsoft Windows 3.1 or later. Both versions of Eudora run well under Windows 95.

- Ethernet card or modem for serial connection. You don't need a fast modem to run Eudora.

- WinSockAPI 1.1 compliant networking package. Don't worry about this technical term; if you are able to run on the Internet, you have this package.

- Connection to the Post Office Protocol version 3 (POP3) server to receive incoming messages.

CHAPTER 2: GETTING STARTED WITH EUDORA

- Connection to the Simple Mail Transfer Protocol (SMTP) server to transmit outgoing messages.

Tip: Unlike many other e-mail software packages, Eudora need not be translated to work on the Internet. Both POP3 and SMTP are standard Internet products. In other words, if you can connect to the Internet, you should be able to connect with Eudora.

Appendix A shows you how to download Eudora Light for Windows and install it on your system as well as presenting its menus.

COMPOSING A MESSAGE

Let's start exploring Eudora by composing and sending a short message. Select the **New Message** command from the **Message** menu. This displays a *composition window* entitled "No Recipient, No Subject," as shown in Figure 2-1.

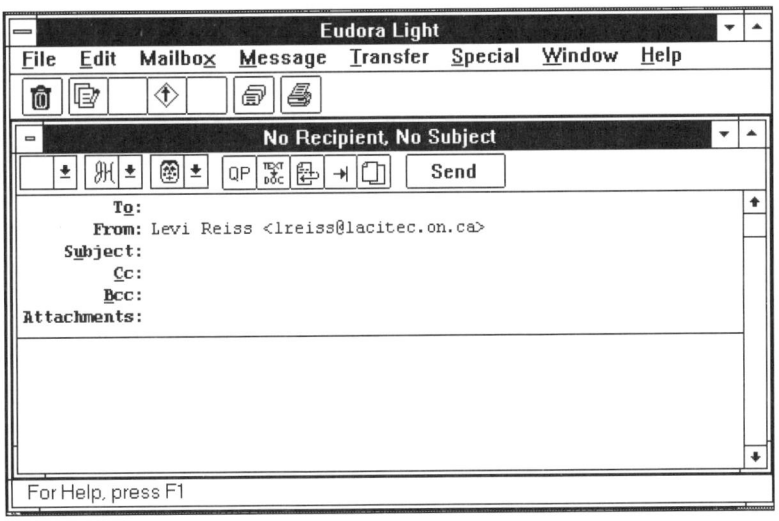

Figure 2-1. Message composition window.

19

You can select the menu and the menu item with the mouse or by using the keyboard as follows. The M in the **Message** menu is underlined, which signifies that you can select the menu by pressing the ALT–M keys. The N in the **New Message** command is underlined; you can select it by pressing the N key, or by pressing the CTRL–N keys. Here CTRL–N is a shortcut, shown to the right of the **New Message** command. Usually, but not always, the first letter in a menu or menu item is underlined. Now that you know what underlining means, and how to make selections from the keyboard as well as the mouse, let's return to the message composition window shown in Figure 2-1. The center of the window includes the *message header* that "introduces" the message. There are six message header fields, starting with To:.

The blinking vertical cursor known as the *insertion point* appears at the start of the To: message header field. When you type or otherwise enter text, the text appears at the insertion point. While you could enter the recipient's e-mail address now, read the following tip and leave this field until further notice.

Tip: Don't complete the To: field until you are actually ready to send the message. This precaution prevents you from sending the wrong message to the right person, or perhaps from sending the right message to the wrong person. Remember, once a message is sent, you cannot get it back.

Eudora automatically completes the From: message header field with the sender's POP3 server account address. While you are in the message composition window, you cannot change its contents.

Use the TAB key or the mouse to place the cursor in the Subject: field. Then enter a short description of your message, such as "Testing." For this first message, skip the Cc:, Bcc:, and Attachments: fields and cross the horizontal line to access the message body area. Then enter your message, such as: "Levi, can you read me?" Your composition window will resemble Figure 2-2. You are now ready to send your first e-mail message, once you address it.

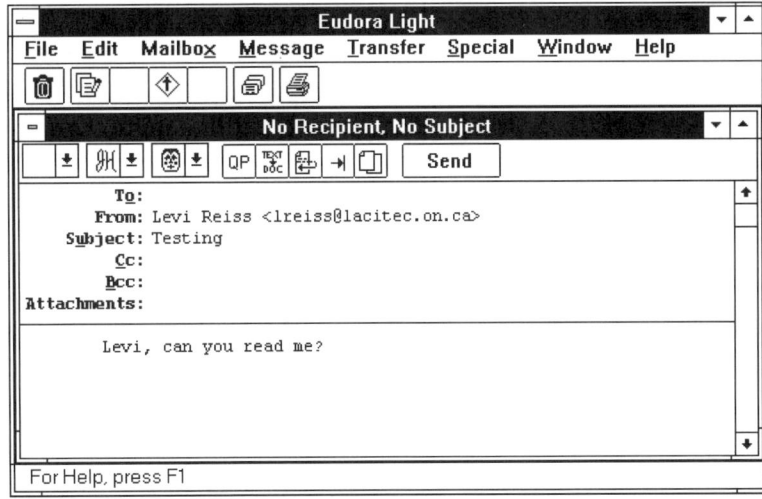

Figure 2-2. Test message.

The easiest way to experiment with Eudora is by sending yourself a message. You can type your own e-mail address in the To: field or you can use the mouse to select the contents of the From: message header field, copy it by pressing the CTRL–C keys, and then paste it into the To: field by pressing the CTRL–V keys. We added the word "recipient" to the To: field to distinguish between the message sender and the recipient without actually changing the e-mail address.

SENDING A MESSAGE

The Send button is located in the upper right-hand corner of the composition window. Click on this button to send the message. As soon as you press the button, the composition window closes. You won't have to guess what happens to your message; a progress window appears on the screen, as shown in Figure 2-3. As its name indicates, the progress window informs you of the message's progress in accessing the network on its journey to the recipient. In this test, the recipient is the sender, so the message shouldn't take too long to reach its destination. Let's see how we can check for its arrival.

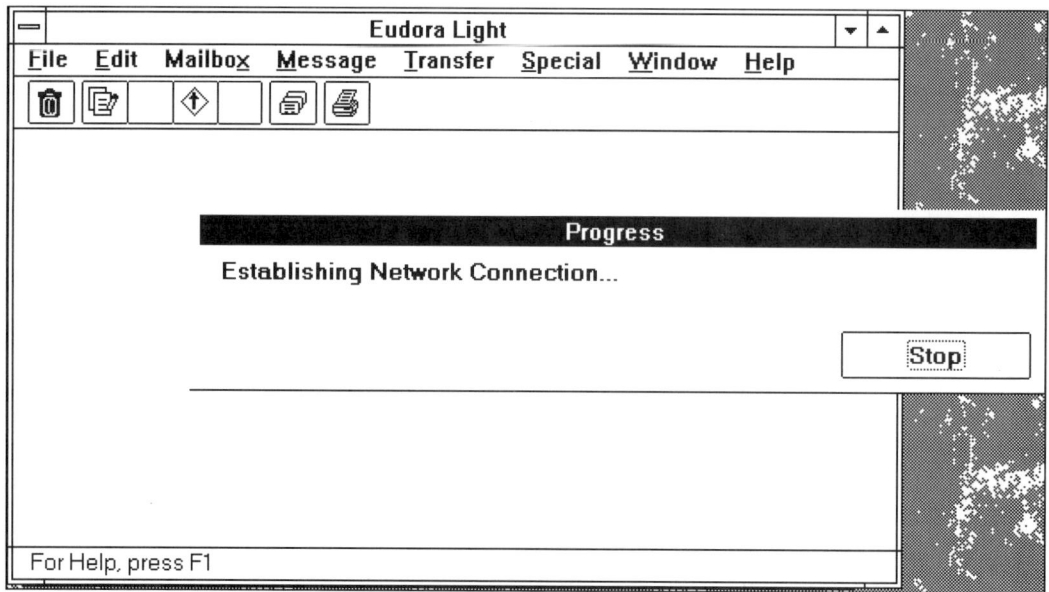

Figure 2-3. The Progress window appears when a message is sent.

CHECKING FOR AND RECEIVING MAIL

You can check for new mail automatically or manually. Chapter 4 describes how to direct Eudora to check for your mail automatically. For the time being, check your mail manually by selecting the **Check Mail** command from the **File** menu.

The first time you check for mail after launching Eudora, the system will request that you enter your POP server password, which may or may not be your regular password. Figure 2-4 shows the Enter Password window. To protect your password, the entry does not appear on the screen; instead asterisks (*) are displayed.

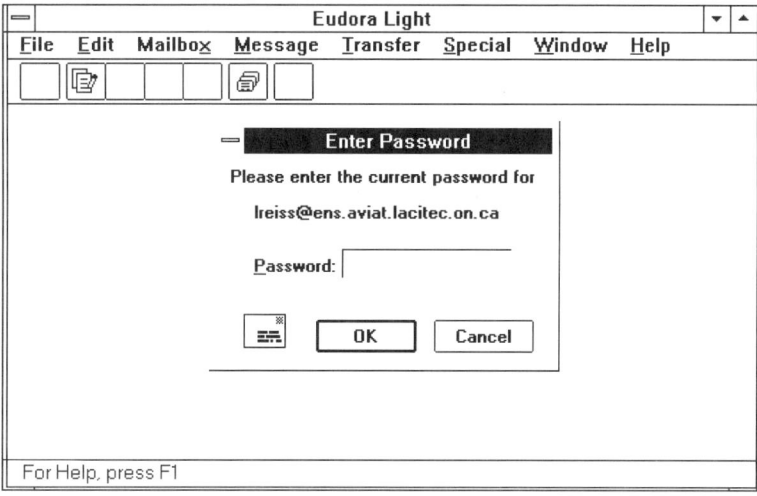

Figure 2-4. The Enter Password dialog box.

THE EUDORA USER'S GUIDE

You can't use e-mail unless you have a functioning POP3 password. Figure 2-5 shows what happens if you make a mistake, such as entering an O for a 0, or vice versa. Memorize your password, but don't post it or write it down. The nuisance of working with passwords is a small price to pay to help maintain e-mail security and network security in general.

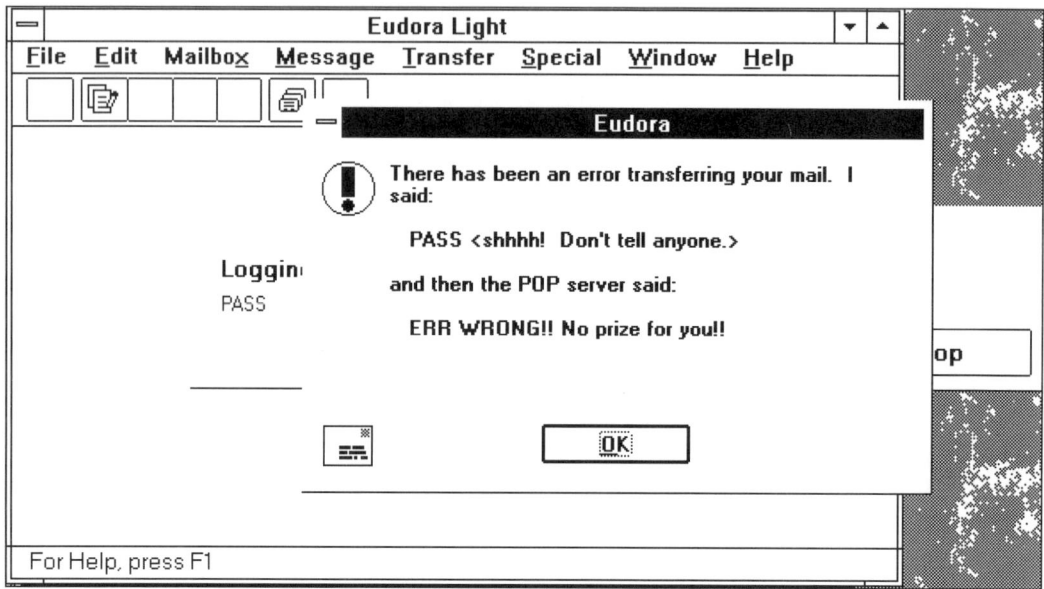

Figure 2-5. This box appears when an incorrect password has been entered.

Sometimes the mail check generates a No New Mail message. Mail delivery is not instantaneous, especially if your message comes from someone other than yourself. Click OK, wait a while, and try again. Of course, if you don't get the message, you might have made a mistake in the recipient's address.

24

When the mail is delivered, the Progress window briefly appears, followed by the New Mail! alert, which is usually audible. The "New Mail!" alert is shown in Figure 2-6.

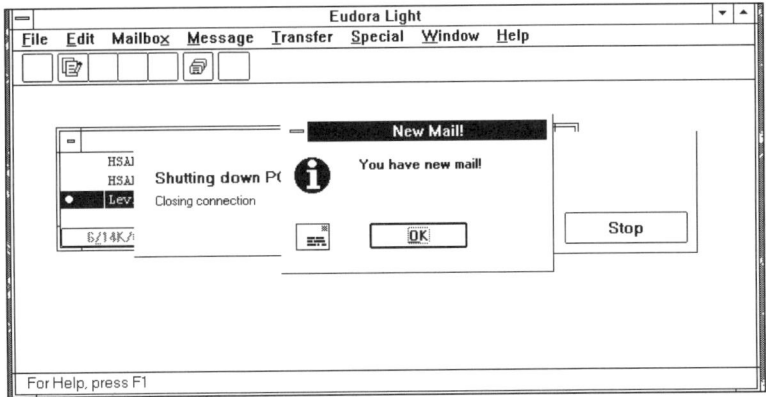

Figure 2-6. The New Mail! alert.

Click OK to display the In Mailbox window, which includes a one-line summary of your message, as shown in Figure 2-7. The first column shows the message status; a bullet (•) specifies that it has not been read. The second column shows the message priority; a blank specifies normal priority. The third column shows the sender's name. The fourth column shows the time and date that the message was sent. The fifth column shows the message size in kilobytes. The sixth and final column shows the message subject as entered by the sender.

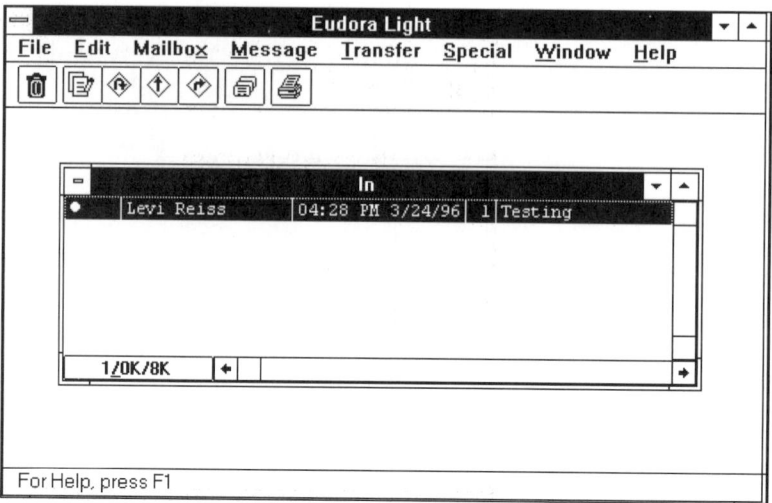

Figure 2-7. The In Mailbox window.

Double-click on a message summary entry to display that message on the screen. Close the message box by clicking on the down arrow in the upper right corner of the window or by pressing the CTRL–F4 keys. You also can close the message box by clicking on the close box in the upper left-hand corner of the message window or by selecting the **Close** command from the **File** menu.

When the message is closed, the In Mailbox reappears. Because the message was read, the bullet in the first column is gone. Incoming messages are stored in the In Mailbox until deleted or transferred to another mailbox.

To change the In Mailbox into an icon, click on the down arrow in the upper right corner of the Mailbox window. Click on the icon to generate a pull-down menu as shown in Figure 2-8. Double-click on the icon to restore it. Press the CTRL–F4 keys to remove the icon from the screen.

CHAPTER 2: GETTING STARTED WITH EUDORA

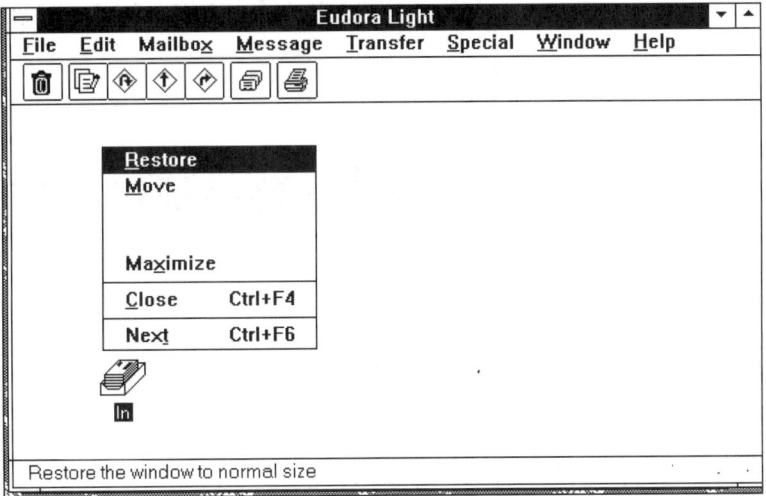

Figure 2-8. Clicking on the In Mailbox icon generates this pull-down menu of options.

REPLYING TO A MESSAGE

It's fairly simple to reply to a message that you have received. First of all, open the In Mailbox by double-clicking on its icon. Highlight a message by clicking on it and then selecting the **Reply** command from the **Message** menu.

Warning: Don't select the **Reply To** *command from the* **Message** *menu, which works with the Quick Recipient list, discussed in Chapter 3.*

Eudora displays a composition window containing the sender's address in the To: message header field and your address in the From: message header field. The message

27

body includes the time and date when the initial message was sent and the text of the original message. Each line of the original message is prefixed by the > character. Move the cursor past the end of the text and enter your reply as shown in Figure 2-9.

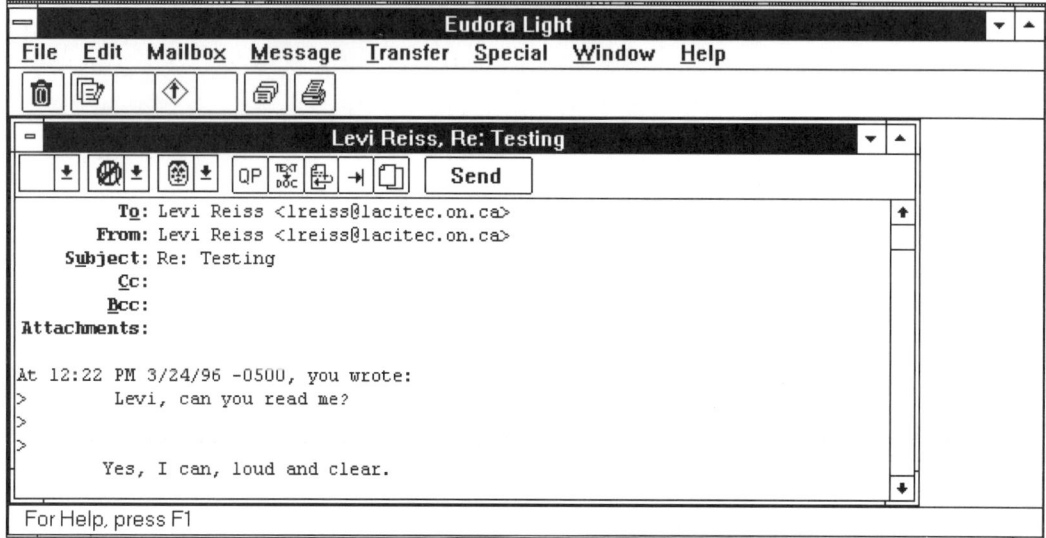

Figure 2-9. Replying to a message.

Warning: It is possible to edit the text of the original message. Of course, fairness dictates that you inform your recipient of your changes and not pretend to be quoting directly. It's a good idea to save a copy of the original message.

Before sending this message, let's see how to save it.

Tip: You don't have to reply to each and every message. Doing so can lead to information overload.

SAVING AN OUTGOING MESSAGE

There are several reasons for saving an unsent message. You shouldn't risk losing your text before sending it, especially if it's long. If you are writing a message in anger, give yourself a chance to cool down before sending it. And sometimes it's just not possible to complete a message at a single sitting.

Saving the message is quite easy. Select the **Save** command from the **File** menu. The composition window remains open and the message is saved in the Out Mailbox. Notice the bullet (•) in the far left column of the message summary, as shown in Figure 2-10. You can make changes to any of the message header fields except the From: field, and you can change the message text.

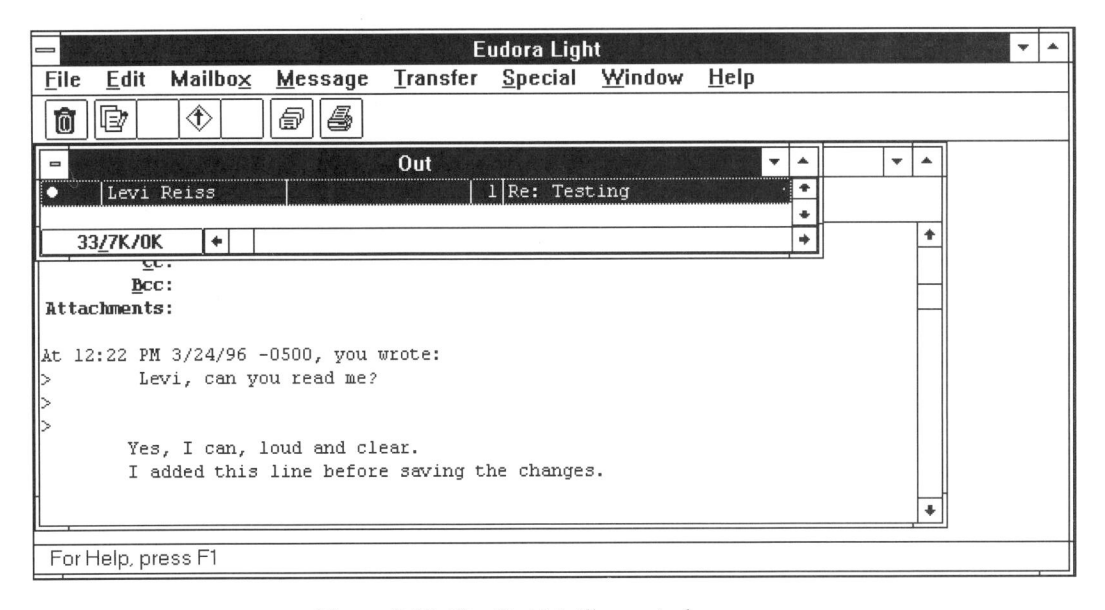

Figure 2-10. The Out Mailbox window.

THE EUDORA USER'S GUIDE

Tip: Avoid information overload and wasted disk space. It's a good idea to keep a copy of messages as they are sent but to have a strict policy on message deletion and archival to keep storage under control.

Let's see what happens if you don't save your changes. Edit the message and select the **Close** command from the **File** menu. Eudora prompts you to save the changes, as shown in Figure 2-11. Your options are Yes to save the changes and exit the message window, No to exit the message window without saving the changes, and Cancel to return to the document. If the message has never been saved, selecting No discards it.

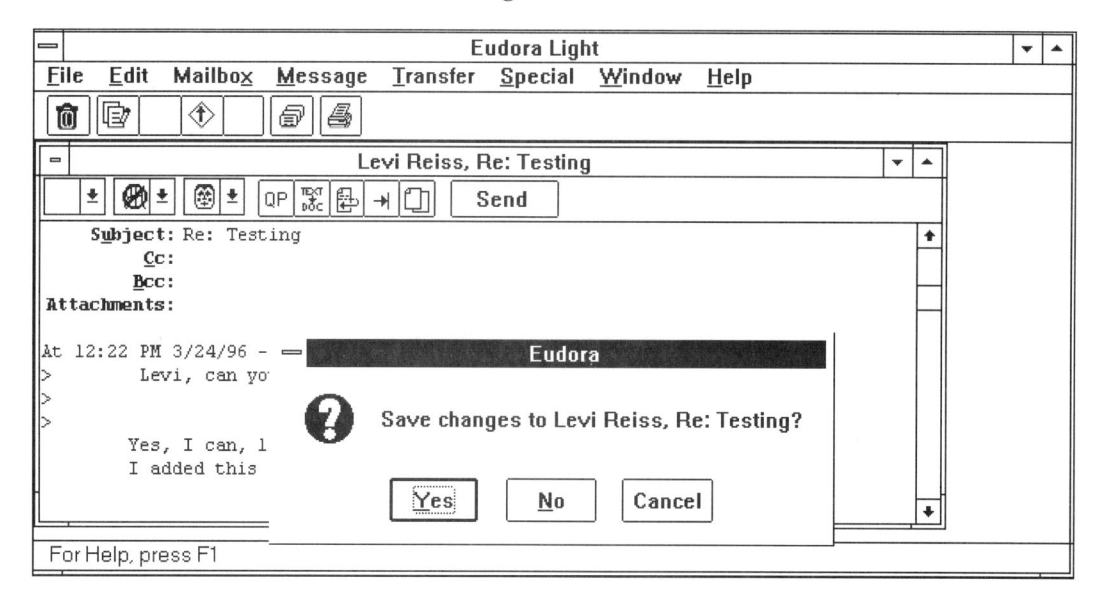

Figure 2-11. Eudora window prompting that message be saved.

MAIN WINDOW ICON

You don't need to keep the Eudora window open to find out if you have mail. Look closely at the Windows Desktop icon to know if you have received mail and if you have messages awaiting delivery. These icon images are familiar to those with a rural mailbox:

Normal

The mailbox is closed and the flag is down. This icon image indicates that you have no new mail and that no messages are awaiting delivery.

New Mail

The open mailbox contains a letter, and the flag is down. You have new mail. To access it, double-click on the icon to start Eudora.

Queued Messages

The mailbox is closed and the flag is up. You have messages queued for delivery.

New Mail/Queued Messages

The open mailbox contains a letter and the flag is up. You have new mail, and outgoing messages are queued for delivery.

Tip: One excellent way to waste time is starting Eudora whenever you see the New Mail icon. Unless you are expecting special mail, continue what you are doing and get your mail later, perhaps just before your coffee break.

MAIN WINDOW TOOLBAR

The Main window toolbar appears under the menu titles. It contains the following seven buttons, reading from left to right: Trash, New Message, Reply, Forward, Redirect, Nicknames, and Print. Each toolbar button launches a common action that also could be launched from a menu.

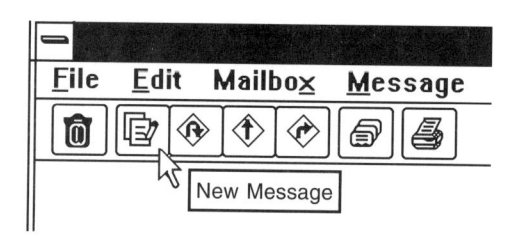

Tip: Save yourself time and effort. Learn to use the toolbar buttons.

There is no need to memorize the list of toolbar buttons or guess what the button image represents. Let the mouse pointer sit on a button for a few seconds to display the button name (toolbar tip) under the button and a longer description of the button's action in the message bar at the bottom of the screen.

Note: Chapter 4 shows how you can turn off the main window toolbar and the toolbar tips. We strongly recommend, however, that you display both of these useful objects. You never know when you may need them.

Trash Button

The Trash button transfers the current message or messages to the Trash Mailbox, whose contents can be permanently deleted by activating the **Empty Trash** option of the **Special** menu.

New Message Button

The New Message button opens the message composition window shown in Figure 2-1. This chapter presents a quick overview of sending messages. Sending messages is discussed in greater detail in Chapter 3.

Reply Button

The Reply button replies to the current message or message summaries, as shown in Figure 2-9. This chapter presents a quick overview of replying to messages. Replying to messages is discussed in greater detail in Chapter 5.

Forward Button

The Forward button forwards the current message or message summaries. Forwarding messages is discussed in greater detail in Chapter 5.

Redirect Button

The Redirect button redirects the current message or message summaries. Redirecting messages is discussed in greater detail in Chapter 5.

Nicknames Button

The Nickname button displays the Nicknames window. A nickname is a short, easy-to-remember alias for an e-mail address. Nicknames and their use are discussed in Chapter 3.

Print Button

The Print button prints a current message, signature file, or Ph window. (See Chapter 9).

CREATING AN OUTGOING MESSAGE

You've already had the experience of creating an e-mail message. Let's examine the composition window shown in Figure 2-1 in greater detail. Remember, you can generate this window by clicking on the New Message button in the Main window toolbar or by selecting the **New Message** command from the **Message** menu. We'll next examine the title bar, the icon bar, and the six fields of the message header.

TITLE BAR

The title bar's contents are similar for incoming messages and outgoing messages. Reading from left to right, the title bar contents for incoming messages are the sender's name, the time and date of message delivery, and the message subject. For outgoing messages, the contents include the addressee's name, the time and date the message was sent, and the message subject. Before new messages are sent or queued, their title bar reads No Recipient, No Subject, even if you have entered the message subject. Queued messages are time- and date-stamped only when they are sent.

ICON BAR

The icon bar appears immediately under the title bar. Use the icon bar objects to control settings for the current message without affecting general message settings, as specified in the Sending Mail Settings dialog box described in Chapter 3. When a button is turned on, it looks slightly depressed (no pun intended) and is surrounded by a small shadow. When it is turned off, it protrudes slightly from its background.

The icon bar contains three combo boxes and six buttons. To a large extent these combo boxes and buttons, described next, are independent.

Priority Combo Box

Select the Priority combo box to change the message's reference priority. Eudora offers five priorities ranging from lowest to highest. Most messages have normal priority. Chapter 3 discusses message priorities in greater detail.

THE EUDORA USER'S GUIDE

Signature Combo Box

Select the Signature combo box to append your signature automatically to the end of your outgoing messages. Signatures are used to verify that you actually sent the message and that the message was not modified since it was signed. Chapter 3 discusses message signatures in greater detail.

Attachment Type Combo Box

Select the Attachment Type combo box to specify the format of documents attached to your outgoing messages. Eudora encodes attachments in the widely used Multipurpose Internet Mail Extensions (MIME) or Bin Hex, which is mostly used with Macintosh e-mail programs or with older versions of Eudora.

Quoted-Printable Encoding Button

Press the Quoted-Printable encoding button when sending messages or attachments containing special characters or long lines of text. You should make sure that this button is always on.

Text as Document Button

Press the Text as Document button to incorporate attached plain text files directly into the message that they accompany.

Word Wrap Button

Press the Word Wrap button so you don't need to press the ENTER key at the end of each line in an outgoing message. This selection causes Eudora automatically to wrap text to the next line, generating lines approximately 76 characters long.

Tabs in Body Button

Press the Tabs in Body button to direct the TAB key to insert tabs when pressed anywhere in the message body. If this button is off, pressing the TAB key places the cursor at the To: field of the message header.

Keep Copy Button

Press the Keep Copy button to direct Eudora to keep a copy of each sent message in the Out Mailbox. Each entry in the Out Mailbox window is a message summary containing an S in the first column. Saved messages are kept until deleted or transferred to another mailbox or folder. It's a good idea to keep a copy of messages as they are sent but to have a strict policy on message deletion and archival to keep storage under control.

Send or Queue Button

The final button in the icon bar is either Send or Queue depending on the Immediate Send option in the Sending Mail Settings dialog box, discussed in detail in Chapter 3. Pressing this button either sends the message on the spot or queues the message to be sent later. In either case, once the button is pressed, the message window closes.

MESSAGE HEADER

Outgoing message headers contain six fields: To:, From:, Subject:, Cc:, Bcc:, and Attachments:. The contents of the From: field are supplied by Eudora and cannot be modified. A special procedure, described below, is required to complete the Attachments: field. The other message header fields may be directly edited.

Access the desired message header field by clicking the mouse or pressing the TAB key. You can use standard Windows **Edit** menu commands to fill or modify these fields. For example, to send a message to yourself, select the contents of the From: field, press the CTRL–C keys to copy this value, and press the CTRL–V keys to paste it into the To: field. The description of each field follows:

To:

The To: message header field contains the addressee's e-mail address, or a nickname. Chapter 3 discusses nicknames in detail. Separate multiple addresses by commas.

From:

The From: message header field contains the sender's e-mail address. This value is automatically entered by Eudora and cannot be edited directly. You can, however, change this field by entering the desired address in the Return Address field of the Personal Information Settings dialog box.

Subject:

The Subject: message header field briefly describes the message contents. It is a breach of netiquette to leave this field blank. Specifying an appropriate subject name reduces the likelihood that your message will be ignored or deleted without being read.

Cc:

"Cc" stands for "carbon copy." This message header field specifies the e-mail address or nickname of the person(s) destined to receive a copy of the message. Separate multiple addresses by commas. Leave this field blank if so desired.

Bcc:

"Bcc" stands for "blind carbon copy." This message header field is similar to the Cc: field except that it lists message recipients who are not identified. In other words, if you send a message to A, a carbon copy to B, and a blind carbon copy to C, A will know that B received a copy of the message but neither A nor B will know that C received a copy. Separate multiple addresses by commas. Leave this field blank if so desired.

Attachments:

The Attachments: message header field lists documents that accompany the message. Use the **Attach File** option of the **Message** menu to attach a document. Delete an attachment from a message by first clicking on the attachment title and then pressing the DELETE key. Leave this field blank if so desired. Chapters 3 and 4 discuss message attachments and their deletion in greater detail.

MESSAGE BODY

Use the area below the horizontal line to enter the message text. Standard Windows editing keys such as CTRL–C (Copy), CTRL–X (Cut), and CTRL–V (Paste) are available. It is recommended that you press the Word Wrap button to avoid pressing the ENTER key at the end of every line. Failure to do so may result in long lines that the recipient cannot read.

AUTOMATIC AND MANUAL MAIL CHECKING

The POP server is the computer that receives your mail and stores it while awaiting transfer to Eudora running on your PC. You can specify your POP server account in the POP Account setting in the Getting Started Settings dialog box, discussed in detail in Chapter 4. As discussed in the beginning of this chapter, you may check the POP server for new mail automatically or manually. In either case, the POP server asks for your password before performing the first mail check in a given Eudora session.

AUTOMATIC CHECKING

Eudora can automatically check for mail at a frequency that you specify. To do so, access the **Special** menu, select the

Settings option, select **Checking Mail**, and finally enter a number (e.g. 15) in the box entitled Check for mail every ? minute(s). In this case, if Eudora is up and running, it will check for new mail every 15 minutes.

Tip: Don't specify a value less than 15 minutes or you will overload the POP server and the system in general.

Note: If automatic checking is set, the **Check Mail** *command under the* **File** *menu displays the next time that an automatic check is scheduled to occur.*

Depending on the settings in the Getting Attention Settings dialog box, discussed in detail in Chapter 4, Eudora has different ways of notifying you that mail has arrived. Among these ways are emitting a sound, changing the mailbox image in the Eudora icon, and displaying a window on the screen.

You can always start Eudora by double-clicking on its icon. However, unless you are expecting urgent mail, it may not be necessary to launch Eudora every time you are notified that mail has arrived.

MANUAL CHECKING

Check for mail manually as desired by selecting the **Check Mail** command from the **File** menu. A progress window helps you pass the time while awaiting results of the mail check. New mail will be transferred automatically from the POP server to Eudora on your computer, again accompanied by a progress window.

MAIL RECEPTION

Unless you specify otherwise, you receive your mail in the In Mailbox. Each message is shown in a one-line message summary. All the mailboxes list the message summaries in order of receipt; the most recent message is at the bottom of the list. To open the In Mailbox, select it from the Mailbox menu. As stated previously, a bullet (•) in the first column of the message summary denotes an unread message. You may open the message by double-clicking on its message summary. Incoming messages are saved indefinitely in the In Mailbox until they are deleted or transferred to another mailbox.

QUITTING EUDORA

To quit the Eudora program, select the **Exit** command from the **File** menu. As will be discussed in Chapter 3, if you have queued messages, or messages scheduled to be sent within the next 12 hours, Eudora asks if you want to send them. If the "Empty Trash on Quit" option in the Switches Setting dialog box is turned on, exiting Eudora also empties your Trash Mailbox.

SENDING E-MAIL

It didn't take very long to get started using Eudora. The next step is mastering the ins and outs of sending mail. In this chapter, you'll learn how and when to queue mail or send it immediately, how to attach just about any kind of file to your text, how to use nicknames to save typing and create custom mailing lists, and how to use the related Quick Recipient list. Furthermore, you'll find out how to get nicknames and the Quick Recipient list to work together and, just as importantly, how not to confuse them. Do you want your correspondents to take your e-mail seriously? Two helpful features are message priorities and signatures. The chapter closes with an examination of the Sending Mail and Attachments settings that let you customize Eudora to meet your specific mail-sending needs.

THE EUDORA USER'S GUIDE

SENDING A MESSAGE

Eudora lets you send a message immediately or queue one or more messages to be sent later. It is fairly obvious why you would want to send mail as soon as you compose it. Queueing your mail can save you money, especially if you are a slow typist and pay for your connect time by the hour or, as many of us do, by the minute. Once you have decided to send or queue, access the **Settings** command in the **Special** menu. Then look at the Immediate Send check box in the Sending Mail Settings window, shown in Figure 3-1. To change the contents of the check box, simply click on it or on its name.

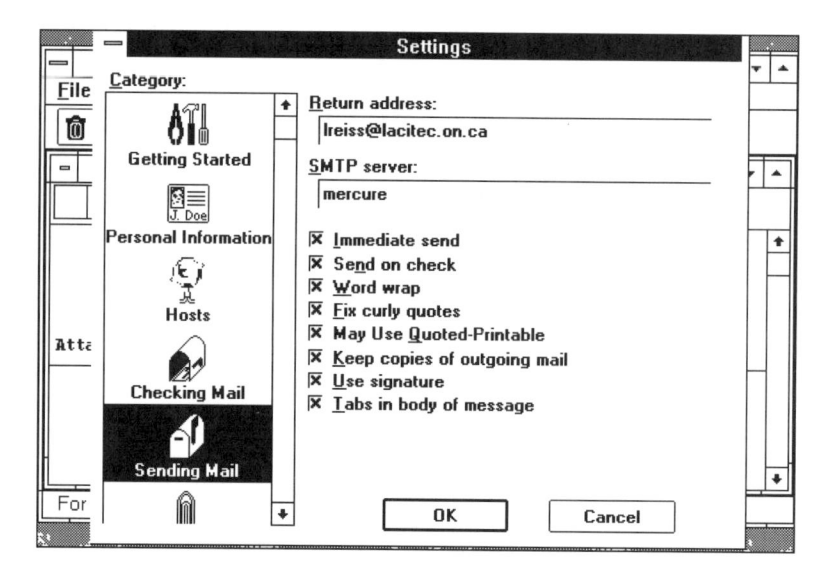

Figure 3-1. The Sending Mail Settings window.

44

IMMEDIATE SEND (SEND BUTTON)

Placing an **x** in the Immediate Send check box of the Sending Mail Settings window displays the Send button at the right end of the message composition window's icon bar. This button is shown in Figure 3-2. This setting also enables the **Send Immediately** command in the **Message** menu. Use the button, the menu selection, or the CTRL–E hot keys to send your message. Eudora displays a progress window to inform you of your message's transmission.

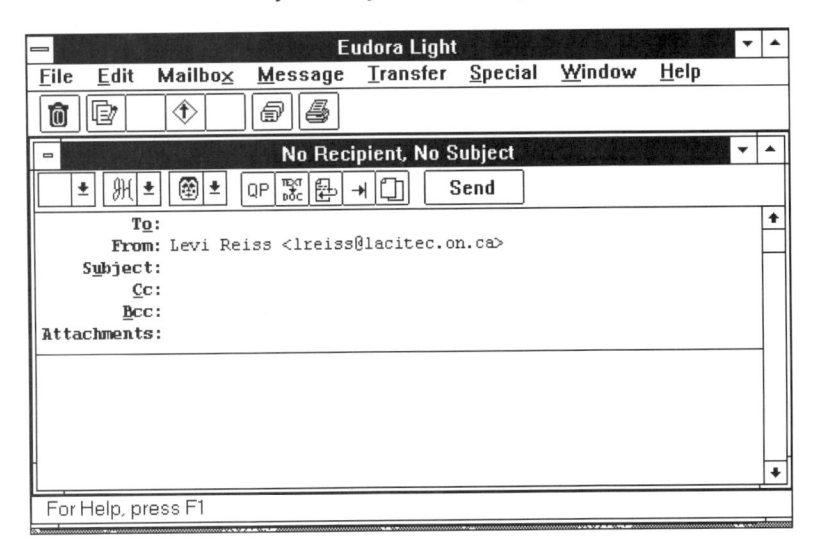

Figure 3-2. Note the Send button at the right end of the message composition window's icon bar.

DEFERRED SEND (QUEUE BUTTON)

While you may choose to send most messages as you compose them, it can be more efficient to compose a group of messages and send them all at once. A deferred send is necessary if Eudora is up and running but is not connected to the network. In other words, network unavailability is no excuse for not working on your e-mail backlog. Furthermore, you can schedule message transmission when you want; for example, in the middle of the night to take advantage of lower connect charges.

Turning off the "Send" option in the Sending Mail Settings window displays the Queue button at the right end of the message composition window's icon bar, as shown in Figure 3-3. This setting also enables the **Queue For Delivery** command in the **Message** menu. Use the button, the menu selection, or the CTRL–E hot keys to send your message. Queueing your message closes the message window, saves the message in the Out Mailbox, and places a Q in the first column of the message summary.

When you are ready to send the queued message(s), access the **File** menu and select the **Send Queued Messages** command. As always, a progress window lets you know how the message transmission is going.

CHAPTER 3: SENDING E-MAIL

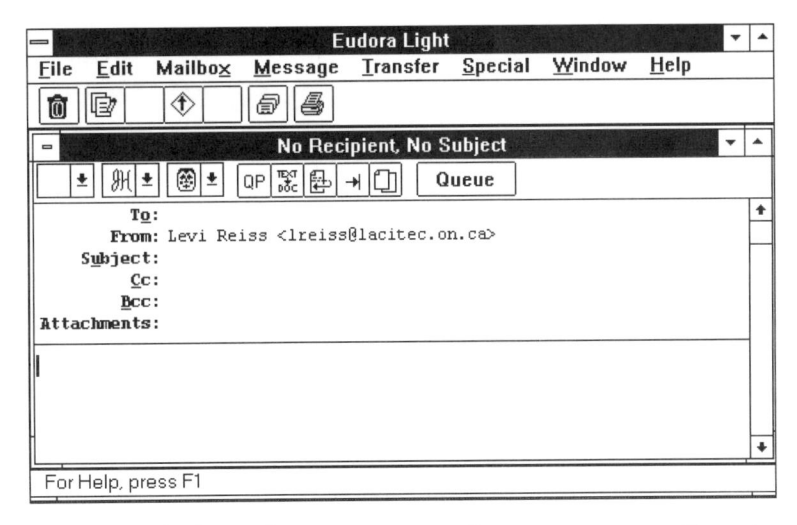

Figure 3-3. The Queue button appears on the message composition window's icon bar when the Send option in the Sending Mail Settings window is turned off.

SCHEDULING MESSAGE TRANSMISSION

Eudora provides several message deferral options. First access the **Message** menu, select **Change**, and then select **Queueing** to display the Change Queueing window as shown in Figure 3-4.

THE EUDORA USER'S GUIDE

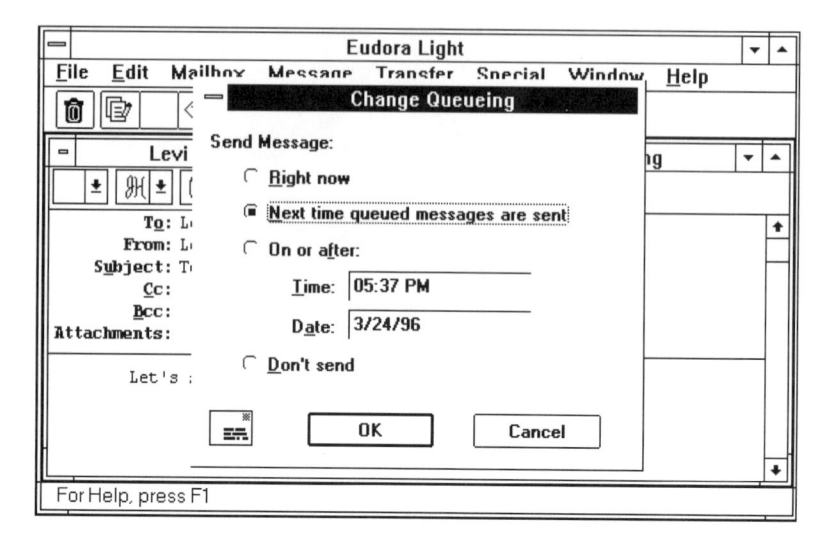

Figure 3-4. The Change Queueing window.

Let's look at the four choices this window offers:

- Specifying the "Right now" option sends the message immediately. In other words, you changed your mind about queueing the message.

- Specifying the "Next time" queued messages are sent option does exactly that: this message goes out with the first queued message. Of course, if all queued messages are so marked, it is possible that no message will be sent.

- Specifying the "On or after" option lets you set the time and date for message transmission. As you may guess, this option will not actually launch Eudora at the specified moment. It won't even warn you that Eudora is not running. The message is sent the first time Eudora runs after the designated time and date.

- Specifying the "Don't send" option holds the message until further notice. This option can be interesting if you are awaiting confirmation before sending one or more messages. The message status changes from queued (Q) to saved (•). The message remains in the Out Mailbox until deleted or re-queued and sent.

CONVENIENTLY SENDING QUEUED MESSAGES

Why use a separate step to send queued messages? Two convenient times for doing so are when checking for messages and when exiting Eudora. The Sending Mail Settings window includes the "Send on check" option. Turn this on, and checking your mail kills two birds with one stone. The window shown in Figure 3-5 is displayed when exiting Eudora with queued messages, unless these messages are scheduled for sending on or after a specified time and date.

THE EUDORA USER'S GUIDE

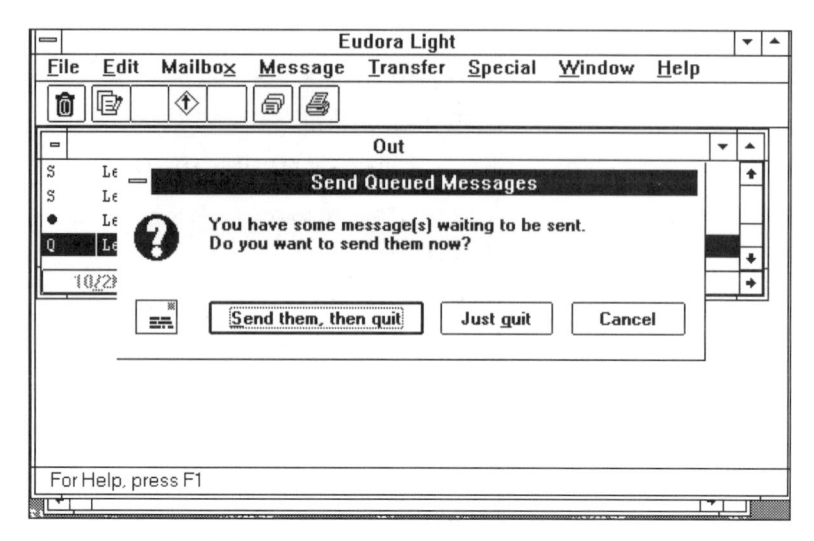

Figure 3-5. This dialog box appears when there are unscheduled queued messages at the time Eudora is exited.

If the message is scheduled to be sent within the next 12 hours, Eudora warns you as shown in Figure 3-6. However, if the message is scheduled to be sent more than 12 hours in the future, no warning appears.

EDITING A QUEUED MESSAGE

Just because a message is queued doesn't mean that it can't be edited. To do so, simply open the Out Mailbox and double-click on its message summary. The queued message appears in the composition window ready for editing. When you have finished editing the message, save it and change its queuing if so desired. Eudora warns you if you attempt to close the message composition window without saving an edited message.

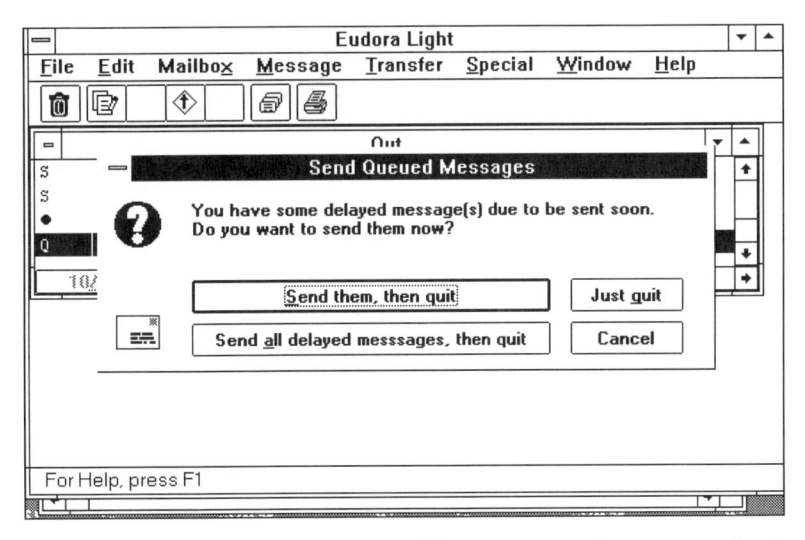

Figure 3-6. This dialog box appears if there are queued messages scheduled to be sent within 12 hours of your exit from Eudora.

SAVING OUTGOING MESSAGES

To save a copy of messages after they are sent, turn on the "Keep copies of outgoing mail" option in the Sending Mail Settings window. You also may press the Keep Copy button in the icon bar. Either method saves the message and creates a message summary entry in the Out Mailbox. The message summary includes an S (for Saved) in the first column. If you have not specifically saved the message, after sending it Eudora transfers the message to the Trash Mailbox.

ATTACHMENTS

Straight text alone can be so boring. Sometimes you want to add punch to your e-mail by including graphics, sound, and animation. You can attach any type of file to your Eudora messages by selecting the **Attach File** command from the **Message** menu. This displays the Attach File window shown in Figure 3-7. This is a fairly standard Windows file open window in which you can specify the file name, change the directory or drive, or list files of a chosen type. Once you have selected the file, click on the OK button to attach it to the message. The file's complete path name is placed in the message header Attachments: field. The attached file does not appear within the message text. Repeat this process to attach several files.

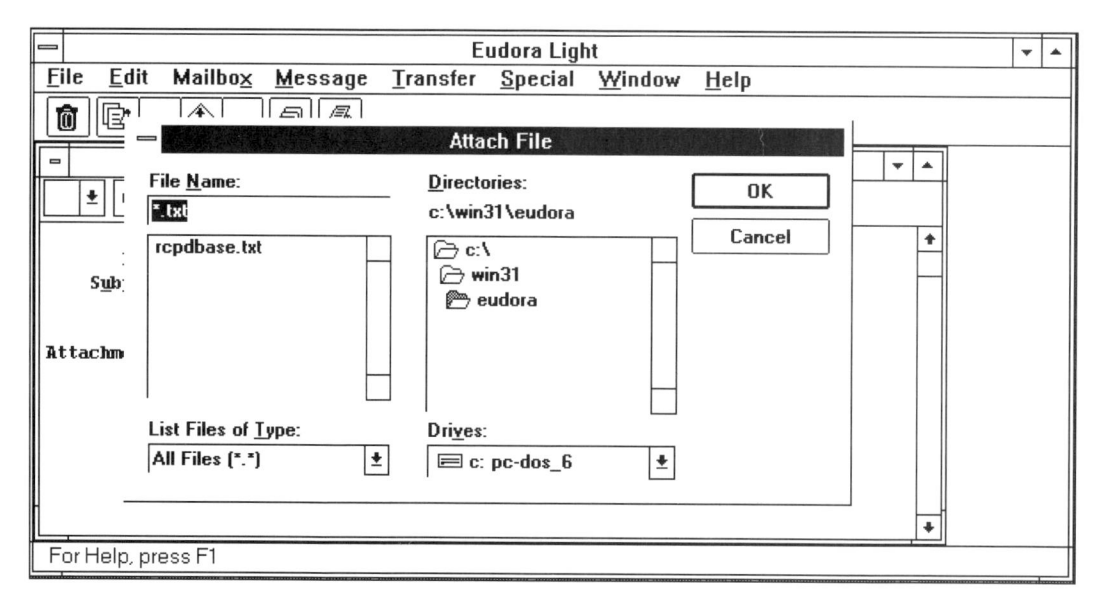

Figure 3-7. Eudora's Attach File window.

Warning: You cannot attach a file by manually editing the Attachments: field.

Attached files are formatted differently depending on the file itself and dialog box or button settings. First consider plain text files, also known as ASCII files. Such files can be simply added to the message as if they were typed in. To do so, turn on the Put text attachments in the body of message option of the Attachments Settings window, or turn off the Text as Document button in the icon bar.

If you have specified other selections for plain text files, or if your attached files are not plain text files, they are formatted according to the message icon bar's Attachment Type combo box. Eudora encodes these attachments in either the widely used Multipurpose Internet Mail Extensions (MIME) or Bin Hex, an encoding method mostly used with Macintosh e-mail programs and older versions of Eudora.

DETACHING A FILE

Perhaps you changed your mind about attaching a given file to your message. For example, you heard the music clip and realized that your party wouldn't like it, or didn't have the software to hear it. Not to worry. Detach the file by first clicking on its name in the composition window's Attachments: field. Then, press the DELETE or BACKSPACE key or select the **Clear** command from the **Edit** menu.

CREATING AND USING NICKNAMES

E-mail addresses can be long and difficult to type. They may include a combination of upper case and lower case characters. If you get one measly letter wrong, the mail won't be delivered. Why struggle? Use nicknames.

A *nickname*, also known as an *alias*, is an easy-to-remember replacement for an e-mail address or group of addresses. Nicknames can replace e-mail addresses in the To:, Cc:, and Bcc: message header fields. It's a good idea to set up a nickname for people with whom you correspond a lot, especially if their e-mail addresses are long or complicated.

Select the **Nicknames** command from the **Window** menu to display the Nicknames window shown in Figure 3-8. (We already filled in our nickname.) The Nickname: field contains your nicknames; the Address(es): field shows the e-mail address or *expansion* for the selected nickname; and the Notes: field displays any comments made for that nickname, for example a phone number or a list of the members associated with a group nickname. The Sample Notes: field does not appear in your outgoing mail.

CREATING NICKNAMES

When you want to create a nickname, simply click on the **New** button in the Nicknames window. This displays the New Nickname window shown in Figure 3-9.

CHAPTER 3: SENDING E-MAIL

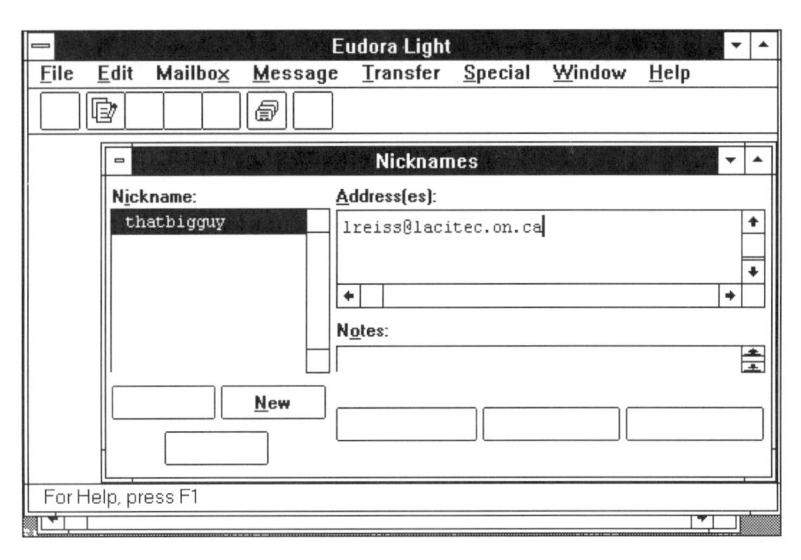

Figure 3-8. Eudora's Nicknames window.

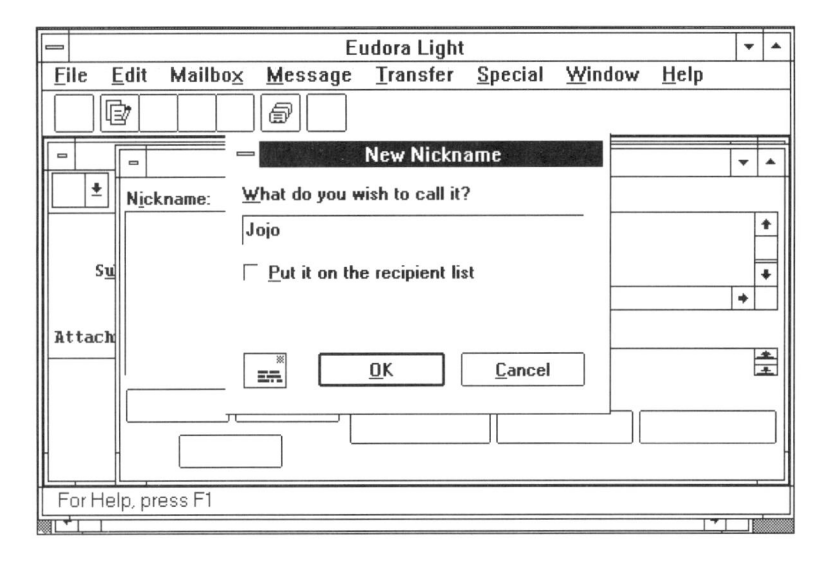

Figure 3-9. The New Nickname window.

55

Enter the new nickname. If you want, click on the "Put it on the recipient list" option to insert this nickname into the Quick Recipient list, discussed in the final section of this chapter. Confirm your entries by clicking on OK. The new nickname appears in the Nickname: field of the Nicknames window. The blinking vertical cursor appears in the Address(es): field, waiting for you to enter this person's complete e-mail address. Add the individual's proper name by placing it in parentheses after the e-mail address. The proper name then appears in the To: field of mail that you send.

To create a group nickname, type two or more e-mail addresses or nicknames in the Address(es): field of the Nicknames window. Separate these entries by commas or by pressing the ENTER key.

Note: You may use the ENTER key to separate e-mail addresses in the Nicknames window, but nowhere else in Eudora.

CHANGING AND REMOVING NICKNAMES

To change a nickname, select **Nicknames** from the **Window** menu. Click on the desired nickname in the Nickname: field to select it, and then click on the Rename button to display a Rename Nickname window, which is similar to the New Nickname window. You may change the nickname and add or remove it from the Quick Recipient list. Confirm your changes by clicking on OK.

Suppose that you want to keep the nickname but change its associated notes or e-mail address(es). Simply select the desired nickname and edit the information. To remove a nickname first select it and then click on the Remove button. This automatically removes it from the Quick Recipient list. To save your new or modified nicknames select the **Save** command from the **File** menu. Eudora warns you if you attempt to close the Nicknames window without saving your changes.

MAKE NICKNAME COMMAND

The **Make Nickname** command simplifies nickname creation in some cases. For example, to create a group nickname from several existing nicknames, select them in the Nicknames window by holding the CTRL key while clicking on the desired nicknames. Then select the **Make Nickname** command from the **Special** menu. Complete the resulting new nickname dialog box by entering the group nickname. Confirm by clicking on OK.

To create a nickname from a message's address list, first select the message. Then select the **Make Nickname** command from the **Special** menu. Complete the resulting new nickname dialog box by entering the group nickname. Confirm by clicking on OK. By selecting multiple message summaries, you can create a nickname for all the addresses.

ADDRESSING MAIL VIA THE NICKNAMES WINDOW

You may have noticed the To:, Cc:, and Bcc: buttons in the Nicknames window shown previously in Figure 3-8. You can initiate mail messages by selecting one or more nicknames and then clicking on the To: button. This displays a new composition window whose To: field contains the selected nickname or nicknames. Use the To:, Cc:, and Bcc: buttons to insert additional nicknames into the corresponding message header fields.

Note: When addressing messages using the Nicknames window To:, Cc:, and Bcc: buttons, hold the SHIFT key to insert the full nickname expansion in the message field.

FINISH NICKNAME OPTION

The **Edit** menu's **Finish Nickname** command menu may reduce your typing in the To:, Cc:, or Bcc: message header fields. You type the unique initial portion of the nickname, and Eudora finishes typing in the nickname. It works as follows.

Start typing the nickname into the To:, Cc:, or Bcc: message header fields. Enter enough characters to make the nickname unique. Select the **Finish Nickname** command from the **Edit** menu, and Eudora enters the rest of the nickname. Let's say that you have two similar nicknames starting with the letter *J*, namely Janet and Jane-Ellen. Type *Jane-*, make the menu selection, and Eudora completes the nickname. If, however, you type only *Ja* and select the **Finish**

Nickname command from the **Edit** menu, Eudora extends your entry to *Jane* and then beeps. It doesn't know which person you want.

Note: To generate a nickname's expansion (e-mail address), press and hold the SHIFT key while finishing a nickname.

QUICK RECIPIENT LIST

The Quick Recipient list, shown in Figure 3-10, lets you access frequently used e-mail addresses or nicknames without typing. The four **Message** menu commands associated with the Quick Recipient list include the word "To." For example, the **New Message To** command creates a new message addressed to an e-mail address or nickname appearing on the Quick Recipient list.

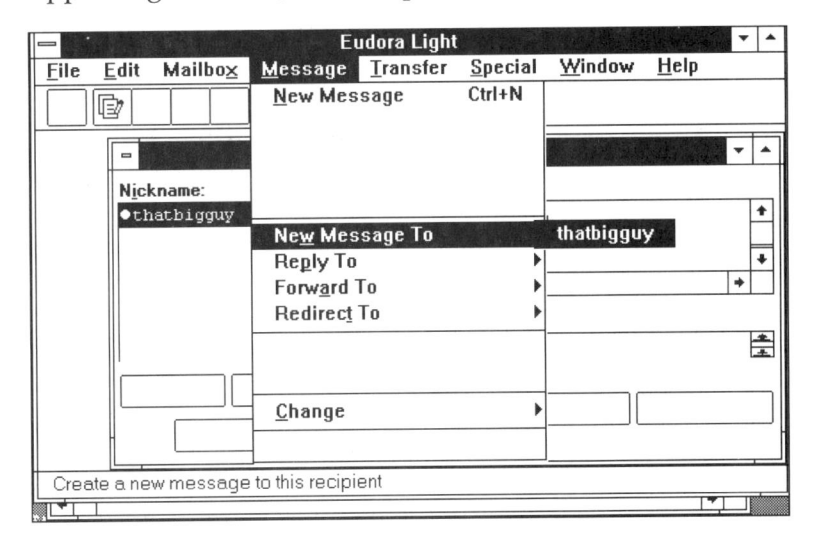

Figure 3-10. The Quick Recipient list.

ADDING A NICKNAME TO THE QUICK RECIPIENT LIST

It's easy to add a nickname to the Quick Recipient list. First access the Nicknames window. Then select a nickname, and place the mouse pointer over the margin to the left of the nickname. The cursor becomes a miniature menu. Click the mouse once and a bullet (•) appears in the margin, indicating that the nickname is now on the Quick Recipient list. When creating a nickname, immediately add it to the list by checking the Put it on the recipient list in the **New Nickname** window, as was shown in Figure 3-9.

ADDING AN E-MAIL ADDRESS TO THE QUICK RECIPIENT LIST

To add an e-mail address to the Quick Recipient list, select the address and then access the **Add As Recipient** command of the **Special** menu.

USING THE QUICK RECIPIENT LIST

Selecting the **New Message To**, **Reply To**, **Forward To**, or **Redirect To** commands of the **Message** menu displays the Quick Recipient list. Launch the desired action by clicking one of these four commands and then selecting a recipient

CHAPTER 3: SENDING E-MAIL

from the list. Eudora fills the To: message header field with the selected recipient.

To add multiple nicknames or addresses contained in the Quick Recipient list to the To:, Cc:, and Bcc: message header fields, place the blinking insertion point in the receiving field. Then, select the desired recipient using the **Insert Recipient** command of the **Edit** menu. Eudora inserts the recipient's nickname or address, adding a comma if necessary to separate the inserted value from any existing field contents.

REMOVING A QUICK RECIPIENT FROM THE LIST

To remove a nickname or e-mail address entry from the Quick Recipient list, first select it using the **Special** menu's **Remove Recipient** command. Releasing the mouse button deletes the selected recipient. An alternative deletion method is clicking the margin to the left of the nickname. The bullet disappears, and the entry is no longer on the list.

Note: Removing or renaming a nickname removes it or renames it on the Quick Recipient list. However, removing a nickname from the Nicknames window deletes it from the Quick Recipient list.

Nicknames and the Quick Recipient List

Sometimes people get confused by two separate but related Eudora functions, Nicknames and the Quick Recipient list.

A nickname is an abbreviation for one or more e-mail addresses. The Quick Recipient list adds addresses to message header fields via the **Message** menu. Quick Recipient list elements may or may not be nicknames. Nicknames may or may not be on the Quick Recipient list.

RESENDING REJECTED MESSAGES

Mail transport agents are computer programs that route e-mail messages across networks. If they cannot deliver a given e-mail message to the intended recipient, they retransmit it to the original sender after adding an error message that may help determine why the transmission failed, as shown in Figure 3-11.

Tip: The most likely reason a message fails to arrive is an error in the recipient's address.

To resend the message, select the **Send Again** command from the **Message** menu. This deletes any error messages and restores the original message format. Make any necessary changes before resending the message.

CHAPTER 3: SENDING E-MAIL

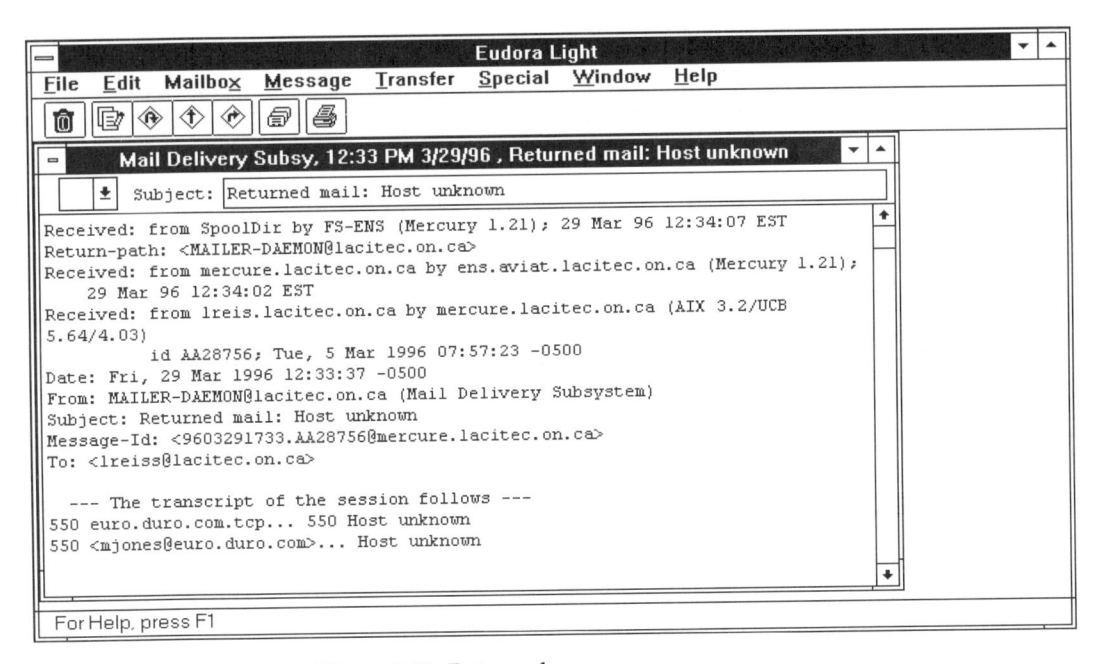

```
-                          Eudora Light                            ▼ ▲
File  Edit  Mailbox  Message  Transfer  Special  Window  Help
[toolbar icons]
-      Mail Delivery Subsy, 12:33 PM 3/29/96 , Returned mail: Host unknown    ▼
          ↓   Subject: Returned mail: Host unknown
Received: from SpoolDir by FS-ENS (Mercury 1.21); 29 Mar 96 12:34:07 EST
Return-path: <MAILER-DAEMON@lacitec.on.ca>
Received: from mercure.lacitec.on.ca by ens.aviat.lacitec.on.ca (Mercury 1.21);
    29 Mar 96 12:34:02 EST
Received: from lreis.lacitec.on.ca by mercure.lacitec.on.ca (AIX 3.2/UCB
5.64/4.03)
          id AA28756; Tue, 5 Mar 1996 07:57:23 -0500
Date: Fri, 29 Mar 1996 12:33:37 -0500
From: MAILER-DAEMON@lacitec.on.ca (Mail Delivery Subsystem)
Subject: Returned mail: Host unknown
Message-Id: <9603291733.AA28756@mercure.lacitec.on.ca>
To: <lreiss@lacitec.on.ca>

   --- The transcript of the session follows ---
550 euro.duro.com.tcp... 550 Host unknown
550 <mjones@euro.duro.com>... Host unknown

For Help, press F1
```

Figure 3-11. Returned message.

MESSAGE PRIORITIES

Eudora message priorities are for reference purposes only and do not affect how it actually handles messages. Five priority levels are available, ranging from 1 (highest) to 5 (lowest). Priorities appear in the second column of the message summary using the following symbols:

    ^^   Highest priority

    ^   High priority

    <blank> Normal priority

63

v   Low priority

v̌   Lowest priority

New messages are usually created with normal priority. To change a message's priority, select the desired priority from the Priority combo box located in the message composition window's icon bar. Alternatively, select one or more message summaries, hold down the CTRL key and press a number key from 1 (highest priority) to 5 (lowest priority). When you send mail with a priority other than normal, Eudora adds an X-Priority: header showing the message priority.

Note: Only Eudora users will see your message priorities. This may be a good reason for them to switch to Eudora.

CREATING A SIGNATURE FILE

A *signature* is a brief message that Eudora can automatically add to the end of outgoing messages. A signature contains the sender's full name and e-mail address and may include other information such as a telephone number and postal address. Signatures personalize your e-mail.

Tip: Don't go overboard creating a long message. What you may find clever, others may find a waste of time.

Create a signature by selecting the **Signature** command in the **Window** menu. Then enter your signature text in the ensuing blank Signature window as shown in Figure 3-12. Close the window, saving the changes. You can modify this file as desired.

CHAPTER 3: SENDING E-MAIL

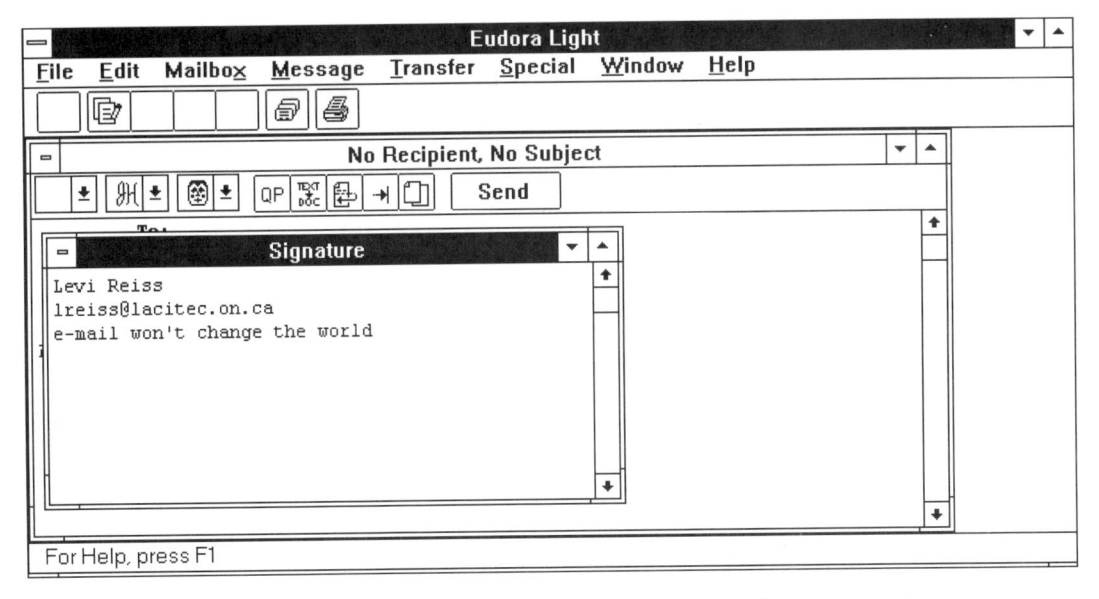

Figure 3-12. Create a signature to personalize you e-mail.

To sign an outgoing message, click on the Signature icon in the icon bar.

Note: You can't see the signature in your outgoing message, but your recipients will.

SENDING MAIL SETTINGS

The Sending Mail Settings window shown in Figure 3-13 determines how Eudora sends your outgoing mail messages. The default values of individual settings appear in brackets in the discussion below. Access these settings via the **Settings** command in the **Special** menu.

THE EUDORA USER'S GUIDE

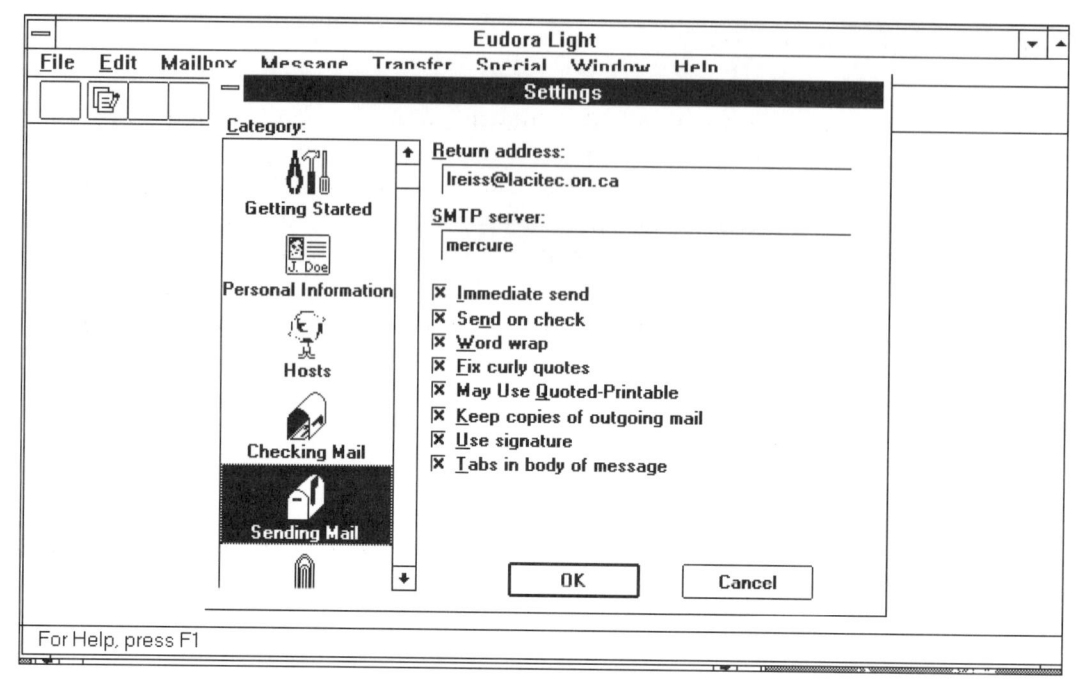

Figure 3-13. The Sending Mail Settings window.

Return address: [none]

If you wish to receive returned mail at an address other than your POP account, enter it here. Of course, try sending mail to this address before specifying it. Otherwise, you may find that nobody sends you mail.

SMTP server: [none]

Specify the name of the computer to use as your SMTP server. If this field is blank, Eudora uses your POP server as your SMTP server.

Immediate send [on]

When this box contains an ✘, the Send button appears at the right of the icon bar of the message composition window. Clicking the Send button sends the message immediately to the SMTP server. When this box is blank, the Queue button appears at the right of the icon bar of the message composition window. Clicking the Queue button places the message in the Out Mailbox, with a Q in the first column of the message summary.

Send on check [on]

When this box contains an ✘, every time that Eudora checks the POP server for new mail, it automatically sends all messages queued in the Out Mailbox.

Word wrap [on]

When this box contains an ✘, Eudora automatically wraps text to the next line with line breaks occurring at approximately 76 characters per line. This selection makes your mail more legible to recipients using line-oriented mail systems. You should keep this option on.

Fix curly quotes [on]

When this box contains an ✘, Eudora replaces all "smart" quotation marks in message text or attachments with "conventional" quotation marks before transmission. This option allows messages to be sent without using quoted-printable encoding. It is not required when corresponding with people who have MIME encoding.

May Use Quoted-Printable [on]

When this box contains an **x**, Eudora uses quoted-printable encoding if necessary; for example, when sending messages containing special characters or long lines of text. When this box is blank, quoted-printable encoding is not used.

Keep copies of outgoing mail [on]

When this box contains an **x**, a copy of each sent message is kept in the Out Mailbox, with an S in the first column of their message summaries. If this box is blank, Eudora places the copies in the Trash Mailbox after sending messages.

Use signature [on]

When this box contains an **x**, Eudora automatically appends an existing signature file to the end of outgoing messages. Signatures are used to personalize your messages.

Tabs in body of message [on]

When this box contains an **x**, pressing the TAB key anywhere in the message body inserts tabs. When this box is blank, pressing the TAB key places the cursor at the To: message header field.

RECEIVING E-MAIL

Now you know the ins and outs of sending mail. In this chapter, you'll complete your knowledge of receiving mail. Of course, before you process received mail, you must know whether you have any mail. Then you'll see how to create and process mailboxes and folders to handle large volumes of mail. Which letters are interesting? Eudora provides several features for locating desired text within you mail. Part of mail processing is sorting your messages in virtually any desired order. The chapter examines the Checking Mail and Getting Attention settings that let you customize Eudora to meet many of your message-processing needs and concludes by telling you how to receive attachments.

CHECKING FOR AND RECEIVING MAIL

You receive your mail on the POP server whose address you specify in the Getting Started Settings dialog box. The mail is stored there until you transfer it to Eudora running on your computer. You must specify your POP server password before you can check for mail, either automatically or manually, as described next.

AUTOMATIC CHECKING

Eudora can automatically check for mail at a frequency that you specify. First select the **Settings** command in the **Special** menu. Then select the "Checking Mail" option and enter a value such as 15 in the Check for mail every ? minute(s) field, as shown in Figure 4-1. This directs Eudora to check for mail every 15 minutes even if you are running other applications.

Tip: Do not choose a value less than 15 minutes. You need to avoid placing too great a load on your POP server and the system in general.

Note: When automatic checking is turned on, the **Check Mail** *option of the* **File** *menu displays the next time that an automatic check is scheduled to occur.*

CHAPTER 4: RECEIVING E-MAIL

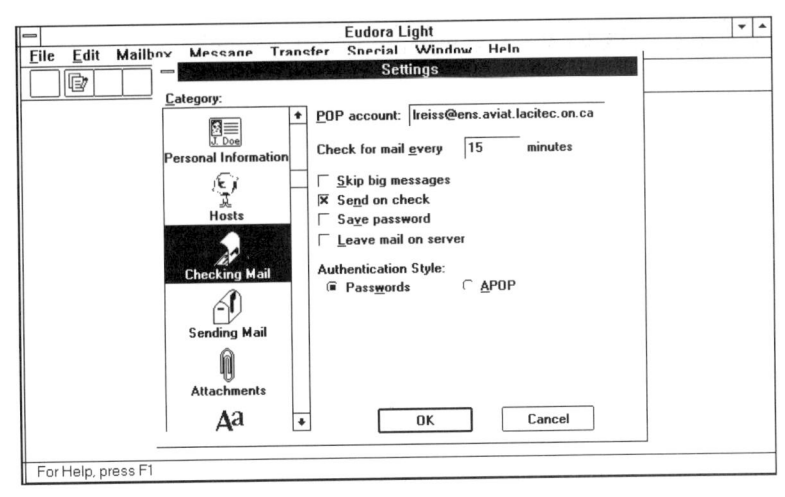

Figure 4-1. Setting Eudora to check for mail automatically every 15 minutes.

How does Eudora notify you of new mail? You decide by selecting one or more of the following Eudora actions: opening the In Mailbox, making a special sound, or generating an alert dialog from the Getting Attention Settings dialog box. Recall from Chapter 2 that if Eudora has been minimized into an icon, the icon image indicates when you have new mail. The New Mail! window is shown in figure 4-2.

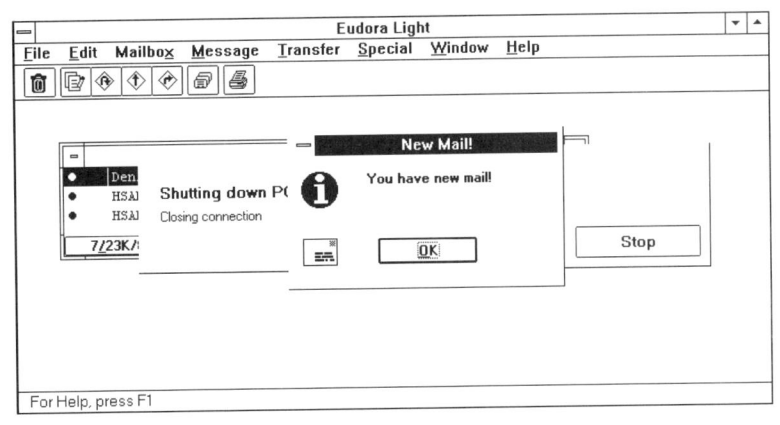

Figure 4-2. New Mail! dialog box.

71

At any time you can use one of the following methods to activate Eudora to read you new mail: double-click on the Eudora icon, select it from the task list, or pressing the ALT + TAB keys.

Tip: Save yourself time by not activating Eudora whenever new mail arrives.

Usually you'll get your mail in the In Mailbox which lists message summaries in the order of arrival. Look for your latest message at the bottom of the mailbox. Open the In Mailbox by selecting **In** from the **Mailbox** menu. A bullet (•) in the first column of the message summary indicates that the message has not been read. Open a message by double-clicking on its message summary. The In Mailbox holds incoming messages until they are deleted or transferred to another mailbox or folder.

MANUAL CHECKING

No matter what value, if any, you have chosen for the frequency of automatic mail checking, you can always check for mail manually by selecting **Check Mail** from the **File** menu. The first time you check for mail after launching Eudora, the system asks for your POP server password, which may or may not be your regular password. If your password is accepted, a progress window lets you know what's happening with the mail check.

If you are unable to access the POP server, an error message is displayed, such as that shown in Figure 4-3. Verify the POP server field in the Getting Started Settings dialog box. You may have to contact your Eudora system administrator.

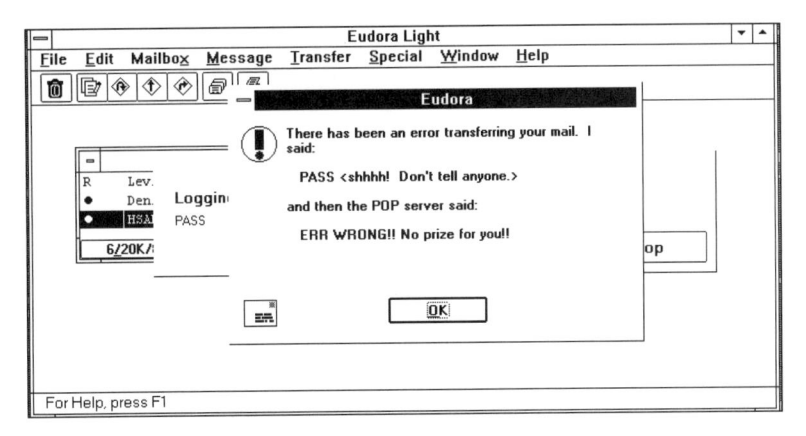

Figure 4-3. Eudora error message.

LEAVE MAIL ON SERVER OPTION

After checking the mail, Eudora normally transfers your incoming messages from the POP server to your computer and then deletes them from the POP server. This is usually a good policy. But what if you get your mail via two or more computers? Suppose that on Monday you are in the office and access your mail from your desktop computer but on Tuesday you are on the road and access your mail from that brand-new laptop. On Wednesday you certainly don't want to check both computers to review your mail. You don't have to.

To avoid this problem when using your secondary computer, let's say the desktop computer, select the "Leave mail on server" option in the Checking Mail Settings dialog box. This directs Eudora to keep copies of messages in your POP server account as well as transfer them to the desktop.

The next time you check your mail from the desktop, Eudora transfers only new mail.

When using your laptop computer, turn off the "Leave mail on server" option in the Checking Mail Settings dialog box. This directs Eudora to transfer all your messages from your POP server to the laptop.

Warning: Don't leave too much mail on the POP server, or you may overload it.

SKIP BIG MESSAGES OPTION

It doesn't matter how fast your hookup is, sometimes message transfer is extremely slow, especially if you are in a hurry. Perhaps you have a very chatty correspondent. You don't have to stop everything to download big files, (in this case, over 40 K). Simply turn on the "Skip big messages" option in the Checking Mail Settings dialog box. Eudora then transfers only the first few lines of the message and informs you that the entire message was not downloaded. Use this option when you are in a hurry or when the system is running slowly. If and when you decide that you want the entire message, turn off the "Skip big messages" option in the Checking Mail Settings dialog box, and check your mail again.

Tip: You can always abort a mail check by clicking on the Stop button in the progress window or by pressing the Esc key.

MAILBOXES AND FOLDERS

Do you put all of your snail mail (post office variety) in the same storage area? Of course you don't. You don't have to put all your e-mail in a single storage area either. Eudora provides standard In, Out, and Trash Mailboxes. In addition, it allows you to create mailboxes for mail storage. For example, you can create a mailbox to store e-mail from a given individual. When the number of mailboxes gets out of hand, you can create folders for storing related mailboxes.

For example, let's say that you are promoting a chocolate novelty item to candy stores in your spare time. Why not create a mailbox for the correspondence associated with each prospective client? Some mailboxes would contain a single item, your initial proposal. Others would contain several messages, documenting the ongoing correspondence between you and potential customers. When the candy correspondence becomes sizable, consider creating a special candy sales folder containing all relevant mailboxes. Then, when you need to check correspondence with your dentist, or your golf partner, you can skip the candy mail folder. Let's look at how you can use Eudora to create, delete, move, and rename mailboxes and folders.

CREATING A MAILBOX

Create a new mailbox by selecting the **New** command from the **Mailbox** menu. This displays the New Mailbox dialog box shown in Figure 4-4. Enter the new mailbox name (in our case SweetTooth Inc.) and click on OK. The new mailbox is added to the **Mailbox** and **Transfer** menus, as shown in Figure 4-5. Alternatively, you may use the **Mailboxes command** of the **Window** menu to create mailboxes. Do not add any mailboxes to the chocolates folder at this time.

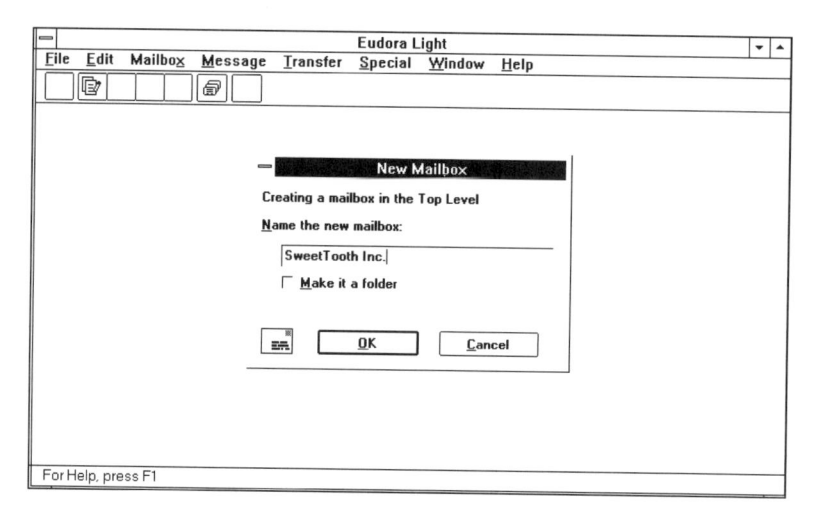

Figure 4-4. New Mailbox dialog box.

Tip: Use this method to create several mailboxes in one sitting.

CREATING MAIL FOLDERS

Select the **New** command from the **Mailbox** menu to create a new mail folder. This displays the New Mailbox dialog box shown in Figure 4-4. This time type the name of the new mail folder (in our case Chocolates), check the Make it a Folder option, and click on OK to confirm.

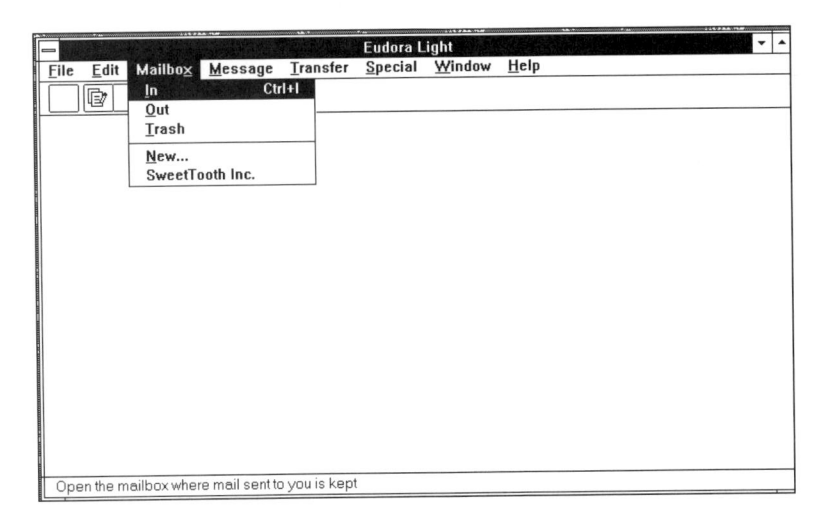

Figure 4-5. The **Mailbox** menu.

The new folder name appears at the end of the mailbox/folder name list in the **Mailbox** and **Transfer** menus, as shown in Figure 4-6. You can tell it's a folder by the arrow to the right of its name. The New Mailbox window appears again. Add a mailbox to this folder now or later, pressing the OK button to confirm. Let's add another top-level mailbox, Chic-choco. Once again, the new mailbox is added to the **Mailbox** and **Transfer** menus.

Alternatively, you may create subfolders by checking the "Make it a Folder" option.

Warning: You cannot transfer mail directly into folders. You must specify the appropriate mailbox.

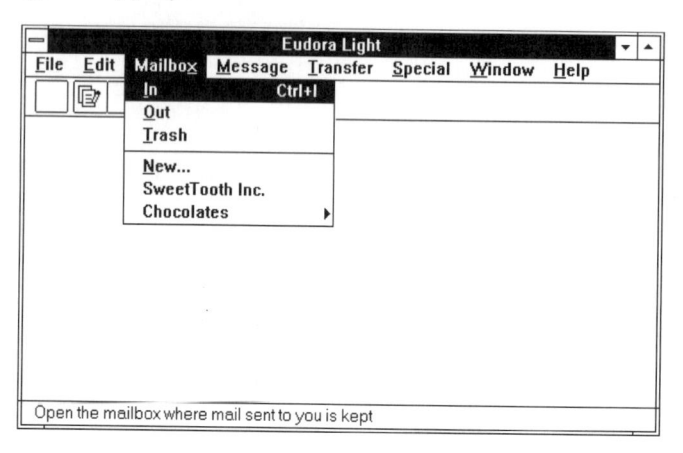

Figure 4-6. The **Mailbox** menu showing a new folder.

OPENING A MAILBOX

Open a mailbox by selecting it from the **Mailbox** menu. If the mailbox is inside a folder, you must first select the folder (from the **Mailbox** menu) and then select the mailbox. Folders may be nested several layers deep.

The Mailbox window title bar displays the mailbox name. As was the case for the In and Out mailboxes, one-line message summaries represent individual messages. Select a message by clicking on its summary. There are several ways to select multiple messages. These methods include:

- dragging the mouse pointer across several summaries,

- clicking on one summary; holding down the SHIFT key, and clicking on another summary to select both these message summaries and all message summaries in between them

- holding down the CTRL key and selecting individual summaries in any order.

Message summaries contain six columns: Status (S), Priority (P), Sender (Who), Date, Size (K), and Subject as shown in Figure 4-7.

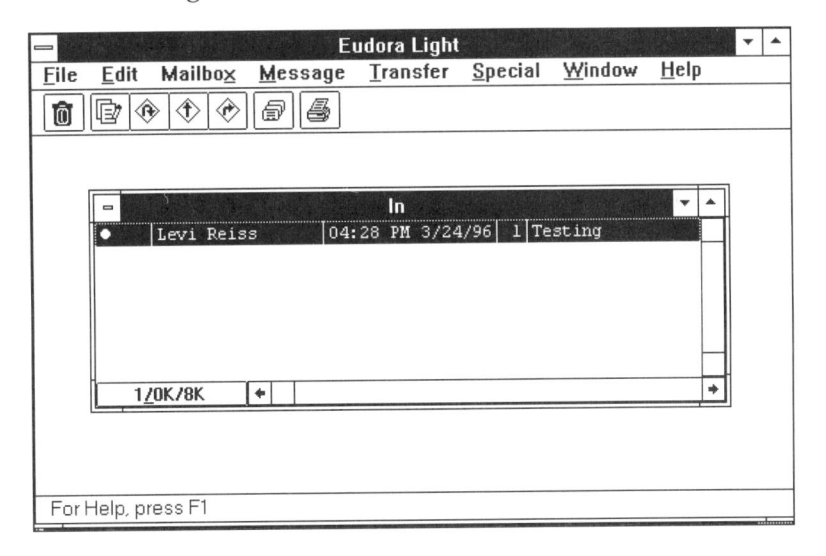

Figure 4-7. Message summary.

The first column, Status, displays the message status, which can be any of the following:

- An unread message, except for the Out Mailbox where it indicates that the message could be queued, but has not been queued.

<blank> A read message, except for the Out Mailbox where it indicates that the message has not yet been queued because it has no recipients.

R   The user has replied to this message.

F   The user has forwarded this message.

D   The user has redirected this message.

S   This outgoing message has been sent.

-   This message was transferred from the Out Mailbox before it was sent.

The second column, Priority, displays the message priority, which is *one* of the following:

$\hat{\wedge}$ Highest priority.

$\wedge$ High priority.

<blank> Normal priority.

$\vee$ Low priority.

$\check{\vee}$ Lowest priority.

Recall that Eudora message priorities are for reference purposes only and do not affect actual message handling. See Chapter 3 for more information about message priorities.

The third column, Sender, shows the sender of incoming messages or the recipient of outgoing messages.

Warning: Bugs in some POP servers/mail transport systems cause Eudora to display the sender of incoming messages as ???@???. This error occurs because the required From: header is missing.

The fourth column, Date, displays the date and time that the message was sent or is scheduled to be sent. The fifth column, Size, displays the size of the message in kilobytes (1K = 1024 bytes). The sixth column, Subject, displays the message subject. While the sender usually enters this value in the Subject: message header field, you can modify it if you so choose.

INCOMING MESSAGE WINDOW

Open a message by double-clicking on its message summary. Press the ENTER key to open the message whose message summary is highlighted. Either method displays the incoming message window shown in Figure 4-8. Message window components are discussed next.

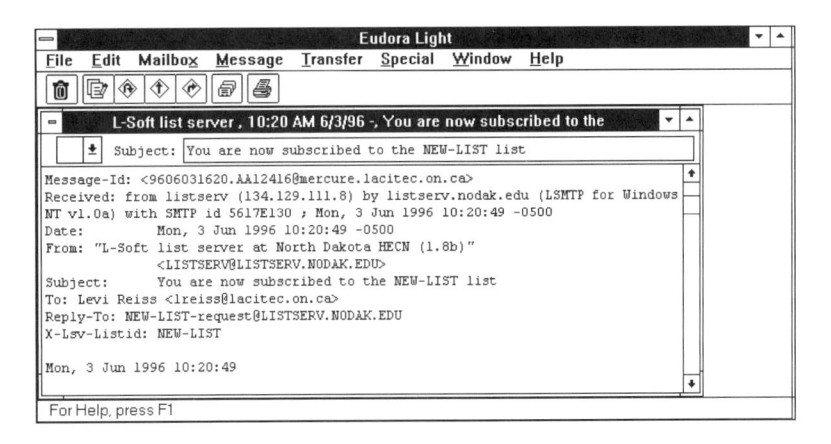

Figure 4-8. Incoming message window.

Title Bar

The title bar displays the sender's name, the time and date of message delivery, and the message subject.

Icon Bar

The icon bar contains the priority popup combo box and the subject text box:

Priority Popup

Most messages have normal priority, denoted by a blank field. Use this combo box to change the priority. Message priorities are discussed in detail in Chapter 3.

Subject

This text box contains the message subject specified by the sender. You can modify the subject if you wish.

Message Body

The message body contains the message header, text, and descriptions of attachments, if any. Double-click on the attachment title to open the attachment.

MESSAGE DELETION

Eudora helps protect against accidental deletions by requiring a two-step deletion process. After selecting the message(s), choose the **Delete** command from the **Message** menu. This step transfers the message(s) to the Trash Mailbox. Then select the **Empty Trash** command from the **Special** menu to delete the selected message(s). If you turn on the "Empty Trash when exiting" option in the Miscellaneous Settings dialog box, exiting Eudora deletes all messages in the Trash mailbox. To delete selected messages from the Trash mailbox, highlight them and select the **Delete** command from the **Message** menu or press the Trash button on the toolbar.

Warning: Deleting a message from the Trash Mailbox permanently eliminates it; there is no associated Undo command.

Another way to reduce the likelihood of accidental deletions is to turn on the "Require confirmation for deletes" option in the Miscellaneous Settings dialog box. Then, if you attempt to delete a never-opened message or an unsent queued message, Eudora asks for confirmation before deleting it, as shown in Figure 4-9.

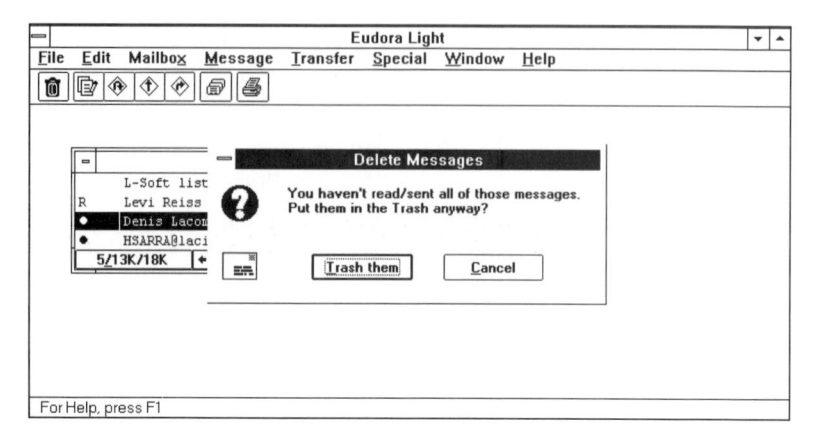

Figure 4-9. Dialog box requesting confirmation before message deletion.

COMPACTING MAILBOXES: RECOVERING STORAGE SPACE

Eudora does not immediately recover the storage space associated with deleted messages. It compacts a mailbox on closing only if one or both the following conditions are met:

(1) The mailbox's wasted space exceeds the space used by active messages in the mailbox.

(2) The wasted space in the mailbox exceeds 5 percent of the free space on its disk drive.

You don't have to wait for Eudora; you can reclaim the wasted space from all mailboxes by selecting the **Compact Mailboxes** command in the **Special** menu.

Tip: Compact individual mailboxes by pressing the Mailbox Size button in the lower left corner of the mailbox window.

FINDING TEXT WITHIN MESSAGES

Who can remember where all their mail is? Try as you might, you can't remember which letter or letters had the price quote on 200 chocolate novelty items. No need to worry or carry out a manual search that could take hours. Just specify the distinguishing word or characters and try the following procedures. First select a message then click on **Find** on the **Edit** menu to display the **Find** command shown in Figure 4-10.

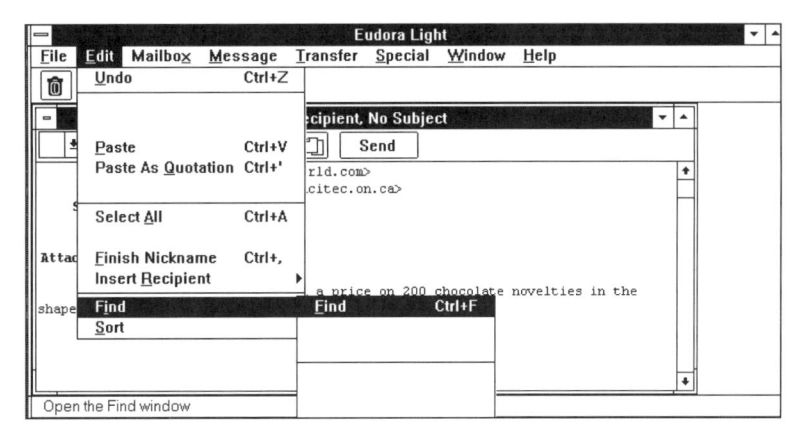

Figure 4-10. The Find Command

THE EUDORA USER'S GUIDE

FINDING TEXT WITHIN ONE MESSAGE

To locate text within a single message, click the "Find" option and enter at the blinking insertion point the characters you are looking for, in this case 200 as shown in Figure 4-11. Then click the Find button. Eudora searches the message for the specified text. Eudora highlights the first occurrence of the text as shown in Figure 4-12. If Eudora doesn't find the text, it displays a results such as that shown in Figure 4-13.

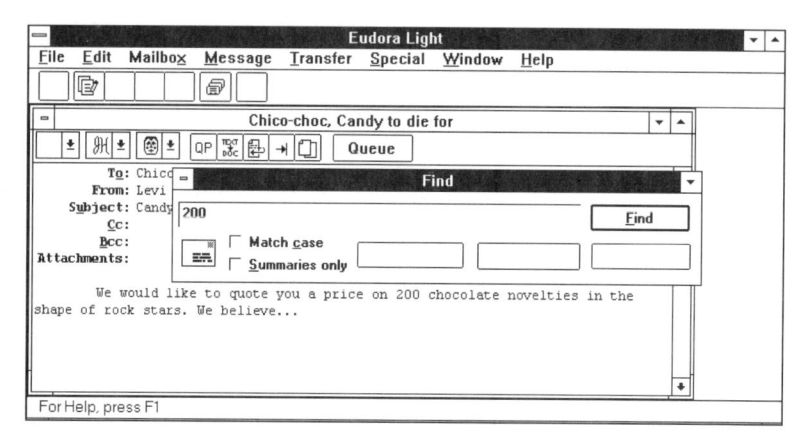

Figure 4-11. The Find dialog box.

There may be several occurrences of the text within a given message. To continue the search within the initial message, click the Find button in the Find dialog box, or select the **Find Again** command in the **Find** submenu. Of course, you need not limit your search to a single message. The following procedures show you how to search multiple messages or even multiple mailboxes.

CHAPTER 4: RECEIVING E-MAIL

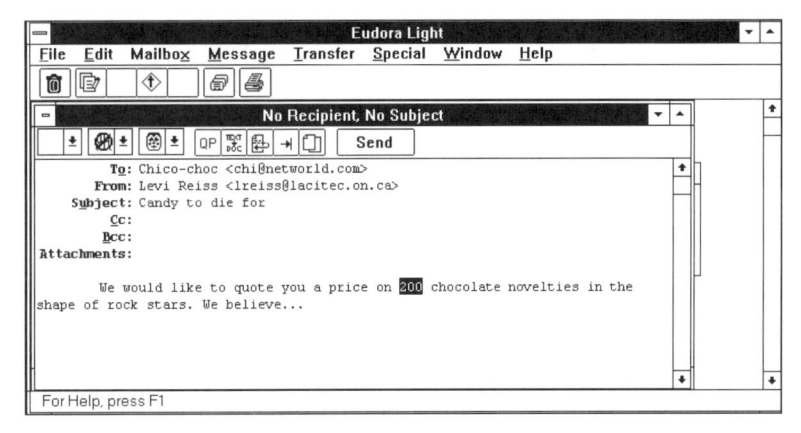

Figure 4-12. Eudora highlighted the first occurrence of the text to be found.

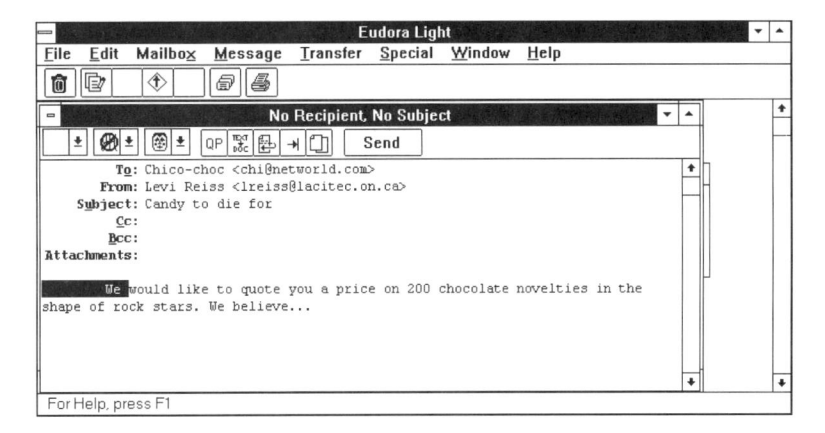

Figure 4-13. Eudora couldn't find the specified text (such as 2000).

87

FINDING TEXT AMONG MULTIPLE MESSAGES AND MAILBOXES

The Find submenu includes the **Next**, **Next Message**, and **Next Mailbox** commands. These functions are also available as buttons in the **Find** dialog box as seen by examining Figure 4-11 closely.

Next

The Next button (or **Find** submenu option **Next** command) searches the current mailbox for the next match of the specified text. The search starts with with the first message.

Next Message

The Next Message button (or **Find** submenu option **Next message** command) searches for the specified text, starting with the message after the current message. The search can continue across all mailboxes.

Next Mailbox

The Next Mailbox button (or **Find** submenu option **Next Mailbox** command) searches for the specified text, starting with the mailbox following the current mailbox. The search continues across all subsequent mailboxes, including the In, Out, and Trash Mailboxes. Mailboxes are searched in the order that they are listed in the **Mailbox** menu. The current mailbox is not searched.

MATCH CASE

Unless otherwise directed, Eudora ignores capitalization when searching for text. Usually it considers 200 chocolate novelties and 200 Chocolate Novelties to be the same. "Check the Match Case" option in the Find dialog box to force Eudora to consider capitalization, in other words to distinguish between 200 chocolate novelties and 200 Chocolate Novelties, perhaps finding one and not the other.

SUMMARIES ONLY

Clicking on this option restricts the search to message summaries. In other words, for a hit the searched text must appear in the message summary Sender: or Subject: fields. Such searches are considerably faster than regular searches.

ENTER SELECTION COMMAND

To avoid typing the search text into the Find dialog box, highlight this text in an existing message, then specify the **Enter Selection** command in the **Find** submenu. Doing so automatically inserts the selected text into the Find dialog box. Start the search by selecting the **Find** option in the **Find** submenu.

STOPPING A SEARCH

You don't have to carry out a search to the bitter end. Sometimes a search takes too long, or perhaps you changed your mind about that particular search. For example, you may remember that you and your correspondents never talked about 200 chocolate novelties. To abort a search, click the Stop button in the progress window or press the Esc key.

SORTING MESSAGES WITHIN MAILBOXES

You can sort the message summaries within a mailbox window in the order of the contents of any of the six message summary columns. First open the mailbox to sort, and then select the desired command from the **Sort** submenu of the **Edit** menu, as shown in Figure 4-14. Releasing the mouse button sorts the message summaries in ascending order, in other words from smallest to largest or first to last. To reverse the sort order (descending order), press the SHIFT key during the sort.

You can sort on multiple columns. For example, to sort messages by sender, and for each sender sorted by date; first select **Sort by Sender**, and then select **Sort by Date**.

Warning: Eudora does not always sort by date properly. This error can be caused by incorrectly formatted date fields or unknown or incorrect time zones. Because Eudora uses

Greenwich Mean Time (GMT) when sorting by date, the messages may only look out of order because the time stamp shows local time where the message originated. For example, a message sent at 9:15 EST is listed before a message sent at 9:00 CST, because 9:15 EST occurs prior to 9:00 CST.

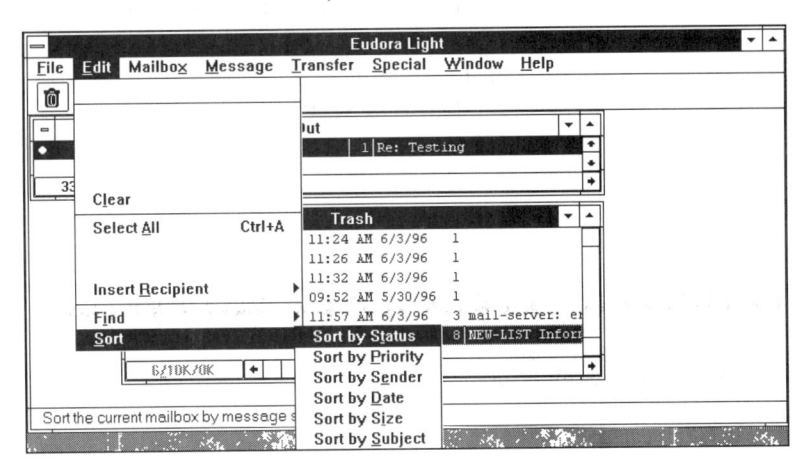

Figure 4-14. Use the **Sort** submenu to choose a sorting method for the message summaries in a mailbox window.

SAVING MESSAGES IN FILES

You should make a habit of saving messages in separate files. To do so first display the message or highlight its message summary. Then select the **Save As** command in the **File** menu to display the Save As dialog box as shown in Figure 4-15. Click on the OK button to confirm.

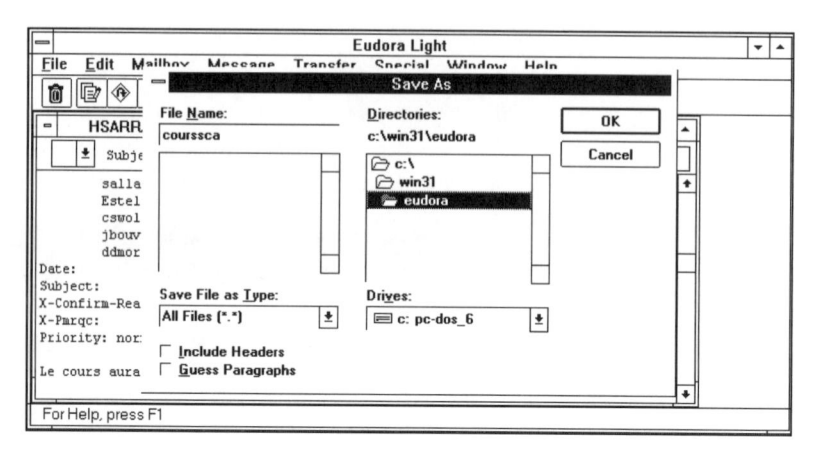

Figure 4-15. The Save As window.

The Eudora Save As dialog box resembles a standard Windows Save As dialog box except for the two check boxes in the lower left corner. The Include Headers box keeps message header information in the saved document. The Guess Paragraphs box directs Eudora to remove unnecessary ENTER key codes from the message, and only keep the ones at the end of each paragraph. As the box name indicates, Eudora can only guess where one paragraph ends and another begins.

*Note: The **Save As** command of the **File** menu can also save multiple messages to a single file. First select multiple messages, and then proceed as before. Eudora breaks up very large messages from the POP server into many smaller messages. Use this method to reconstitute the original message.*

CHECKING MAIL SETTINGS

The Checking Mail Settings box shown in Figure 4-16 controls how Eudora checks for and receives your incoming mail messages.

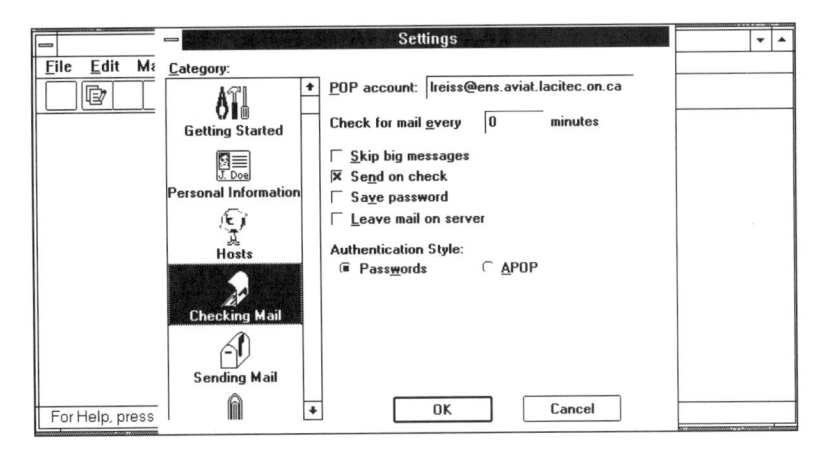

Figure 4-16. Checking Mail Settings window.

POP account: [none]

This text box contains your POP account address.

Check for mail every ? minute(s) [0]

This numeric field specifies the frequency at which Eudora checks your POP server for new mail and transfers new mail to your computer. Avoid overloading your POP server by specifying a value of at least 15 minutes between checks. If Eudora is not running at the scheduled check time, it checks for mail the next time it runs. A 0 value disables automatic checking.

Skip big messages [off]

If this box contains an **x**, Eudora downloads only the first few lines of messages larger than 40 K. Doing so may reduce transmission time considerably. If you want the entire message, turn off the Skip big messages option in the Checking Mail Settings dialog box, and check your mail again.

Send on check [on]

If this box contains an **x**, whenever Eudora checks the POP server for new mail, it automatically transmits all messages queued in the Out mailbox.

Save password [off]

If this box contains an **x**, your password is stored on the computer and need not be entered to check your mail. Don't use this option unless you know your computer is secure.

Leave mail on server [off]

If this box contains an **x**, Eudora saves your mail on the POP server and transfers it to your computer. Use this option if you employ two or more computers to get your mail. Otherwise Eudora deletes your messages from the POP server after sending them.

Authentication Style [Passwords]

Eudora supports two network authentication technologies: Passwords and APOP. Ask your e-mail administrator which one your site uses.

GETTING ATTENTION SETTINGS

The Getting Attention Settings window, shown in Figure 4-17, controls how Eudora informs you when new mail arrives.

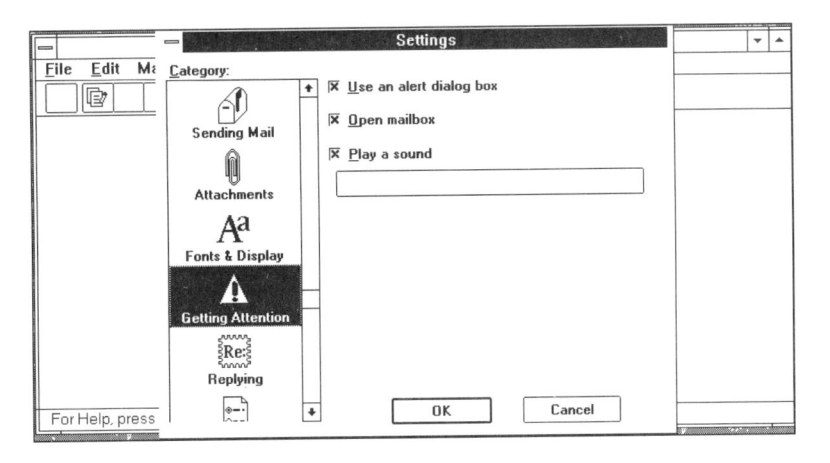

Figure 4-17. The Getting Attention Settings window.

Use an alert dialog box [on]

If this box contains an **x**, Eudora informs you of new mail via an alert dialog box.

Open mailbox [on]

If this box contains an **x**, Eudora automatically opens mailboxes when new mail arrives. It places the mail in the mailbox, scrolls to the end of the mailboxes, and selects the first unread mail message within the last unread group of mail messages. This is not necessarily a new message.

Play a sound [on]

If this box contains an **x**, Eudora makes a sound to announce new mail arrival. Select the sound (*.wav) file by clicking on the field below the "Play a sound" option to display the Select sound file dialog box shown in Figure 4-18.

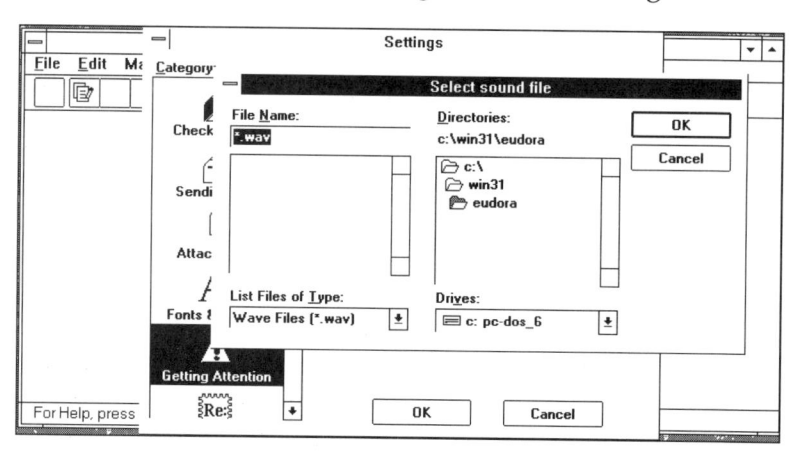

Figure 4-18. The Select sound file dialog box.

RECEIVING AN ATTACHMENT

Attachments are automatically decoded and placed in your Eudora directory upon receipt unless you specify an attachment directory in the Attachments Settings dialog box. To do so, select the **Settings** command from the **Special** menu and select the **Attachments** settings. Then click on the Attachment Directory button to display the Select a directory dialog box, as shown in Figure 4-19. Next, double-click on a directory name to select it, displaying its name above the list. Confirm by clicking the Use Directory button, which closes the dialog box. The selected directory name appears on the Attachment Directory button, as shown in Figure 4-20. To change the Attachment Directory, click on this button to redisplay the dialog box.

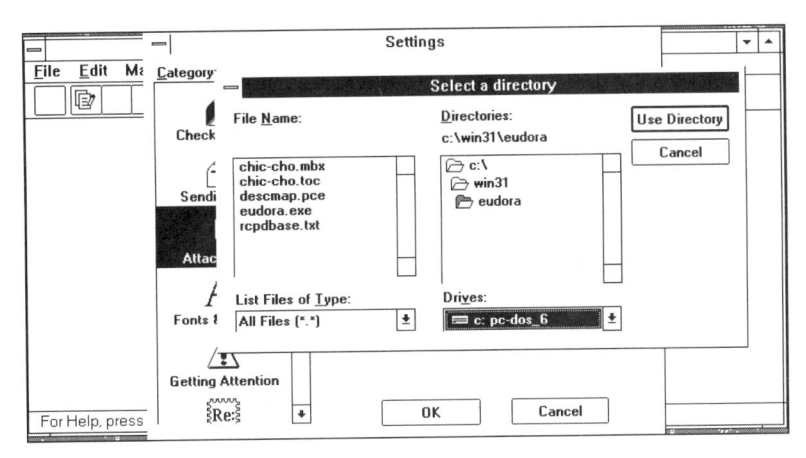

Figure 4-19. The Select a directory dialog box to use when receiving attachments.

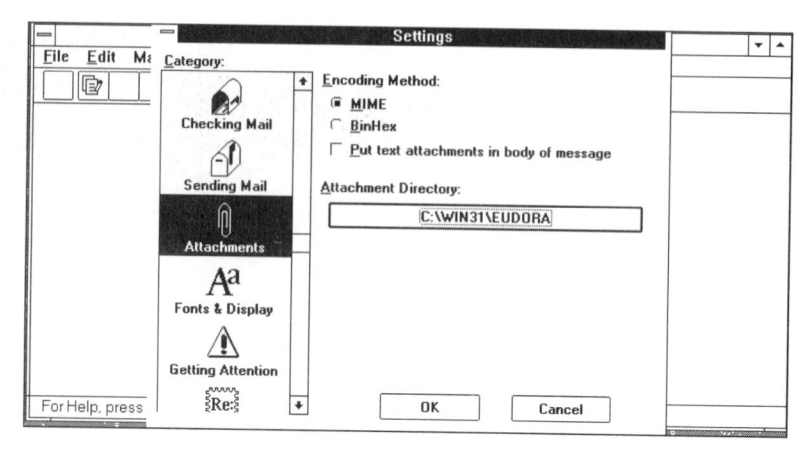

Figure 4-20. The Attachment Settings dialog box showing the Attachent Directroy.

Eudora automatically decodes attachments and saves them in the Attachment directory. The attachments name is recorded in the accompanying message. Multiple attachments with the same name are distinguished by a number appended to the end of the attachment's name.

NON-EUDORA USERS RECEIVING ATTACHMENTS

If you send an attachment to someone using an e-mail package other than Eudora, the attached file is included at the end of the message in either MIME or Bin Hex format, depending on your encoding specification. The recipient must decode it before use.

ANSWERING E-MAIL

Now you know the ins and outs of receiving mail. In this chapter, you'll complete your knowledge of what to do with the mail you have received. You can put this mail in a mailbox, even one that you create on the fly. You'll see Eudora's rich facilities for creating and processing mailboxes, and groups of mailboxes known as folders. After digesting mailbox processing, you'll see how you can reply to, forward, or redirect messages. The chapter concludes with a look at the message reply settings.

TRANSFERRING A MESSAGE TO A DIFFERENT MAILBOX

Mail isn't always in the mailbox you want. It's fairly easy to transfer messages from one mailbox to another. First select the message, and then specify the receiving mailbox via the **Transfer** menu. To copy the message instead of transferring it, press the SHIFT key during the message transfer.

Warning: Don't overdo message copying or you'll have storage and message management problems. Just think how hard your snail mail would be to manage if you could copy it at will.

CREATING A MAILBOX DURING TRANSFER

Interestingly enough, a mailbox does not have to exist for it to receive mail. You can create the mailbox at the beginning of message transfer. To do so, specify the **New** command in the **Transfer** menu. Figure 5-1 shows the New Mailbox dialog box. As its name indicates, this dialog box creates a new mailbox. It is not necessary to transfer any mail at this time. You just select the "Don't transfer, just create mailbox" option. Chapter 4 presented alternative mailbox creation procedures using the **Mailbox** menu or the Mailboxes dialog box in the **Window** menu.

Tip: Use the Mailboxes window to create several mailboxes together.

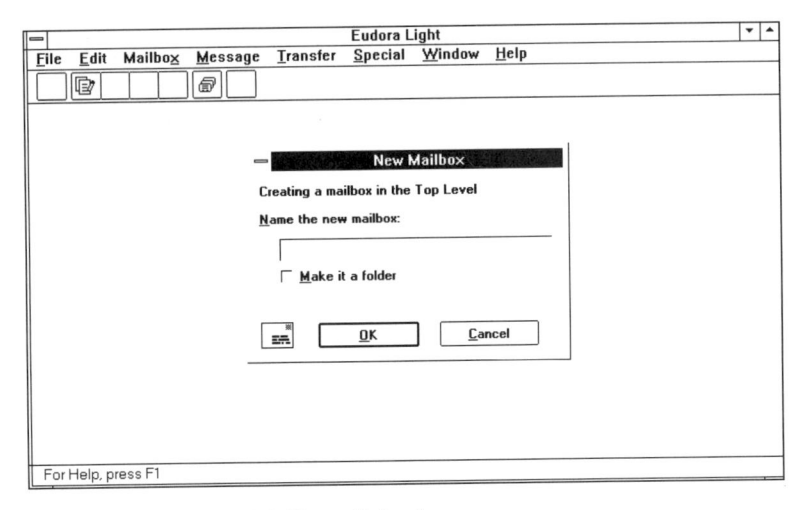

Figure 5-1. The New Mailbox dialog box.

CREATING A MAILBOX FOLDER DURING TRANSFER

As you probably remember, a folder can contain multiple mailboxes. When necessary, folders may be nested; in other words, one folder may contain subfolders, which in turn contain mailboxes.

As for mailboxes, you can create a folder at the beginning of message transfer. Once again, specify the **New** option in the **Transfer** menu to display the New Mailbox dialog box, previously shown in Figure 5-1. This time, enter the new mail folder name and check the "Make it a folder" option. Then click on OK to confirm.

Eudora won't let you place messages directly in folders; they must be contained in mailboxes. So you can't transfer your message until you create a mailbox to hold it. First enter the mailbox name (Candies) into the New Mailbox dialog window. Then click on OK to confirm. Figure 5-2 shows the mailbox name list associated with the **Mailbox** and **Transfer** menus. Note that the new folder name appears after the mailboxes but before any existing folders. As discussed in Chapter 4, an arrow to the right of a list entry denotes a folder instead of a mailbox.

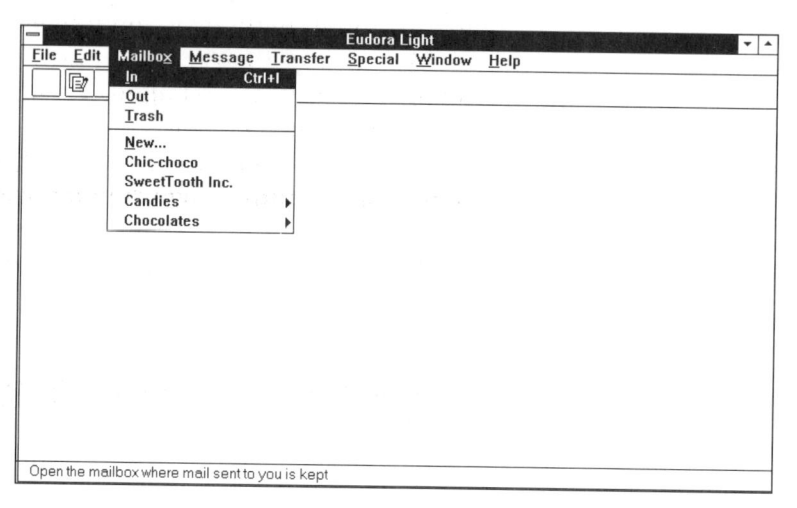

Figure 5-2. The mailbox name list associated with the **Mailbox** and **Transfer** menus.

MAILBOXES WINDOW

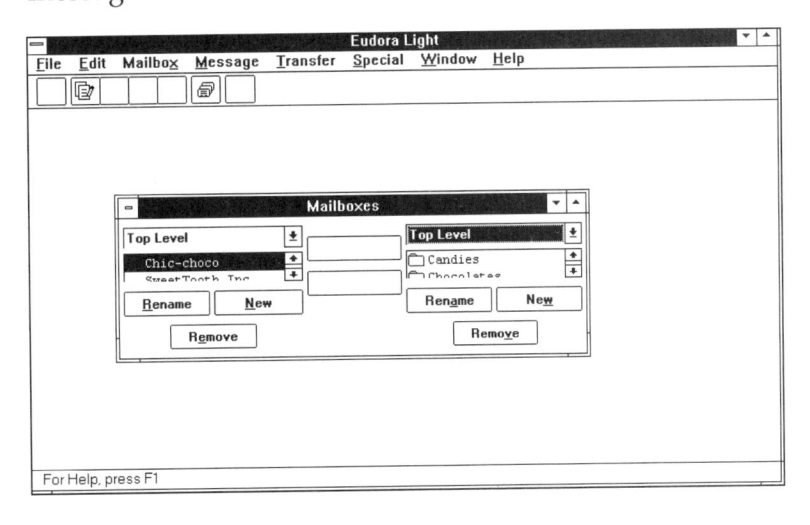

Figure 5-3 shows the **Mailboxes** window menu. Use this window to create new mailboxes and folders and to remove or rename them. This versatile window also lets you move mailboxes and folders from one folder to another.

On closer examination you see that the Mailboxes window includes two subwindows with scroll bars. These subwindows list your mailboxes and folders, identified as usual by a folder icon in their left margin. Unlike the **Mailbox** and **Transfer** menus, the Mailboxes window list does not contain the In, Out, and Trash Mailboxes. For ease of use, there are two sets of Rename, New, and Remove buttons, as well as two Move buttons, which point from one list to the other.

Double-clicking on a mailbox opens its mailbox window. Use the open mailbox window to process individual mail messages.

Figure 5-3. The Mailboxes window.

LOCATING A MAILBOX OR FOLDER

If you have many mailboxes and folders, you may need to use the scroll bar on the right side of the list to display the remaining mailboxes and folders. Double-clicking on a folder changes the list's current title to the folder name and displays the folder's mailboxes and subfolders. To go from a subfolder to the folder that contains it, select the folder from the list title popup menu.

CREATING A NEW MAILBOX OR FOLDER

You can create mailboxes and folders via the Mailboxes window as well as via the **Transfer** menu. After opening the Mailboxes window, double-click in either list on the folder that will contain the new mailbox or folder. Its name and present contents are displayed as shown in Figure 5-4.

Click on the New button to display a dialog box in which you enter the new name as shown in Figure 5-5. Because Jan's candies names a mailbox and not a folder, don't place an **x** in the "Make it a folder" option. Click on OK to confirm. The new mailbox or folder name appears in its parent folder listing and in the **Mailbox** and **Transfer** menus.

CHAPTER 5: ANSWERING E-MAIL

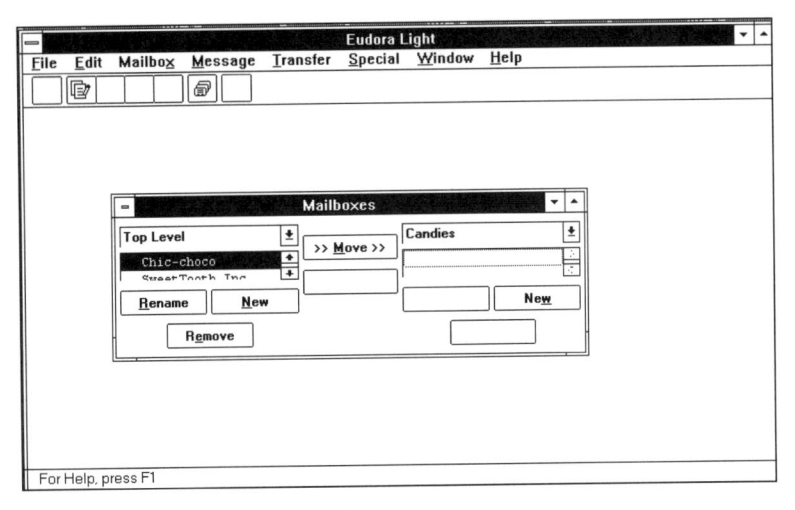

Figure 5-4. Creating a new folder.

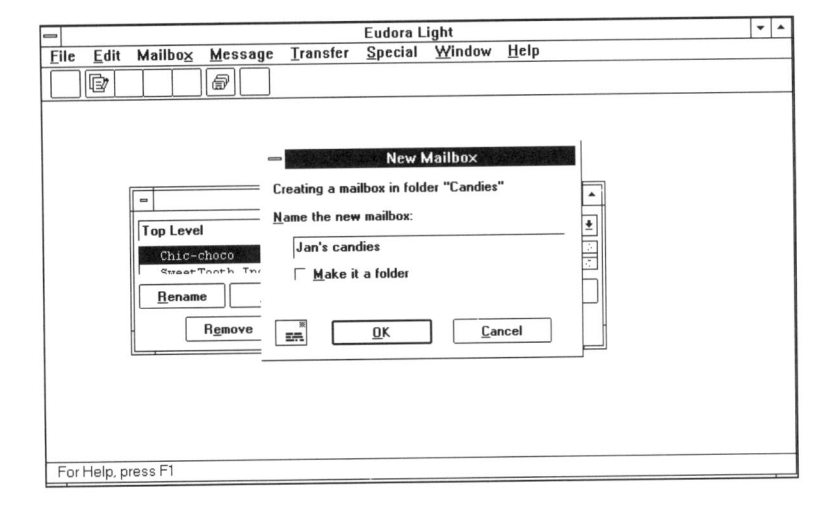

Figure 5-5. Naming a new mailbox to add to the Candies folder.

MOVING A MAILBOX FROM ONE FOLDER TO ANOTHER

One way to reorganize your mail structure is to move a mailbox from one folder to another. In this case, we'll move the Jan's candies mailbox from the Candies folder to the Chocolates folder. Although we are going from right to left, we could have moved from left to right.

You must use the Mailboxes window to change a mailbox's parent folder. First locate the mailbox to be moved in either list. Then double-click on the destination folder in the other list. This displays the destination name and contents, as shown in Figure 5-6. Select the mailbox to be moved and click on the Move button as you point from the source list to the destination list. Figure 5-7 shows the new mailbox location.

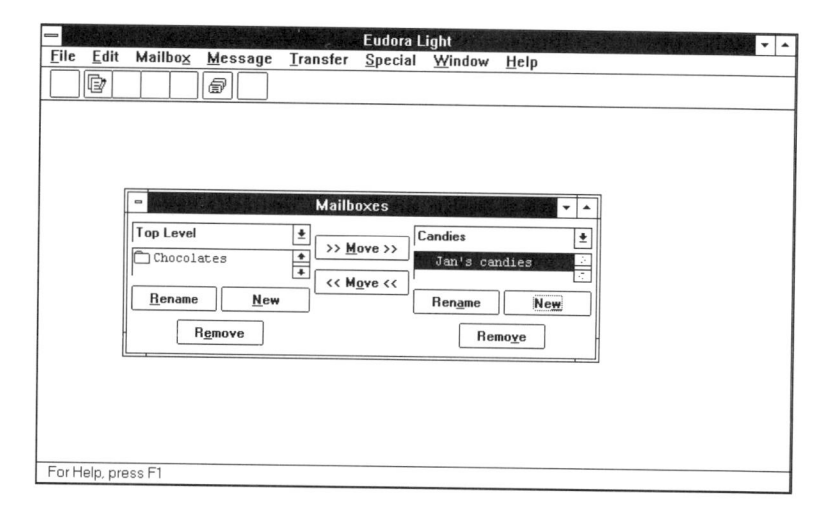

Figure 5-6. Moving a mailbox from one folder to another.

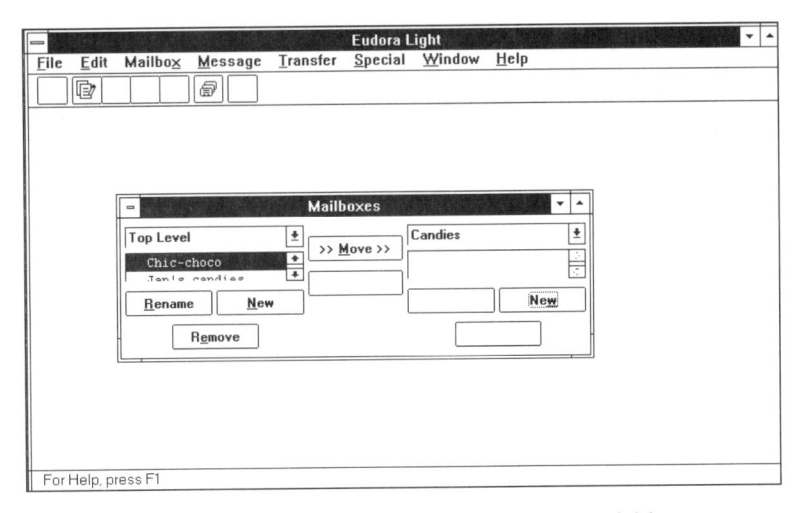

Figure 5-7. The Jan's candies mailbox is now in its new folder.

REMOVING A MAILBOX OR FOLDER

Sooner or later the folder–subfolder–mailbox population explosion will get to you and you'll want to remove mailboxes or folders. Let's remove the mailbox for Jan's candies, after putting some mail but before even reading the mail. First open the Mailboxes window, and then select from either list the objects to be removed. Then click on the Remove button under the list. If any messages remain in the mailbox, Eudora warns you by displaying a dialog box as shown in Figure 5-8. If you still want to go ahead with mailbox deletion, click on the Remove it button. To speed the deletion process, press the CTRL key while selecting several mailboxes or folders. Eudora displays the confirmation dialog box as each mailbox or folder is to be removed. If you are sure of what you are doing, click on "Remove all" to delete all the selected items immediately.

THE EUDORA USER'S GUIDE

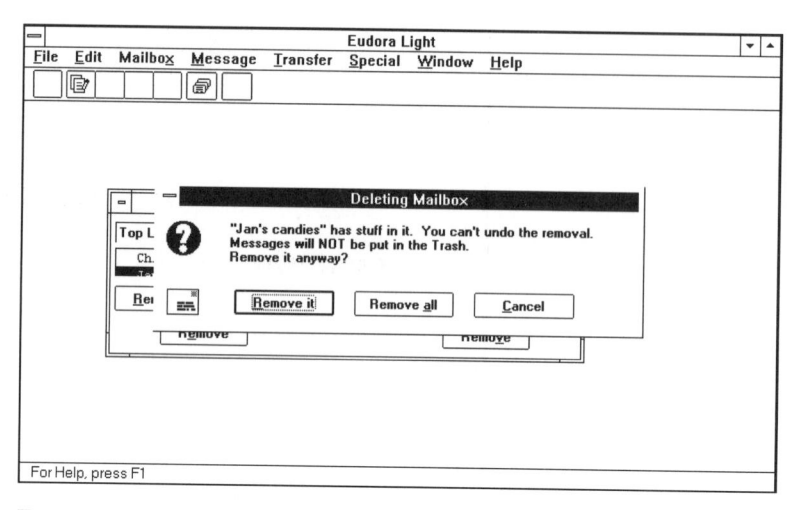

Figure 5-8. Eudora warning before deleting a mailbox that is not empty.

Warning: Removing a mailbox or folder removes all objects (messages, mailboxes, or folders) within the selected item. Once the object is gone, you can't get it back.

RENAMING A MAILBOX OR FOLDER

Did you ever think that a name wasn't clear enough? For example, due to an expansion of our product line, we might change a mailbox name from Candies to Goodies. Use the following simple procedure to change a mailbox or folder name. First open the Mailboxes window; then, from either list, click on the desired mailbox or folder; and finally click on the Rename button. This displays a dialog box. Enter the new name, as shown in Figure 5-9, and click on Rename to confirm the name change.

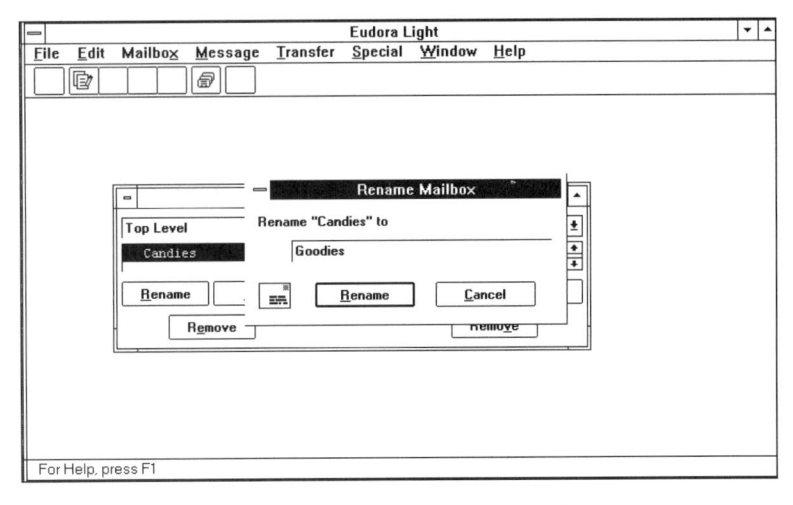

Figure 5-9. Renaming the Candies mailbox to Goodies.

PROCESSING INCOMING MESSAGES

You can process incoming messages with the **Reply**, **Forward**, and **Redirect** commands in the **Message** menu. These commands are similar to, but distinct from, the **Reply To**, **Forward To**, and **Redirect To Message** menu commands that process the Quick Recipient list as discussed in Chapter 3.

REPLYING TO A MESSAGE

As its name indicates, the **Reply** command in the **Message** menu replies to the current message. It first creates a new message window whose To: message header field contains the address of the original sender. Its message body includes the original message text at the beginning of the message body area. Each line of the original message starts with a >. While you can edit or delete this text, it is common courtesy to clearly indicate that you have made changes to the original message. Add your reply to the bottom of the message and perhaps save it before sending. When you have replied to an incoming message, its message summary contains an R, as shown in Figure 5-10. Note that the date shown indicates when the original message was sent, not the reply date.

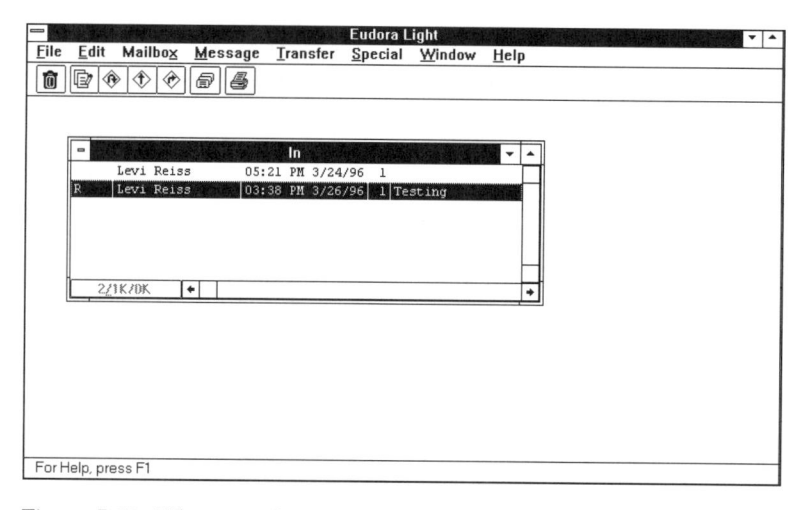

Figure 5-10. When you have replied to a message, an R appears to the left of its message summary in the In Mailbox.

MODIFIED FORMS OF REPLY

The **Reply** command contains several options which we describe next. For example, you can reply to all recipients of the original message, including a reply to yourself. Doing so precludes the need to save a copy of the message.

Reply to all

The Replying Settings dialog box contains the option "Reply to all" by default. If this little square contains an **x**, anyone who received the original message gets the pleasure of reading your reply. You may want to choose this option to continue an ongoing discussion. If this little square is blank, only the original sender receives the reply. This option is good for maintaining confidentiality. To reverse the box's action, press the SHIFT key while selecting **Reply** from the **Message** menu. For example, if the Reply to all by default box contains an **x**, but you hold down the SHIFT key while selecting **Reply** from the **Message** menu, only the original sender receives a reply. The SHIFT key lets you treat messages individually without having to change the general settings.

Including yourself

What does Reply to all mean? Does *all* include you, or doesn't it? You decide by filling or leaving blank the "Include yourself" option in the Replying Settings dialog box. If this box contains an **x**, sending a reply to all sends a copy of the message to you as well. If this box is blank, sending a reply to all does not send you a copy of the message.

Note: Eudora determines who you are via the "me" nickname if you have one. If you don't have such a nickname, Eudora determines who you are by examining the contents of the POP Account: and Return Address: fields in the Settings dialog box.

Cc: original To: recipients

Let's say that you want to reply to all who received the original message. The question remains whether the addresses of recipients other than the sender should be placed in the Cc: message header field of the new message. To do so, place an **x** in the "Put original To: recipients in Cc: field" option of the Replying Settings dialog box. Here, only the address of the original sender is placed in the To: field.

FORWARDING A MESSAGE

Did you ever get a message that you wanted to pass on (forward) to another party? Forwarding a snail mail message requires that you add postage, and perhaps place the letter in a new envelope to avoid misdirection. It can be complicated to forward a snail mail message to a dozen recipients at once. Eudora makes it easy to forward messages to other users. Simply select any message you received and select the **Forward** command in the **Message** menu. This creates a new message window and transfers to it the header and body of the original message. Each line of the original message starts with a >. While you can edit or delete this text, it is common courtesy to clearly indicate that you have made changes to the original message. Then complete the To: message header field with the address of the person to receive the forwarded message. The From: message header field contains your address, which indicates that you have forwarded the message. Figure 5-11 shows an example of a forwarded message (in the interest of brevity, the forwarded message was cut). When you have forwarded an incoming message, its message summary contains an F, as shown in Figure 5-12.

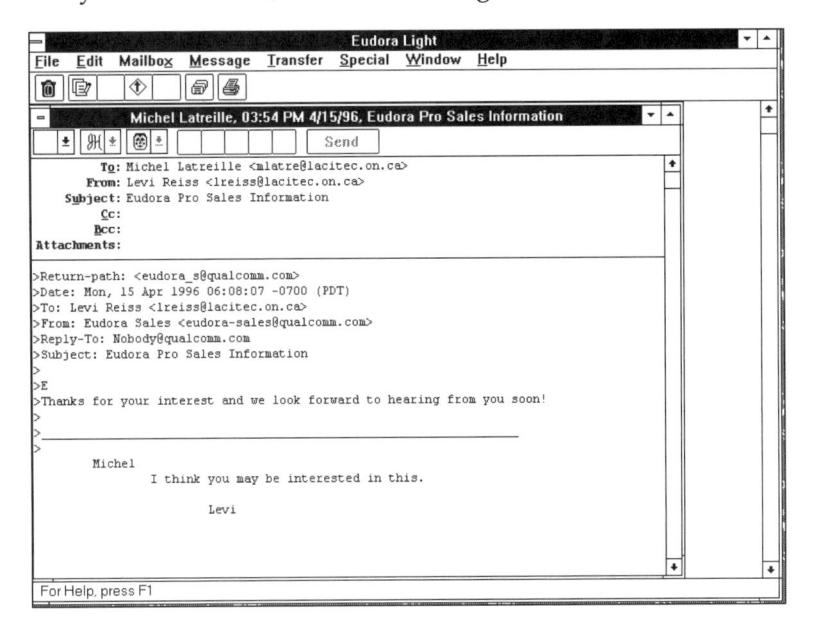

Figure 5-11. A forwarded message, with additional text from the original recipient (Levi).

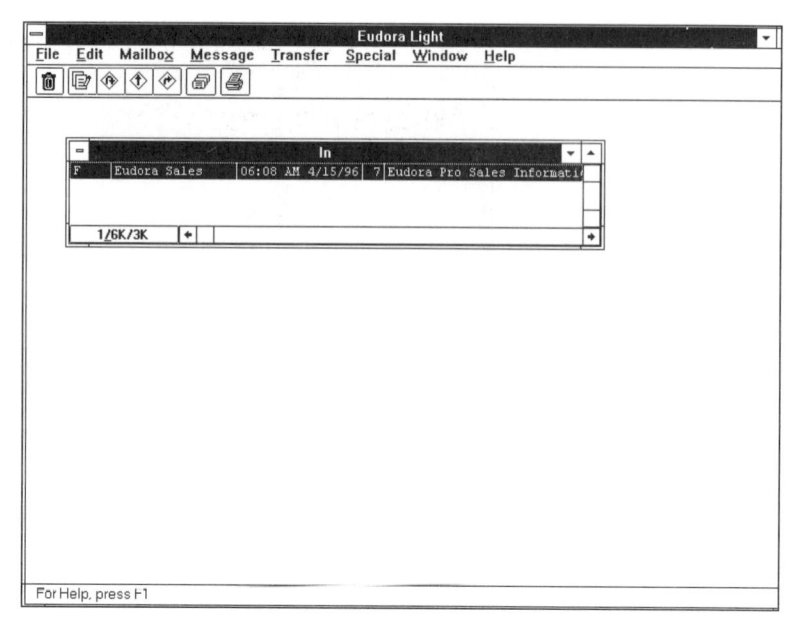

Figure 5-12. When you have forwarded an incoming message, an F appears in its message summary in the In mailbox.

REDIRECTING A MESSAGE

Did you ever receive a message that was really for someone else? Such messages should be *redirected*, not forwarded. To redirect a message that you received, select the **Redirect** command in the **Message** menu. This displays a new message window whose To: message header field you will complete with the address of the correct recipient, as shown in Figure 5-13.

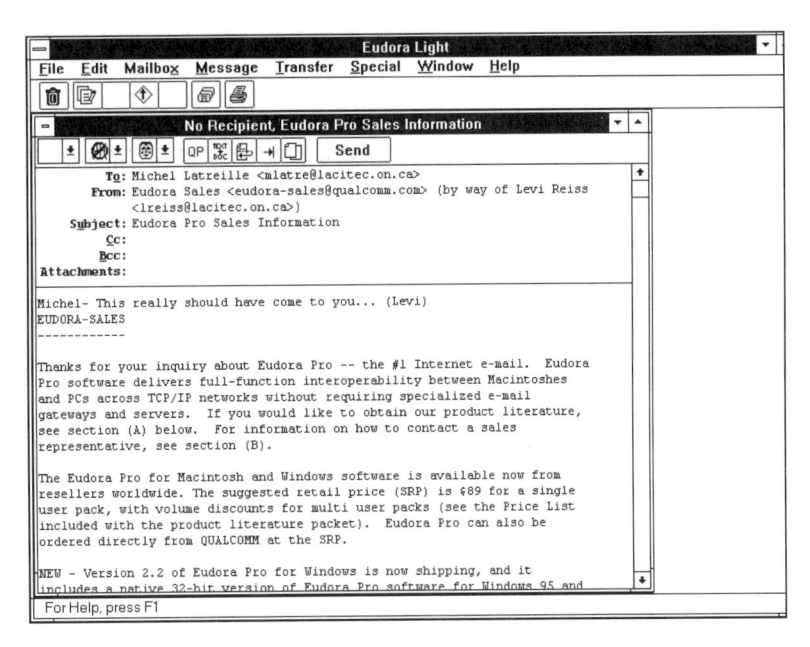

Figure 5-13. Redirecting a message to the intended recipient.

The address in the From: message header field is that of the original sender, not your address. Furthermore, there are no > characters at the beginning of each line of the original text. As when forwarding or replying to a message, you can edit the existing text, or add more. Once again, common courtesy dictates that you clearly indicate the changes and additions you made. When you have redirected an incoming message, its message summary contains a D, as shown in Figure 5-14.

THE EUDORA USER'S GUIDE

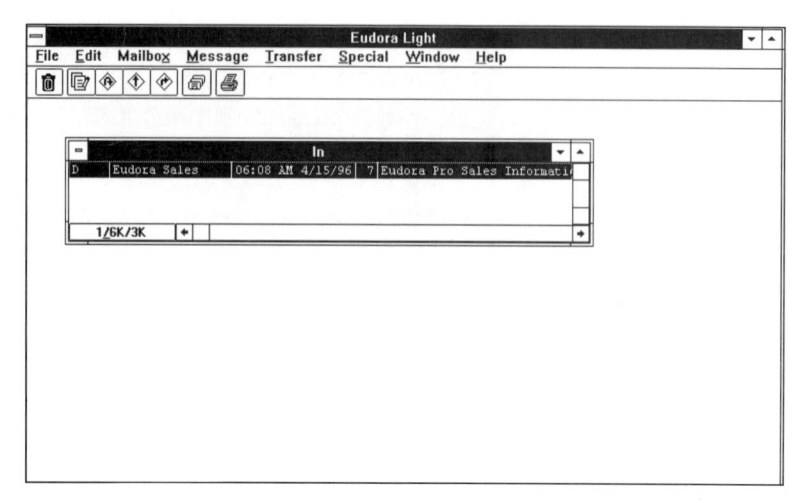

Figure 5-14. The D for this message summary indicates that the message was redirected.

Redirect and Signatures

You can add your signature only to a message that you have created. Eudora adds your signature if the address in the From: message header field exactly matches your return address setting or your POP account address if you have not entered a return address in the Personal Information Settings dialog box.

Easy Repeat ("Canned") Messages Using Redirect

Let's say that you like to send a given message to many people, perhaps one of those infamous Christmas newsletters announcing all the wonderful things that happened to your family during the past year—Anne got that promotion, and Joey will be starting medical school next fall.... To save yourself some effort, keep a "canned" copy of the message and send it easily using the **Redirect** command. First compose a new message whose To: message header field is blank. Save this message in the Out Mailbox or in a special mailbox. To send the message, open it or highlight it, add a personal greeting if you wish, select the **Redirect** command in the **Message** menu, complete the To: field, and send the message.

REPLYING SETTINGS

The Replying Settings dialog box, shown in Figure 5-15, controls how Eudora processes your replies to incoming messages.

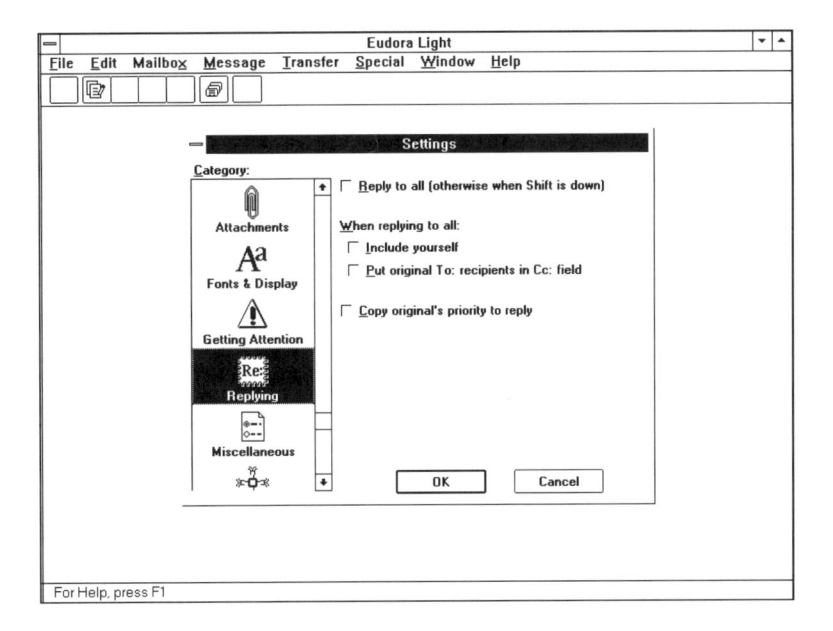

Figure 5-15. The Replying Settings dialog box.

Reply to all (otherwise when Shift is down) [off]

If the Reply to all box contains an **x**, activating the **Reply** command in the **Message** menu creates a message addressed to the original message sender and all recipients. If this box is blank, only the original sender gets a reply. Holding down the SHIFT key when activating the **Reply** command effectively reverses the setting.

When replying to all: Include yourself [off]

When the "Include yourself" option box contains an **x**, specifying Reply to all sends a message to you. When the "Include yourself" option box is blank, specifying Reply to all does not send a message to you. The Reply to all section earlier in this chapter explains how Eudora determines who you are.

When replying to all: Put original To: recipients in Cc: field [off]

If this box contains an **x**, Eudora moves the addresses of all original message recipients from the To: message header field to the reply's Cc: message header field. The original sender's address is placed in the reply's To: message header field.

Copy original's priority to reply [on]

If this option is on, your reply retains the original message's priority. In general, new messages are created with normal priority, even if they are replies to messages whose priority is other than normal. You can always manually change a message's priority.

JOINING THE E-MAIL CULTURE

By now you are probably close to mastering the mechanics of Eudora, have little or no hesitation in sending and receiving messages, and are familiar with the ins and outs of mailboxes and folders. Yet there remain many things to learn about electronic mail in general, and Eudora in particular. It's time to consider the proper ways to employ this mighty tool. E-mail gives you power a poison-pen artist could only dream of. In a large sense, the world is at your fingertips. You know how to use Eudora, but you must also know how not to abuse it. You'll also want to become familiar with the not-so-secret but often baffling language shared by e-mail aficionados.

Before we set down some behavioral guidelines, often called netiquette, and learn some tricks that help you join the "in" crowd, we may well ask ourselves the following questions:

- Why is this trip necessary?

- Does electronic mail really necessitate a special code of behavior?

- Why can't we just type our merry way?

THE SPECIAL NATURE OF ELECTRONIC MAIL

As any parent of teenagers can tell you, the telephone opens the door to new cultural patterns. It changed the way we communicate. The same is true of electronic mail. Even infrequent users must take note of e-mail's special characteristics. These include uncontrolled reception list, undying permanence, disrespect for organizational hierarchy, message proliferation, and—perhaps most importantly—the likelihood of misunderstanding. As you become a devotee of electronic mail, you may find additional characteristics.

UNCONTROLLED RECEPTION LIST

When you make that special phone call, it is quite unlikely that your party will record the conversation and send a tape to dozens of people. While photographers can capture a face-to-face meeting on film and transmit it halfway around the world, such behavior is usually the domain of spy novels and divorce courts. E-mail is very different.

Anyone who has worked through Chapter 5 can forward or redirect your message to multiple correspondents quite rapidly. All recipients can repeat the process, leading to information glut. When writing a friend, do you feel the need to comment on your boss or your mother-in-law? Maybe you should think about Ccing him or her. At least you'll know that he or she got an unaltered copy of your message.

UNDYING PERMANENCE

When you make that special phone call, it is unlikely that the other party will record the conversation and replay it 14 years later much to the chagrin of you and your loved ones. Surreptitiously recorded telephone conversations may not be admissible in court. Face-to-face meetings are, by their very nature, volatile, although they may leave lasting scars. E-mail is very different.

Those little squiggles on the screen don't look very permanent. It's easy to believe that once the power is off, they will disappear forever. They do, sometimes. Don't forget that electronic mail can be easily stored on hard disk files with a life expectancy measured in decades. It's quite simple to save an e-mail message to diskette, and pop it into a shirt pocket to be resurrected at will. What can be easier than printing an e-mail message? The fancier your printer, the more official your message looks. Worst of all, an unscrupulous person can edit a message ever so slightly and alter its meaning.

Who owns the message you sent—you, your intended recipient, or your company? If you sent the message during working hours on its network does your company own the message? The answer to the ownership question remains unclear. Be safe; don't assume that you own the message.

Be as safe as you can

To be really safe, follow a simple rule. Don't put anything in e-mail that you aren't willing to see on the front page of your local newspaper, attributed to yours truly.

DISRESPECT FOR ORGANIZATIONAL HIERARCHY

Most organizations require that internal communications follow a strict hierarchy. If you are a disgruntled clerk, don't even bother to telephone the company president. Her secretary won't let you get through. Forget a face-to-face meeting; except for the annual Christmas party, the president hasn't been seen in the employee cafeteria since the spring of 1981. Furthermore, her assistant opens all her correspondence. E-mail is very different.

Few such shielding mechanisms exist for electronic mail. Once you know the president's full e-mail address, there is probably no chained dog or electronic barrier stopping you from addressing her majesty. Her e-mail address could be secret, but in most organizations it is formed the same way as e-mail addresses belonging to mere mortals (perhaps the first letter of her first name, followed by ...). E-mail systems such as Eudora Pro can be set up to filter messages. For example, it may automatically redirect mere employees' correspondence addressed to the president into her assistant's In mailbox. Arguably, most organizations have not yet introduced such message filtering.

E-mail's lack of access control has negative aspects. As a consumer, I may be bombarded with electronic junk mail, junk faxes, good old-fashioned junk mail, and those wonderful, unsolicited dinner-time phone calls. There is already a demand for unlisted electronic mailboxes. Totally uncontrolled communication means nobody knows what's going on, and it inevitably leads to misunderstanding and unnecessary duplication of efforts.

The Impact of E-mail

What is the general impact of e-mail? Proponents claim that e-mail democratizes office communication. Detractors talk about the anarchy of e-mail. In a sense, they are both right.

MESSAGE PROLIFERATION

We all know about the famous chain letters, which claim that in less than 6 weeks you will receive 5,210 color postcards from exotic destination, or, even better, thousands of silver dollars. Yet how many people have ever received a single picture postcard, to say nothing of silver dollars from a chain letter? Electronic mail is very different, as the following example shows.

The vice president of sales at a major company wants each of his nine sales managers to comment on a proposed new product. He fires up the e-mail software and sends every sales manager a message including the nine full e-mail addresses, plus his own. The sales managers all respond to the vice president and send a copy of their response to the entire mailing list. We now have 100 e-mail messages, and the discussion is just beginning. Think of all the possibilities; for example, the Cleveland Sales Manager informs the Atlanta Sales Manager that she agrees with his message dated May 8, except for paragraph 2, where she feels that he is underestimating.... Of course, Atlanta replies, and then Chicago joins in the melee.

Many systems automatically send a copy of the response to all people listed in the original message. Special effort is required to restrict the reception list.

Many people spend an hour or two a day simply reading and deleting their (mostly unwanted) e-mail. If your message has a poorly chosen subject header, your message risks deletion before ever being read. If you join too many newsgroups or mailing lists (see Chapter 7), you may not have the time to do any work.

LIKELIHOOD OF MISUNDERSTANDING

Misunderstandings occur in any type of communication. History is full of duels that took place because of imagined slights. Face-to-face conversations and to a lesser extent telephone conversations enable participants to change their tone of voice or rephrase their comments on the spot, before any lasting damage occurs. A twinkle of an eye or a lilting tone of voice may tell your interlocutor not to take the comments seriously. Electronic mail systems in their original form do not offer these signals. You'll see later in this chapter how to convey emotions in your e-mail.

Next we'll examine some guidelines that reduce misunderstandings. Apply them judiciously and they will help you become a member in good standing of the electronic mail culture.

E-MAIL ETIQUETTE

Communication inevitably leads to misunderstanding. Even Dear Abby and Ann Landers can't solve all interpersonal communication problems, and, as you have seen, e-mail brings new communications challenges.

We consider two overlapping categories of e-mail etiquette: that involved in sending messages and that associated with receiving and replying to messages.

MESSAGE-SENDING ETIQUETTE

Remember, the message you send to X today may reach virtually anyone with an e-mail address a lot sooner than you think. These suggestions may reduce your embarrassment now, and in the unforeseen future.

Assume Your Messages Are Permanent

We cannot stress this point enough. Unlike snail-mail love letters, which are probably yellowing in some shoebox or landfill, your e-mail love letters can be resurrected and retransmitted to that special someone in a few keystrokes. So can your marketing studies.

Clearly Identify Yourself and Your Affiliations

Let people know who you are, and include your affiliations where relevant. As in other communications, distinguish your personal views from those of your organization. A good signature can help. Eudora Pro lets you create multiple signatures, ideally one for business and another for personal correspondence.

Create Single-Subject Messages Whenever Possible

Suppose that you have two very different things to say to a given correspondent. Should you send one or two messages? We suggest that you send two separate messages, instead of a single composite message. Here are some reasons why:

The message subject is the best way to catch a busy recipient's attention. A composite subject title may be meaningless and cause the message to remain unread.

The recipient can process the different messages independently, perhaps saving one and deleting the other.

It is easier and more direct to reply to a given message, rather than to relevant parts of a composite message.

Don't Be Insulting

Avoid nastiness in your electronic mail. Does your correspondent seem totally incapable of doing the slightest computer tricks? Perhaps he or she is among the thousands of newbies who first joined the Internet today. If you can't make your point without getting personal, perhaps you can't make your point at all. Don't let everybody in on this secret.

Don't Shout

Sending a message in all uppercase characters is known as "shouting". Just like shouting over the phone or in a face-to-face meeting, it's considered poor form. It is hard on your correspondents' eyes, if not on their ears.

Keep Your Intended Audience in Mind

It makes a big difference who is at the other end of the Send button—your boss, an old college buddy, or your grandnephew. The level of formality and the choice of language and style definitely depend on the recipient. Just as in face-to-face conversations, you can joke with some e-mail recipients and not with others. Be very careful when using humor, especially if you are communicating across wide cultural or age differences.

Keep Your Recipient List to a Minimum

In high-security situations information is available only on a need-to-know basis. We feel that the need-to-know policy is often a good idea, even when security is not at question. Too many messages fill too many hard disks and clog too many thought processes.

Label Your Emotions and Opinions

Your recipient won't see those little body language clues or hear changes in the tone of voice suggesting that your comments are tongue in cheek. If you can't keep your emotions out of your correspondence, at least label them. When you are giving an opinion, state so clearly. If you force people to guess, they may guess incorrectly.

Watch the Send Button

One problem with e-mail is the ease with which people send messages. One false click, and a poorly spelled, poorly written message becomes part of your permanent record. Your recipient may well feel that you just didn't care enough to give your best effort.

MESSAGE RECEIVING AND TRANSMITTING ETIQUETTE

The good manners associated with sending messages also apply when receiving and replying to them. Consider also the following points.

Assume That the Sender is Competent and Honest

Once you accuse the other party of incompetence or dishonesty, it's almost impossible to get the debate back on a calm, rational level. Avoiding accusations is not enough. If you think that your interlocutor is incompetent or dishonest, you won't address the issues that he or she is raising. Keep an open mind and you might even learn something from his or her point of view.

Avoid Excessive Emotions

If a message makes you emotional, reread it carefully. Perhaps the other party was only joking when he said, "Only an absolute moron would like ABC's new line of printers." You might feel that only an absolute moron would make such a statement, but why should you care? How important is clearing the record? Few rational people will consider you a moron for your opinions, but if you escalate the debate, they may wonder about your intelligence, or at least your sense of priorities.

The old advice of counting to 10 before getting mad is still valuable. Its corollary, write a nasty letter but don't send it, is dangerous. All of us have pressed the Send button by accident at least once. If you absolutely must respond, first put Eudora in the Message Queueing mode.

Don't Get Sidetracked

It is pointless to get carried away and give your viewpoint on all subjects. If you absolutely must start a new subject, do it in a separate message with a new subject header. Think twice before doing so.

Don't Ignore Messages Intended for Others

Accidents happen. Be a sport—it only takes a minute to scan a message, realize that it is not for you, and return it to the sender with a quick explanatory note. Doing so prevents the sender from misinterpreting the intended recipient's lack of reply, and it helps to ensure that the intended message finally arrives. This policy has an added benefit; you can read the entire message without feeling guilty. You can always tell yourself, "I was only trying to find the recipient's address to forward it."

Identify the recipient's emotions and opinions

Drive defensively on the information superhighway. React but don't overreact to the other party's errors and breach of etiquette.

CHAPTER 6: JOINING THE E-MAIL CULTURE

Pare the response list

Just as you shouldn't automatically dash off a response to a given message, don't automatically send your response to all recipients listed in the initial message. Stop message proliferation. Your non-recipients would thank you if they knew.

SMILIES AND EMOTICONS

E-mail enthusiasts are not the kind of people to lament the lack of visible and audible signals to accompany their typed messages. They addressed this very real need by developing **smilies**, also known as **emoticons**, inventive combinations of standard keyboard characters that look like sideways faces. For example, :-) denotes a smile. The colon : represents eyes, the dash - represents a nose, and the closing parenthesis) represents lips. Place this smilie at the end of a sentence and your informed interlocutor will know that you and your message are smiling. Or you could type :_) to indicate that your comments were tongue in cheek.

Smilies not only help reduce misunderstandings, they also serve to bond e-mail enthusiasts. There is nothing like a shared, semisecret language to draw people together. Learn to use smilies correctly and you are on the way to joining the "in" crowd.

The Internet is an excellent place to find smilies. Surf for a short time and you'll even see smilie-covered T-shirts for sale. The following list comes from Kevin at

`http://www.ozemail.com.au/~kread/smilies.html`

131

THE UNOFFICIAL GUIDE TO SMILIES AND ABBREVIATIONS

Kevin divides smilies into several categories. Try not to use the abusive ones.

Basic Smilies

Smilie	Usage
:-)	Standard smilie. Just joking, implies humor.
;-)	Winking smilie. Used when you make a sarcastic remark.
:-(	Sad smilie. Used when you didn't like something, or to imply sadness.

Popular Smilies

Smilie	Usage
:-!	Foot in mouth.
:-#	Wears braces/been hit in the mouth.
:-$	Put your money where your mouth is.
:-&	Tongue-tied.
:-/	Skeptical.
:-O	Yelling.

:_)   Tongue in cheek.

Smilies with Emotion

Smilie	Usage
:-<	Very sad.
:-D	Laughing.
:-@	Screaming.
:-|	Hmmm .... Don't know what to think.
:-P	Sticking your tongue out.
:-X	My lips are sealed.
:-e	Disappointed.
;-)	Say no more (nudge nudge, wink wink).
:-*	Kissing.
:-)))	Very emotive (suggested by Kay, Trieste, Italy).

Abusive Smilies

Smilie	Usage
(:|	Egghead.
~-)	Cock-eyed.
%-6	Brain dead.

:-t	Very cross.
:>)	Big nose.
:-+	Oooohhhhh !!!.

Miscellaneous Smilies

Smilie	Usage
|-|	Asleep.
|-)	Falling asleep.
|-O	Bored.
.-)	One-eyed.
:,(	Crying.
|^o	Snoring.
(-:	Left-handed.
8-)	Wearing sunglasses.
B-)	Wearing horn-rimmed glasses.
@@@:-)	Marge Simpson.

Abbreviations

To be a member of the e-mail culture, you'll need to know a plethora of abbreviations. Kevin includes many popular ones.

CHAPTER 6: JOINING THE E-MAIL CULTURE

Abbreviation Usage

IMHO	In my humble opinion.
LOL	Laughing out loud.
OTF	On the floor.
OTFL	On the floor (laughing).
ROTFL	Rolling on the floor (laughing).
BRB	Be right back.
BTW	By the way.
CYA	See you.
CYL8TER	See you later.
FYI	For your information.
NE1	Anyone.
NEway	Anyway.

If you know of any more or have a different use for a smilie, please feel free to drop Kevin an e-mail. He promises to add all new ones right away. Please send your contributions to mailto: kread@ozemail.com.au.

The Ten Commandments for Computer Ethics

Arlene Rinaldi is a well-known writer on netiquette, etiquette as applied to the Internet. You can read about her book, *The Net: User Guidelines and Netiquette,* on the Internet by accessing http://www.fau.edu/rinaldi/net/ten.html. In it she quotes "The Ten Commandments for Computer Ethics" from the Computer Ethics Institute.

1. Thou shalt not use a computer to harm other people.
2. Thou shalt not interfere with other people's computer work.
3. Thou shalt not snoop around in other people's files.
4. Thou shalt not use a computer to steal.
5. Thou shalt not use a computer to bear false witness.
6. Thou shalt not use or copy software for which you have not paid.
7. Thou shalt not use other people's computer resources without authorization.
8. Thou shalt not appropriate other people's intellectual output.
9. Thou shalt think about the social consequences of the program you write.
10. Thou shalt use a computer in ways that show consideration and respect.

Permission to duplicate or distribute this document is granted with the provision that the document remains intact or if used in sections, that the original document source be referenced.

7

ACCESSING INTERNET SERVICES

Mailing lists and USENET newsgroups are two valuable, if sometimes neglected, ways of applying Eudora to access the Internet. An Internet mailing list resembles a conventional mailing list. It is a collection of e-mail addresses of individuals and organizations with similar interests. Send a message to anyone on the mailing list, and you automatically send it to all members of the list. You don't need any software other than Eudora to receive information that was sent to your mailing list. This information is processed like regular Internet e-mail. Later you will see that special software is used for managing mailing lists.

USENET is a global interactive news service. While not formally part of the Internet, USENET is closely associated with the Internet. USENET consists of about 20,000 discussion groups known as "newsgroups." Depending on their interests—and the time and money they are willing to spend—individuals subscribe to one or many newsgroups, read newsgroup articles, and "post" their viewpoints. As always when accessing the Internet, netiquette, as described in Chapter 6, is essential when dealing with newsgroups. While you'll need software besides Eudora to participate in USENET newsgroups, you can use Eudora to find newsgroups and post your viewpoint. Because mailing lists and newsgroups are similar, novices sometimes confuse them. Let's look at their similarities and differences before examining each in detail.

SIMILARITIES

Mailing lists and USENET enable you to read and discuss topics of interest. Both services require an e-mail address and are available via the Internet, using Eudora. Both let you receive a virtually unlimited volume of information. Therefore they require a clear usage policy to avoid information overload and excessive charges. Both allow you to broadcast your opinions to thousands of people and, consequently, open the doors to abuse.

DIFFERENCES

While exceptions abound, the following distinctions between mailing lists and newsgroups often hold true:

- Mailing lists have few restrictions. USENET severely restricts commercial newsgroups.

- Mailing list messages go directly into your In mailbox. (Eudora Pro message filtering can channel mailing list messages to specific mailboxes.) USENET articles go directly to individual newsgroups. You'll need special software, called **newsreaders**, to read these articles.

- Mailing list messages are eternal, lasting until you delete them. USENET news articles have a very limited life span, perhaps one week. Of course, once you read the article, you can store it for an indefinite period.

- Mailing list messages usually go directly to individuals. USENET articles are often reviewed by moderators (some call them "censors") who approve them before individuals receive them.

- No one needs permission to start a mailing list. In contrast, proposed USENET newsgroups generally must go through a lengthy, often painful, approval process before obtaining USENET distribution rights.

MAILING LISTS

The Internet includes several thousands of mailing lists on almost any subject. A mailing list may include a few or literally thousands of members who share an interest (and occasionally, viewpoints) on a particular topic. Many mailing lists have become vehicles for distributing newsletters and journals.

MAILING LIST CATEGORIES

Some mailing lists are a discussion forum, while others summarize mailing list or newsgroup discussions. Mailing lists can be moderated, unmoderated, or closed.

Moderated Mailing Lists

Posting a message to moderated mailing lists and most USENET newsgroups sends it to a moderator (or moderators) for approval before the message reaches individuals. In theory, moderators ensure that messages directly concern the topic. In practice, moderators may censor messages that they find offensive, or sometimes just don't like. Newsletters, journals, and summary mailing lists are often moderated.

Unmoderated Mailing Lists

Most mailing lists are unmoderated; messages go directly from the sender to mailing list members. Sometimes only mailing list members may send a message; in other cases, anyone may.

Closed Mailing Lists

As you might guess from their name, closed mailing lists are available to a select crowd. They provide a forum for specialists to exchange ideas without interference from the "great unwashed". After all, neurosurgeons may wish to discuss interesting cases among themselves without having to deal with my comments.

ACCESSING MAILING LISTS

Processing of mailing list subscriptions may be manual or automated. LISTSERV is the most widely used mailing list software, but other products are available. Majordomo, another popular product, manages mailing lists for Qualcomm, distributors of Eudora.

Subscribing

It's quite easy to subscribe to a mailing list. To do so, send an e-mail message to a special address designated to handle subscriptions. Your request may be processed manually or by software.

Tip: Turn off your message signature before sending a subscription message.

To subscribe to a LISTSERV mailing list, send an e-mail message to an address such as LISTSERV@address. In the message body, type SUB listname yourname, replacing listname by the name of the mailing list, and yourname by your first name, a space, and your last name.

Many mailing lists not managed by LISTSERV use an e-mail address such as listname-request@address. The -request denotes a subscription request. The actual message contents depend on the mailing list.

Warning: Do not send a subscription (or cancellation) message to the mailing list itself. Doing so sends a message to all members of that list.

Whether or not your subscription was processed by LISTSERV, you may be prompted with additional steps required to join the mailing list, as shown in Figure 7-1. Once you receive confirmation that you have joined the list, you can start sending messages.

Tip: Read the subscription documentation for the mailing list of interest. Keep this information. You may need it to cancel your subscription.

Sending Messages

After joining the mailing list, to send a message to everyone on the list, simply send it to the mailing list address.

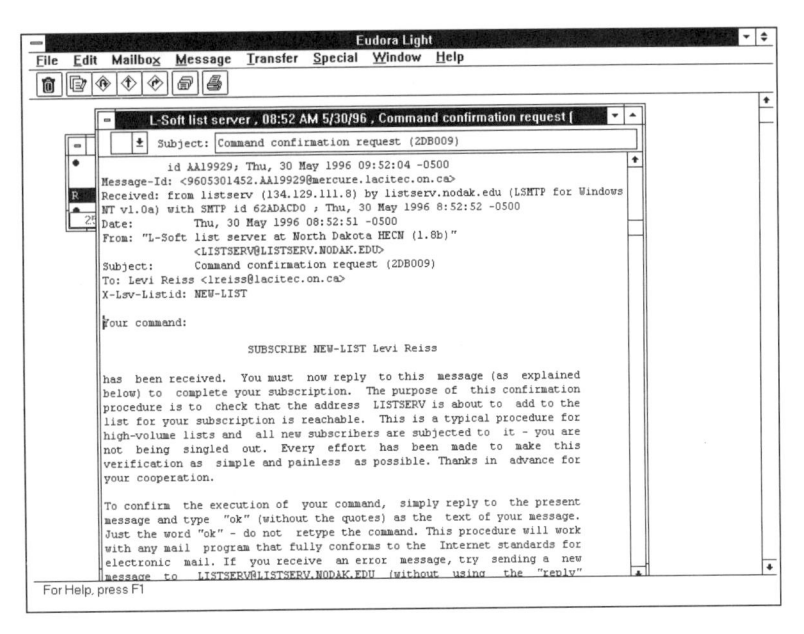

Figure 7-1. Mailing list command confirmation request.

Canceling Subscriptions

To cancel a subscription to a LISTSERV mailing list, send an e-mail message to an address such as LISTSERV@address. In the message body, type SIGNOFF listname, replacing LISTNAME by the name of the mailing list. Many non-LISTSERV mailing lists let you cancel your subscription by a similar process, such as sending a message to listname-request@wherever.

LAUNCHING A MAILING LIST

After a bit of experience with mailing lists, you may want to start your own. Before doing so, carefully consider whether you want the responsibility and the headache. Be prepared to be insulted both professionally and personally. If you decide to go ahead, check with your Internet service provider about the technical and financial details. You just might find that before long "your" mailing list becomes the accepted center of discussion for your favorite topic.

FINDING MAILING LISTS

There are several routes for locating mailing lists that interest you. One quick way is by asking around. Another is via selected newsgroups, discussed in the USENET section. No matter how you find out about the lists, keep the following two warnings in mind.

- Internet addresses change. You may have to do some detective work to find the new address.

- Lists of mailing lists and USENET newsgroups may be quite large, often greater than a megabyte. This means you'll pay a pretty penny if your Internet service provider charges you by character transferred or by connection time.

BITNET LISTS

BITNET is a global network linking universities and research organizations across the globe. Strictly speaking, it is not part of the Internet. It provides thousands of mailing lists, available to Internet users.

The document "List of all LISTSERV lists known to LISTSERV@BITNIC" is a comprehensive summary of over 4,000 special interest lists, as shown in Figure 7-2. For a copy of this list, send a message to listserv@bitnic.educom.edu or listserv@bitnic.bitnet. The message body should read: list global.

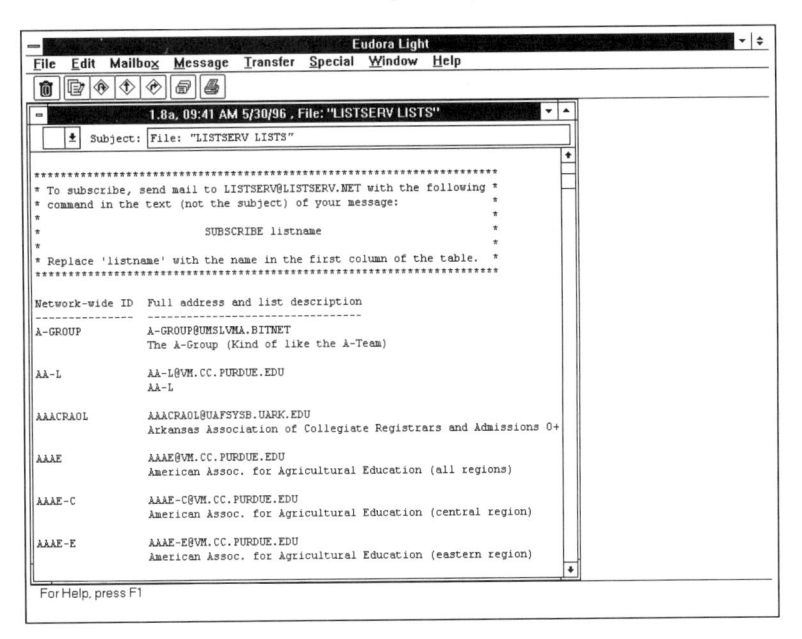

Figure 7-2. List of mailing lists.

New-List Mailing Lists

This mailing list announces new mailing lists, mostly those using LISTSERV software. For a copy of this list, send a message to LISTSERV@VM1.NODAK.EDU. The body of the message should read: SUB NEW-LIST yourname, where, as usual, you specify your own first and last names.

Net-Happenings List

This list gives you an excellent idea of what is taking place on the Internet. For a copy of this list, send an e-mail message to listserv@is.internic.net. The message body should read: subscribe net-happenings yourname, where, as usual, you specify your own first and last names.

Warning: This list is voluminous, generating about 15 to 20 messages daily, whose connection to the Internet may be sketchy at best. Don't subscribe unless you like wading through piles of mail.

USENET NEWSGROUPS

USENET started as an electronic bulletin-board system linking students at Duke University and the University of North Carolina. Subscribers can choose from approximately 20,000 newsgroups. Just like it is physically impossible to collect all new postage stamps, no human can manage to keep up with all newsgroups.

USENET consists of several thousand topic areas known as **newsgroups**, whose variety almost defies imagination. You can subscribe to any of the USENET newsgroups that your Internet service provider carries. Not all providers carry all newsgroups. For example, many service providers do not carry controversial or prurient newsgroups. Many newsgroups are moderated. If a newsgroup is not moderated, you can post to it via newsreader software or via Eudora.

*Tip: Get started by reading "A Primer on How to Work with the USENET Community" and "Rules for Posting to USENET," which are posted regularly on the **news.newusers.questions** and **news.answers newsgroups**.*

NEWSGROUP CATEGORIES

USENET newsgroups are divided into nine major categories. The category is the leftmost part of the newsgroup name. Newsgroup names are read from left to right. The newsgroup **comp.mail** would refer to computer (electronic) mail. The newsgroups **comp.mail.eudora** would refer to Eudora electronic mail in general. The newsgroup **comp.mail.eudora.ms-windows** refers to Eudora electronic mail on MS-Windows computers. The newsgroup names in the following examples are often self-explanatory:

Category	Topic	Example
alt.	alternative	alt.magic
biz.	business	biz.jobs.offered

comp.	computer-oriented topics	comp.mail.eudora. ms-windows
misc.	miscellaneous	misc.forsale. computers.memory
news.	Internet or USENET news	news.lists
rec.	recreational activities	rec.arts.disney. animation
sci.	scientific	sci.med.nursing
soc.	sociological	soc.culture.usa
talk.	debates	talk.politics. medicine

Among these groups, alt. is unique. Because anyone can start an alt. group without prior approval, alt. groups are often controversial.

Sample Messages

USENET messages resemble e-mail messages. Figure 7-3 shows a sample message from the **comp.mail.eudora. ms-windows** newsgroup, the first of 268 messages available at that time. This message was read using Trumpet News Reader software.

Tip: Subscribe to ***comp.mail.eudora.ms-windows*** *or* ***comp.mail. eudora.mac***, *and read the messages regularly. You may find the answer to some of your e-mail problems.*

CHAPTER 7: ACCESSING INTERNET SERVICES

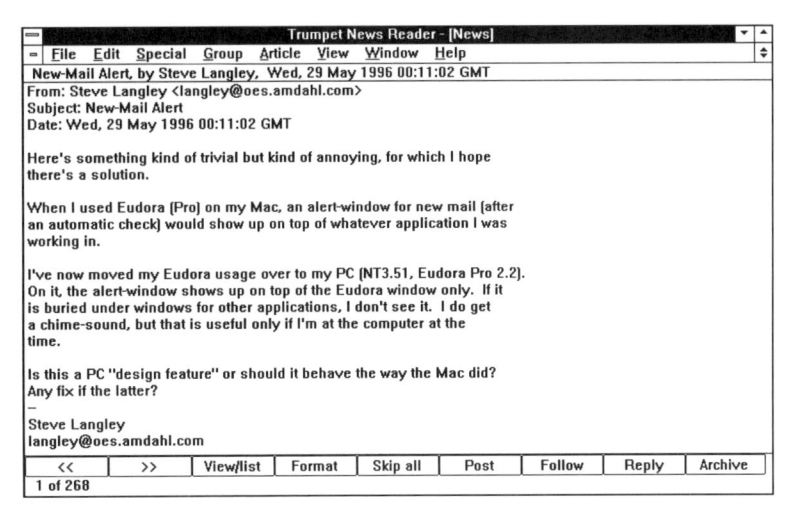

Figure 7-3. Sample message from a Eudora MS-Windows newsgroup.

STARTING A NEWSGROUP

Starting a newsgroup is not a simple process, especially one associated with a major category such as comp. or talk. The first step is sending a message to the moderator of the **news.announce.newsgroups** group and to other newsgroups, explaining why the world needs another newsgroup. This leads to a discussion that might last a month or more. Then a call for votes takes place, and voting lasts about three or four weeks. Acceptance generally requires 66.6 percent of those voting and at least 100 more yeas than nays. Most USENET sites will not carry newsgroups that have not passed this strict acceptance process. After a newsgroup is approved, it is open for subscriptions and postings if the Internet service providers include it in their offerings.

For more information on starting USENET newsgroups, subscribe to **news.announce.newsgroups** and **news.groups**. Proposals for new groups appear in **news.announce.newsgroups**. The debates take place in **news.groups**. These debates are not for the timid. USENET aficionados like to speak their mind and are not always known for mincing their words.

READING THE NEWS

Eudora alone will not give you access to newsgroups. Reading USENET groups requires special **newsreader software**. You can read the news "on-line," with a live connection to your Internet service provider by modem or other link. You also can transfer all articles for subscribed groups, and read them later "off-line," after breaking the connection to the service provider. This method can be less expensive, especially if the messages are transferred to your computer during off hours.

Like the rest of the Internet, USENET exists to help people exchange information. Unlike most of the rest of the Internet, USENET has for the most part resisted commercialization. Nobody will complain if you try to sell appropriate hardware via the newsgroup **misc.forsale.computers.memory**. On the other hand, don't try to sell goods or services on the **soc.culture.usa** or even the **comp.mail.eudora.ms-windows** newsgroup.

Tip: When in doubt, don't flog your goods or services on USENET.

It's a good idea to learn about the USENET culture by following some lively debates before jumping in yourself. When responding to a USENET newsgroup article, you can post a message to the newsgroup or to the person who posted the article.

Tip: Save your postings; you may need to refer to them later.

ROT-13 is a simple method of changing characters in a message (A becomes N, B becomes O, etc.). This code is often used for controversial postings and jokes that some people may find offensive. Check your newsreader to see if it can decode ROT-13 messages.

Many USENET newsgroups periodically post an **FAQ**, or Frequently Asked Questions, list. One excellent source is **rtfm.mit.edu**, in the **pub/usenet/news.answers** directory.

Lists of Newsgroups

Figure 7-4 shows part of a list of USENET newsgroups. Similar listings can be found within the document "List of Active Newsgroups" posted on a frequent basis to the group **news.announce. newusers**. Check with your Internet service provider to obtain a list of the newsgroups it provides. Remember that not all providers distribute all newsgroups.

THE EUDORA USER'S GUIDE

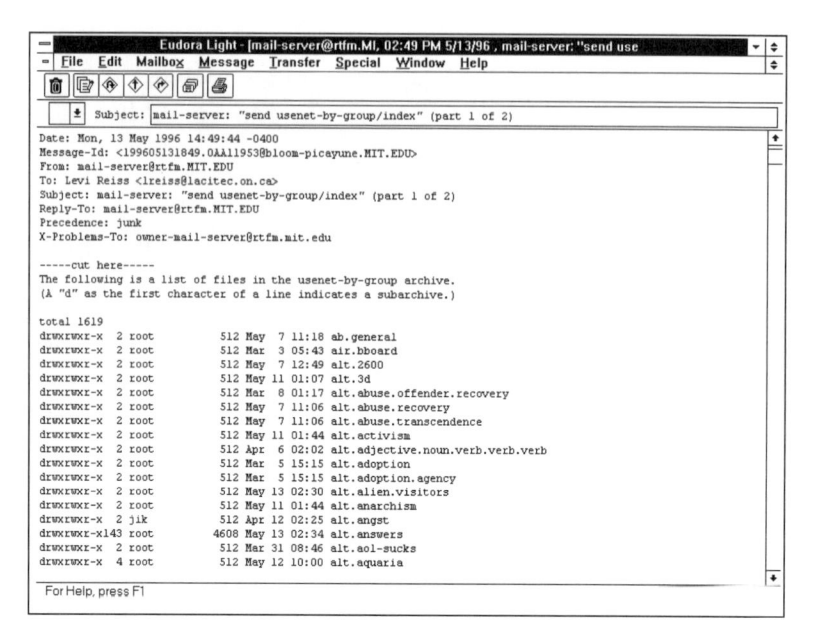

Figure 7-4. A partial list of USENET newsgroups.

BECOMING AN E-MAIL PRO

Now that you are a member in good standing of the electronic-mail culture and are familiar with accessing a wide variety of e-mail services, the time has come to tackle some of Eudora's more complicated features. You'll want to apply them to meet your own e-mail processing needs. Furthermore, once your coworkers become aware of your e-mail knowledge, they may look to you to get them started in e-mail. In these difficult times, your company may look to employees with your experience to take on Eudora duties.

This chapter begins with an examination of the remaining Eudora settings. It then describes the various files associated with Eudora, showing you samples. It presents a few ideas that may make it just a bit easier to share a PC among several e-mail users. It briefly describes the servers Eudora uses to process outgoing and incoming mail. The chapter concludes with explicit directions on how to get more Eudora information and software, much of which is free.

SYSTEM CONFIGURATION SETTINGS

The Getting Started settings provide Eudora with the minimum user account information necessary to send and receive mail. The Personal Information settings identify you to Eudora. The Hosts settings describe your servers to Eudora. The Attachments settings control how Eudora sends and receives attachments. The Fonts & Display settings direct how Eudora displays messages. The Miscellaneous settings manage miscellaneous functions. While these settings may not have merited individual names, don't think that they are not important. The Advanced Network settings control some of Eudora's advanced network functions. Do not modify them before seeing your Eudora support coordinator or service provider.

GETTING STARTED SETTINGS

The Getting Started settings shown in Figure 8-1 include your POP account designating the computer used for incoming mail, your full name, and your connection method.

CHAPTER 8: BECOMING AN E-MAIL PRO

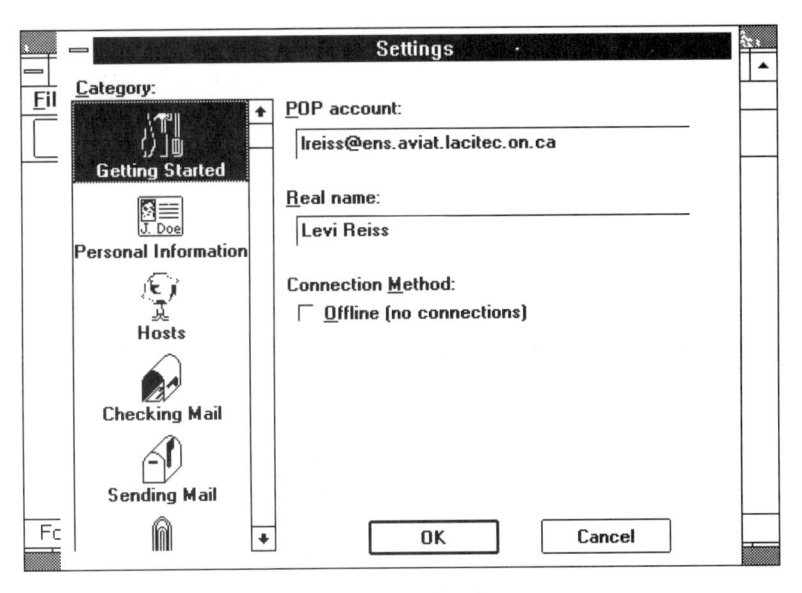

Figure 8-1. Getting Started Settings dialog box.

POP account: [none]

One requirement for using Eudora is an active account on a computer connected to Post Office Protocol version 3 (POP3 or POP) server. This account receives your e-mail messages before they are transferred to the Eudora program running on your PC. Complete this setting with your login name account, followed by the @ sign and the computer's domain name. You should check with your system's e-mail coordinator, but often you can simply enter your usual account number.

Warning: Usually you accept the setting value contained within brackets; for example, the display or printer character size. Here, and for many other settings within this chapter, you must supply a specific value. If you do not have a POP account, you won't get message delivery.

155

Real name: [none]

This setting contains your real name. Eudora automatically copies this name into the From: message header field in your outgoing mail messages, immediately preceding your return address.

Connection Method:

Check the Offline box to prevent Eudora from trying to connect your personal computer to the mail server. Doing so saves connect charges.

Personal Information Settings

The Personal Information settings shown in Figure 8-2 include your POP account designating the computer used for incoming mail, your full name, and your return address.

CHAPTER 8: BECOMING AN E-MAIL PRO

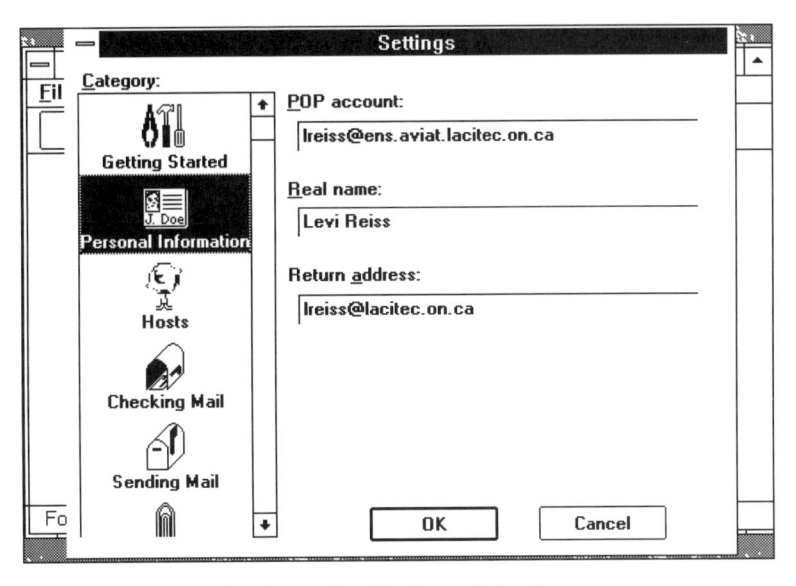

Figure 8-2. Personal Information Settings dialog box.

Return address: [none]

Usually your return address is your POP account address. Enter a different return address, if pertinent.

Warning: Test this return address before sending any mail. If you put my return address here, I'll get your mail, and you won't.

HOSTS SETTINGS

The Hosts settings shown in Figure 8-3 describe your servers to Eudora. They include four servers: your POP account used for incoming mail; your SMTP (Simple Mail Transfer Protocol) server; your Ph server; and your Finger server.

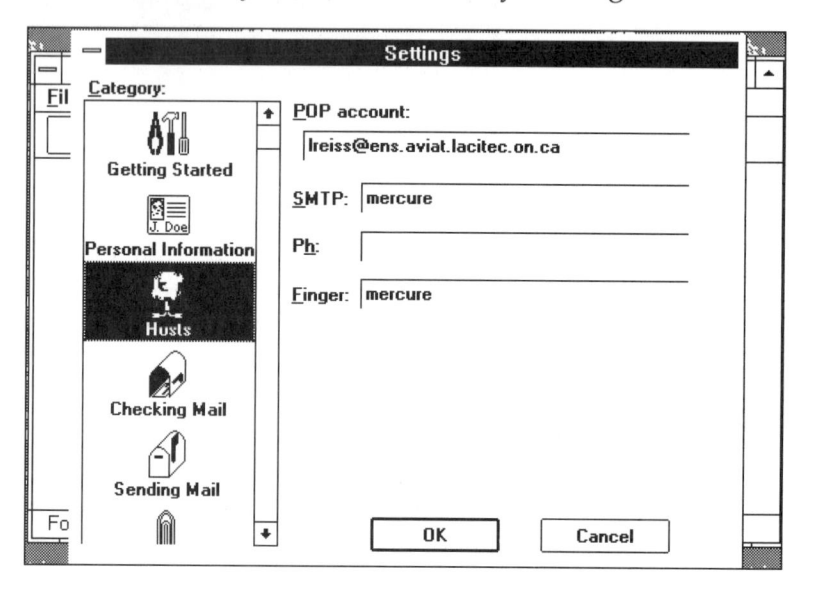

Figure 8-3. Hosts Settings dialog box.

POP account: [none]

This setting contains your POP (Post Office Protocol) account address used as described in the Getting Started settings section earlier in this chapter. You need enter this information only once, but you must enter it to receive mail.

SMTP: [none]

Sending mail via Eudora requires access to a computer with an SMTP (Simple Mail Transfer Protocol) server program. You do not require a login account on the SMTP computer. This field will remain blank if the computer containing your POP account is also an SMTP server. Otherwise, you must specify the name of the computer to use as your SMTP server.

Ph: [none]

Enter the host name of your Ph name server here. The Ph name server is the computer that may help you find information about someone, provided you know his or her name.

Finger: [none]

This setting identifies your Finger server. If it remains blank, Eudora selects your SMTP server to be your Finger server. Your finger server is the computer used to process the **finger** utility, which may help you find information about a person or a company, if you know his, her, or its e-mail address.

ATTACHMENTS SETTINGS

The Attachments settings shown in Figure 8-4 control how Eudora sends and receives attachments. They designate the encoding method and the directory that receives attachments to incoming files.

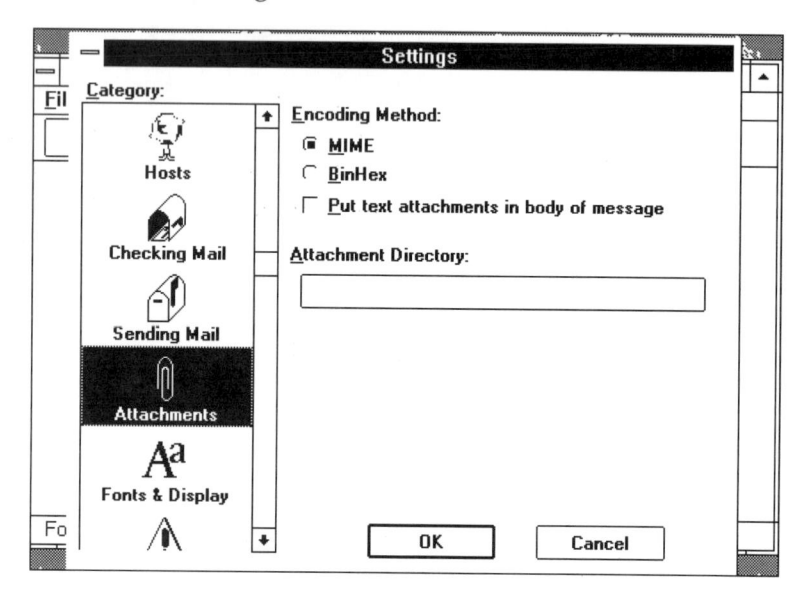

Figure 8-4. Attachments Settings dialog box.

Encoding Method [MIME]

Use this setting to select the format of documents attached to outgoing messages. Eudora encodes attachments in the widely used Multipurpose Internet Mail Extensions (MIME) or Bin Hex, used mostly with Macintosh e-mail programs and older versions of Eudora.

Put text attachments in body of message [off]

When this box contains an **x**, Eudora adds plain text (ASCII) files to the message as if they were typed in.

Attachment Directory: [none]

Use this setting to tell Eudora where to place incoming file attachments. Clicking on the bar displays a dialog box in which you specify the attachment destination directory. By default, attachments arrive in your Eudora directory.

FONTS & DISPLAY SETTINGS

The Fonts & Display settings shown in Figure 8-5 control how Eudora displays messages. They include the screen font settings for text display, the print font, the message window width and height, and several check boxes used for controlling the display of Eudora windows.

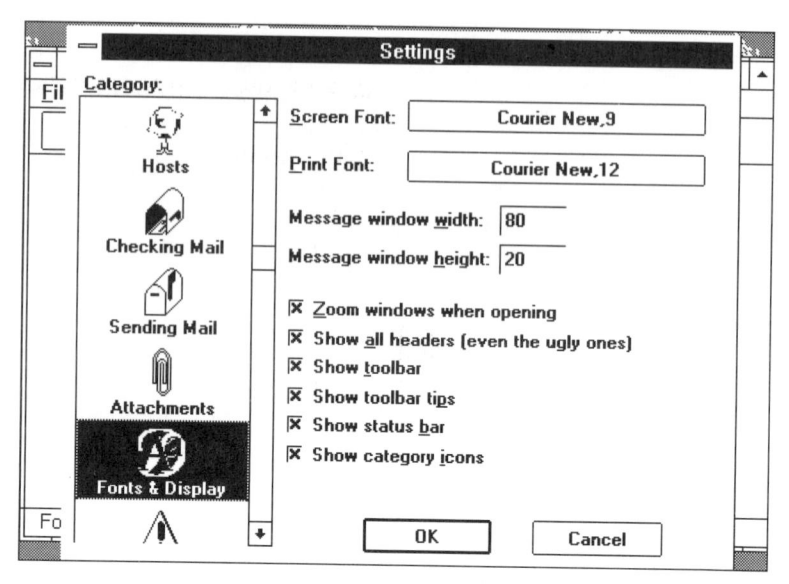

Figure 8-5. Fonts and Display Settings dialog box.

Screen Font: [Courier New, 9]

This field lists the font and point size used to display text appearing in messages and mailbox windows. Change the font by clicking on this field to display the Font dialog box shown in Figure 8-6 and entering appropriate values. Make your changes and click on OK to confirm.

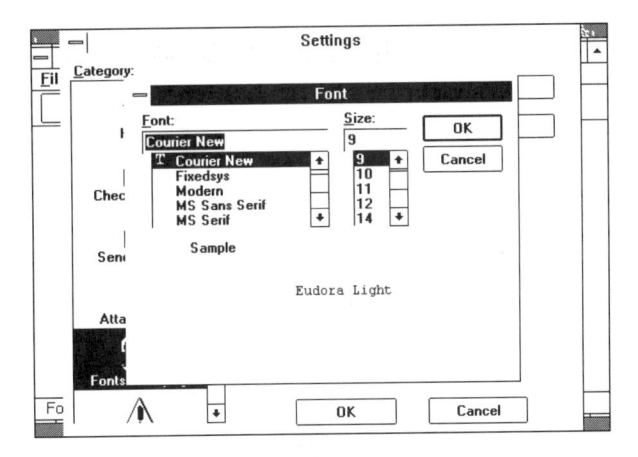

Figure 8-6. Font dialog box.

Print Font: [Courier New, 12]

This field lists the font and point size used to print messages via the **Print** command. Change the font by clicking on this field to display the Font dialog box shown in Figure 8-6 and entering appropriate values. Make your changes and click on OK to confirm.

Message window width: [80]

The Message window width field: specifies the width of your message windows in characters. It does not affect the appearance of your mail. No matter what value appears here, Eudora wraps messages at 76 columns or less before sending them.

Note: When using a proportional font, Eudora sets the window width according to the average width of the characters in the font.

Message window height: [20]

The Message window height field: specifies the height of your message windows in lines. If the "Zoom windows when opening" option (discussed next) is turned on, Eudora automatically adjusts received message window heights to the message text height.

Zoom windows when opening [on]

If this box contains an **x**, new message windows automatically open to their "zoomed" size, which is calculated for each individual window. The zoomed length of message windows is big enough to display the entire message but may not be longer than the Main window. The zoomed width equals the Message window width setting. The Message window height setting specifies the zoomed height of composition windows.

Show all headers (even the ugly ones) [off]

If this box contains an **x**, Eudora displays the entire message header, including routing information, for incoming messages.

Show toolbar [on]

If this box contains an **x**, the main window toolbar is displayed.

Tip: Display this toolbar unless you are really short of window space.

Show toolbar tips [on]

If this box contains an **x**, holding the mouse pointer over a main window toolbar button displays a very brief description of the button's function.

Show status bar [on]

If this box contains an **x**, Eudora displays a status bar at the bottom of the main window. This status bar briefly describes menu items and toolbar buttons.

Tip: Display this status bar unless you are really short of display space.

Show category icons [on]

This option turns on and off the Category icons in the Settings dialog box. Figure 8-7 show the Settings dialog box with the Category icons off.

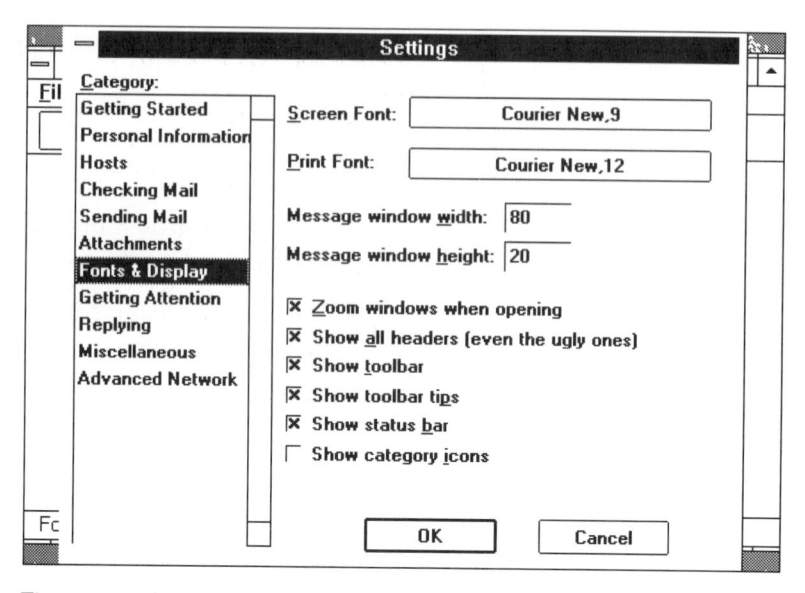

Figure 8-7. The Settings dialog box with the Show category icons option turned off.

MISCELLANEOUS SETTINGS

The Miscellaneous settings shown in Figure 8-8 control miscellaneous functions. They include check boxes associated with message switching, the confirmation of message deletion, and other important functions.

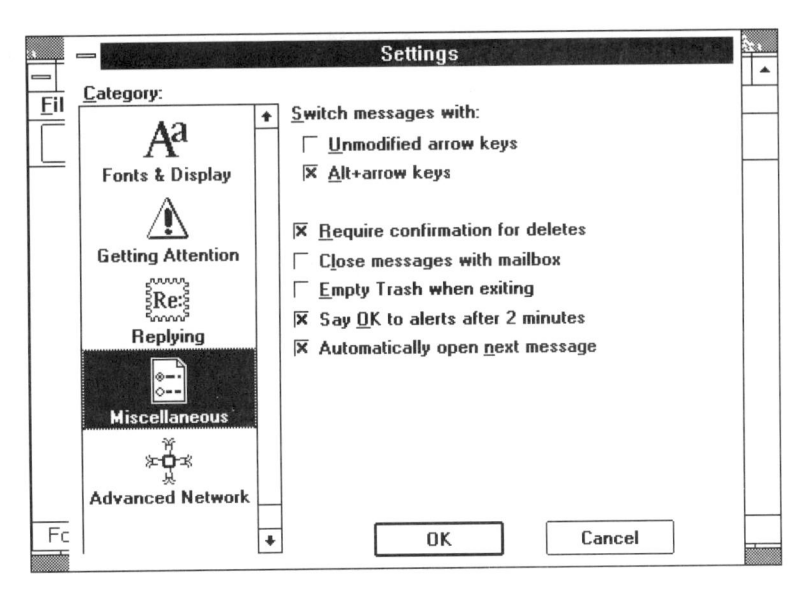

Figure 8-8. The Miscellaneous Settings window.

Unmodified arrow keys [off]

Selecting this option affects the functionality of the keyboard arrow keys when working with an active (highlighted) incoming message window. The up or left arrow key closes the current message and opens the previous message. The down or right arrow key closes the current message and opens the next message. When this option is off, the arrow keys can move the caret in messages.

Note: An active message composition window stops the arrow keys from switching messages.

Alt+arrow keys [off]

Selecting this option also affects the functionality of the keyboard arrow keys. Pressing the ALT key and the up or left arrow key closes the current message and opens the previous message. Pressing the ALT key and the down or right arrow key closes the current message and opens the next message. These changes take place even if the active window is a message composition window.

Require confirmation for deletes [on]

Select this setting and Eudora will alert you if you attempt to delete an unread message, as shown in Figure 8-9. Eudora will also alert you if you attempt to transfer queued messages out of the Out Mailbox.

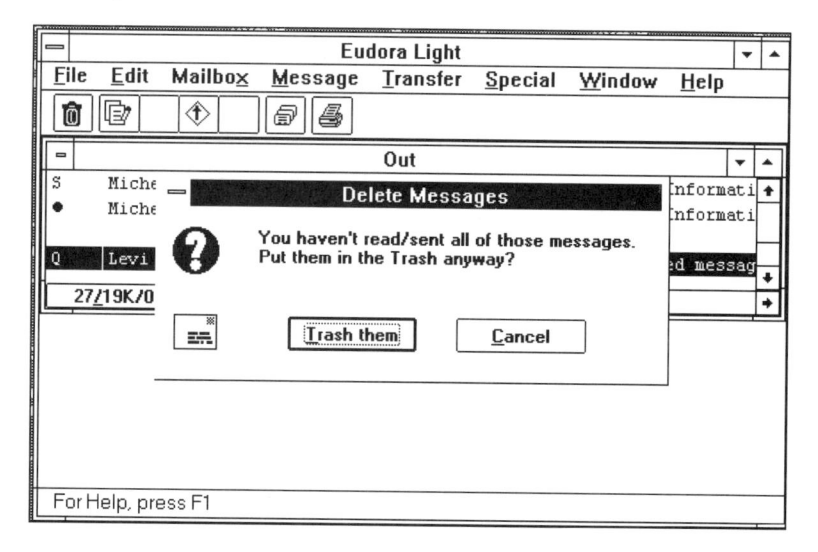

Figure 8-9. Eudora alert that unread messages are to be deleted.

Close messages with mailbox [off]

Select this option to close all open messages in a mailbox automatically when you close the mailbox window.

Empty Trash when exiting [off]

If this option is specified, Eudora will empty the Trash Mailbox when you exit the program. If this option is off, Eudora doesn't empty the Trash Mailbox automatically but only does so if you select the **Empty Trash** command from the **Special** menu. Only experienced users should turn this option on.

*Tip: To remove selected messages from the Trash Mailbox, first highlight them and then specify the **Delete** command in the **Message** menu.*

Say OK to alerts after 2 minutes [on]

Should network trouble occur during mail transfer or mail checking, Eudora notifies you as when receiving new mail. Selecting this option stops notification after two minutes, when Eudora once again attempts mail transfer or mail checking. Use this setting when you have selected automatic mail checking.

Automatically open next message [off]

> When this option is on, deleting or transferring the current message opens the next unread message in the current mailbox.

ADVANCED NETWORK SETTINGS

> The Advanced Network settings shown in Figure 8-10 control some advanced functions associated with Winsock and network functions. Do not modify them before consulting your Eudora support coordinator or Internet service provider.

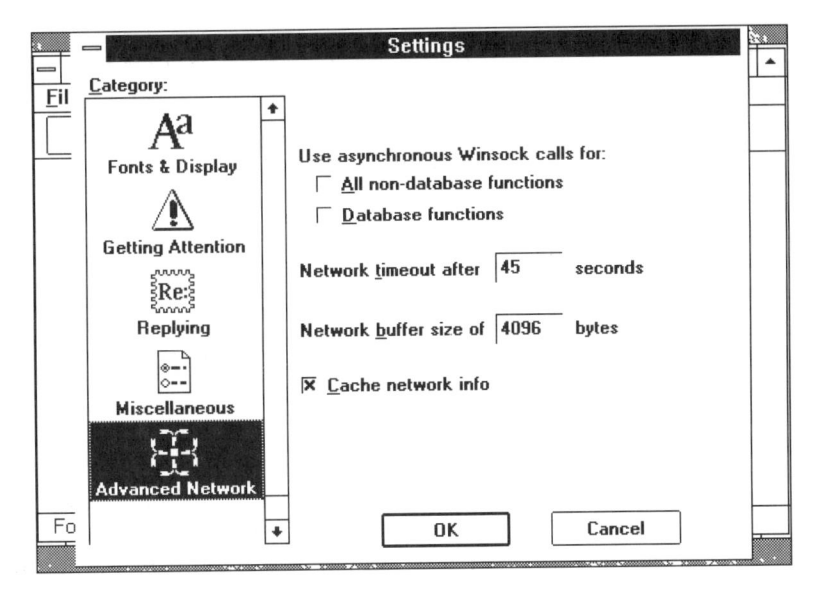

Figure 8-10. Advanced Network Settings dialog box.

Use asynchronous Winsock calls for:

This option allows you to select asynchronous calls for All non-database functions or Database functions when using the Winsock connection method. Winsock calls using TCP/IP stacks may be blocked or asynchronous. Usually the asynchronous method is preferred because of its superior error-handling capabilities. Not all TCP/IP stacks are able to handle asynchronous calls correctly. A specialist may turn this option off if the Winsock connection is not working properly.

Network timeout after ? seconds [45]

This option sets the waiting time (in seconds) before the network connection will time out—in other words, cease.

Network buffer size of ? bytes [4096]

This option sets the size of the buffer (storage area) used to transfer information between your computer and the server.

Tip: If you experience problems when transferring large messages, try decreasing the size of this buffer.

Cache network info

This option stores the results of previous database operations that occurred when the Winsock connection method was active. Selecting this option may increase the speed of performing database functions within a single Eudora session.

MAIL STORAGE

At installation Eudora creates several files in a directory whose name you specified; by default, the EUDORA directory. After installation, Eudora creates additional files as needed for mailboxes, signatures, and other settings. File descriptions and sample contents follow.

eudora.ini

The **eudora.ini** file is fairly large. Among its contents is the value of certain settings. For example, consider the following lines extracted from our **eudora.ini** file:

```
[Settings]

Offline=0

ImmediateSend=1
```

The first line of this code specifies the Settings section of the **eudora.ini** file. The remaining lines define some current settings. For example, the 0 indicates that the Offline connection setting (Getting Started) is not selected; in other words, that Eudora is connected to the server. The 1 indicates that the ImmediateSend setting (Sending Mail) has been selected; a 0 would specify message queueing.

nndbase.txt

The **nndbase.txt** file contains your nicknames. A short example follows:

```
alias thatbigguy lreiss@lacitec.on.ca,
```

nndbase.toc

The **nndbase.toc** file is the table of contents associated with your nicknames file. This file may help Eudora access your nicknames more rapidly.

in.mbx, out.mbx, trash.mbx

Files whose extension is **mbx** hold your mail. One such file exists for each of your mailboxes. An extract of the **in.mbx** file follows:

From ???@??? Sun Mar 24 16:31:00 1996

Received: from SpoolDir by FS-ENS (Mercury 1.21); 24 Mar 96 16:29:25 EST

Return-path: <lreiss@lacitec.on.ca>

Received: from mercure.lacitec.on.ca by ens.aviat.lacitec.on.ca (Mercury 1.21);

   24 Mar 96 16:29:15 EST

Received: from lreis.lacitec.on.ca by mercure.lacitec.on.ca (AIX 3.2/UCB

5.64/4.03)

         id AA15781; Sun, 24 Mar 1996 16:28:52 -0500

Date: Sun, 24 Mar 1996 16:28:52 -0500

Message-Id: <9603242128.AA15781@mercure.lacitec.on.ca>

X-Sender: lreiss@ens.aviat.lacitec.on.ca

X-Mailer: Windows Eudora Light Version 1.5.2

Mime-Version: 1.0

```
Content-Type: text/plain; charset="us-
ascii"

To: Levi Reiss recipient
<lreiss@lacitec.on.ca>

From: Levi Reiss <lreiss@lacitec.on.ca>

Subject: Testing

        Levi, can you read me?
```

While you will probably not often access these files, they can be of use in reconstructing lost messages.

in.toc, out.toc, trash.toc

Files whose extension is **toc** are table of contents files associated with your mailboxes. For example, the **in.toc** file is a table of contents file for the In Mailbox. These table of contents files enable Eudora to access the associated mailbox files more quickly. You will not process these files directly.

lmos.dat

This file contains information about the messages stored on your mail server. A sample follows:

```
Version 1.5.2

#POPSTART <lreiss@ens.aviat.lacitec.on.ca>

2147483647

1
```

```
020F5.CNM207D6443 <9603291733.AA28756@mer-
cure.lacitec.on.ca>-5-Mar-1996-07:57:23-
0500 828103048 delS Nskip Nsave read Nget
1044912772

#POPEND

This be the absolute end !
```

This file is of interest only to technical personnel.

eudora.log, eudoralog.old

Eudora keeps records of all mail transfers in the **eudora.log** and **eudoralog.old** files. When the **eudora.log** file reaches its maximum size (approximately 100K), Eudora creates a new **eudora.log** file, overwriting the **eudoralog.old** file. A sample of this file follows:

```
Fri Jan 12 09:54:27 1996

Version 1.5.2

8:0.0 Dialog: "The POP Account should be a
user name, followed by an '@', followed by
a host name.  For example:\r\n"

8:0.0 Dialog: "      'jeff@pophost.qual-
comm.com'"

8:0.4 Dialog: "Dismissed with 1"

Fri Jan 12 11:48:39 1996

Version 1.5.2
```

CHAPTER 8: BECOMING AN E-MAIL PRO

```
8:0.0 Dialog: "The POP Account should be a
user name, followed by an '@', followed by
a host name.  For example:\r\n"

8:0.0 Dialog: "       'jeff@pophost.qual-
comm.com'"

8:0.3 Dialog: "Dismissed with 1"
```

This file can be of interest in reconstructing your Eudora activities in case of error.

signatur.pce

The **signatur.pce** file contains your signature. An example follows:

```
Levi Reiss

lreiss@lacitec.on.ca

e-mail won't change the world
```

descmap.pce

The **descmap.pce** file contains mappings between mailbox names and DOS 8.3 file names. This file is of interest to Eudora technical personnel.

SHARING A PC

Not everyone has his or her own personal computer. Budget constraints may require several users to cohabitate on a single PC. Don't despair. While Eudora won't eliminate all sharing conflicts, it was designed with computer sharing in mind. Use the following procedure when juggling multiple users on a single computer.

Create an individual mail directory and a separate program item for each user. Choose significant directory names. Specify the appropriate directory name as the first parameter on the Command Line of the Program Item Properties dialog box.

Note: The individual directories can be located on floppy disks, hard drives, or network hard drives. This gives you some measure of security.

MAIL TRANSPORT SERVERS

The software and hardware associated with outgoing and incoming mail may be different. Eudora transfers outgoing mail from your PC to your SMTP server using the Simple Mail Transfer Protocol (SMTP). The SMTP server employs this same software to send your mail to your recipients. Your Post Office Protocol (POP) server collects incoming mail for Eudora, which transfers it to your PC using version 3 of the Post Office Protocol (POP3).

OUTGOING MAIL

As stated above, Eudora sends mail to your party via a two-step process, using the Simple Mail Transfer Protocol. You may wonder why it takes two steps to send outgoing mail. Why not just send the mail directly from your computer to the recipient? Eudora's two-step process is similar to the hub system used by many airlines and courier companies. Direct connections often take more time, because they require that the computer address each recipient individually. The more connections, the greater the likelihood that the line is busy. Furthermore, unlike cities, some computer addresses are hard to find. Instead of making each individual computer responsible for all message transmission details, your computer delivers the messages to a centralized message handler (the SMTP server). This server then handles all the ugly details of outgoing message transmission. A similar two-step method processes incoming mail.

INCOMING MAIL

Recall that you receive mail on your POP server, mail delivered by an SMTP server. Eudora collects your incoming mail from the POP server and uses the POP3 protocol to deliver this mail to your PC.

You may ask the question, why bother with two protocols. Why not use SMTP to receive your mail and not only to deliver it? SMTP works best with computers that are constantly available. Most people don't want to keep Eudora and their own computer up and running around the clock.

Furthermore, SMTP is not a good solution in environments running a variety of computers.

OBTAINING INFORMATION AND SOFTWARE

Do you want more information about Eudora? Do you need Eudora software such as the freeware version of Eudora, and POP3 servers? An excellent source is the distributor's (Qualcomm) own anonymous ftp server, ftp.qualcomm.com. This appears in the quest directory.

EUDORA INFORMATION

Eudora is undergoing constant revision. Perhaps something on your wish list is already in the latest software upgrade. For the latest information about Eudora, send an e-mail message to eudora-info@qualcomm.com. The message text should include "sub eudora your-first-name your-last-name" and nothing else.

OBTAINING A POP SERVER

Do you need a POP server to run on your UNIX system? Qualcomm suggests that you run "popper." Not only does it suggest it, but it also makes several UNIX versions available via anonymous ftp from its ftp site, ftp.qualcomm.com.

VAX/VMS (DEC) systems users may try the "Multinet" package available from TGV, or IUPOP3, available via anonymous ftp from ftp.indiana.edu.

VM/CMS (IBM) system users may access a version of "popper" available via anonymous ftp from vmd.cso.uiuc.edu (cd to the "POPD" directory).

PH SERVER SOURCE CODE

A "Ph" protocol server is available via anonymous ftp from ftp.qualcomm.com. Recall that a Ph name server is the computer that may help you find information about someone, provided that you know his or her name.

PASSWORD CHANGE SERVER

Three sample UNIX servers for Eudora's **Change Password** command are available via anonymous ftp from ftp.qualcomm.com.

WINDOWS SOCKETS PRODUCTS

Demonstration versions of Windows Sockets 1.1 compliant stacks and applications are available via anonymous ftp from sunsite.unc.edu in the micro/pc-stuff/ms-windows/winsock directory. They are also available on ftp.cica.indiana.edu in the pub/pc/wins/winsock directory.

SERIAL LINE IP (SLIP)

You can get information and software for Serial Line IP (SLIP) applications via anonymous ftp from biochemistry.cwru.edu in the /slip directory.

PC SPEAKER

To hear Eudora announce new mail, you must first install the PC speaker driver. This software is available via anonymous ftp from ftp.qualcomm.com. It appears in the SPEAK.EXE file located in the quest/eudora/windows/utils directory. The file is self-extracting and contains all required documentation.

EUDORA PRO FOR WINDOWS

This chapter covers the commercial version of Eudora, namely Eudora Pro. It assumes that you have a basic familiarity with the freeware version, referred to here as Eudora Light, and covers the additions and changes to the product, starting with the most important (after the installation, of course).

INSTALLING EUDORA PRO

It's fairly simple to install Eudora Pro. For example, instead of downloading software from the Internet, you start by opening shrink-wrapped diskettes. Power users can perform a custom installation, described in the following section.

STANDARD INSTALLATION

For a standard installation of Eudora Pro 2.2, carry out the following steps:

1. Exit all current applications.

2. Insert the first diskette into your PC's A: drive.

3. Access Windows Explorer (Windows 95) or File Manager (Windows 3.1) and double-click on the Setup Application file to start the Setup program.

4. After reading the Welcome screen, click on the Next button.

5. Enter your User Code (from the inside cover of this manual or from your Eudora support coordinator), then click on the Next button.

6. Specify the installation directory and then click on the Next button.

Note: If Eudora Pro 2.2 is an upgrade to Eudora Light or an older version of Eudora Pro, select your current Eudora directory to store your messages, mailboxes, folders, and options. Otherwise you may select any directory. Setup automatically installs the 16-bit version of Eudora Pro for Win 3.1 systems and the 32-bit version for Win 95 and Win NT systems. If you are running Win 95 or Win NT but do not have 32-bit TCP/IP software, Eudora displays an error message and asks if you want to install the 16-bit version.

7. Check the displayed settings. If they are correct, click on the Next button. If not, click on the Back button and make the necessary changes.

8. In response to the prompt, insert the second diskette into the A: drive and click on OK. When Setup is complete, the designated directory contains Eudora Pro 2.2.

9. In response to the on-screen question Do you want to view the README file?, click Yes, and then read this file.

10. Exit the README file and Windows Explorer or File Manager, and you're ready to roll.

UNINSTALLING EUDORA PRO

The latest versions of Windows enable you to uninstall Eudora Pro 2.2 easily. In Windows 95, open the control panel, double-click on Add/Remove Programs, select Eudora Pro, and click on Remove. In Windows NT, open the Eudora Pro program group from within the Program Manager, then double-click on the Uninstall Eudora icon.

ADVANCED INSTALLATION

Power users have additional control over the installation process by modifying the **setup.ini** file contained in Eudora Pro diskette # 1.

*Warning: Don't modify **setup.ini** before making a copy of the original file.*

[Version] section

The Setup program normally installs the 16-bit version of Eudora Pro on Win 3.1 systems and the 32-bit version on Windows 95 and Windows NT systems. You can force a different version of Eudora Pro by coding the Version variable in the Version section as in the following example:

```
[Version]

Version=16
```

[Options] section

By default, the Setup program puts mail files and an attachment directory in the user's target install directory. Setting the variable AskForOptionsDirs=1 adds a dialog to the setup process, which prompts the user to enter new directories for attachments and mail. The MailDir and AttachDir values provide defaults for this dialog. For example,

```
[Options]

AsdkForOptionalDirs=1
```

```
MailDir=c:\mymail

AttachDir=c:\mymail\attachments
```

The 32-bit version of Eudora Pro under Windows 95 includes a New Mail notification icon in the Task Bar Tray. Place the mouse pointer over this icon to display a tool tip, which provides you with a message count. Double-click on this icon to bring Eudora to the foreground. The icon disappears when you click the mouse button or press a key inside the Eudora window.

DIFFERENCES RIGHT OFF THE BAT

No matter how you want to use Eudora Pro, you'll see these differences right away. They include the main window toolbar, the right mouse button, the message composition window, and message summaries.

MAIN WINDOW TOOLBAR

The Eudora Pro Main window toolbar shown at the top of Figure 9-1 contains 15 buttons. In comparison, the Eudora Light toolbar contains 7 buttons. Both toolbars appear just below the menu titles. However, the 32-bit version of Eudora Pro allows you to drag the toolbar to any on-screen location.

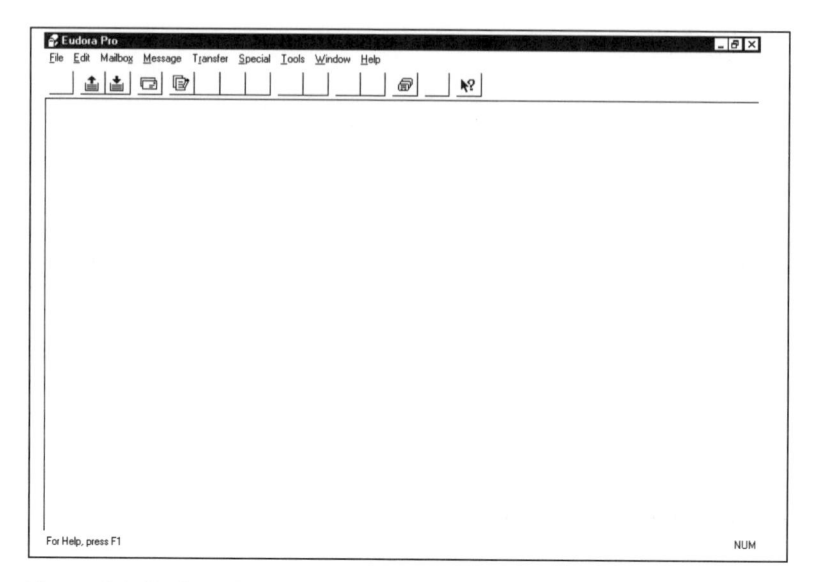

Figure 9-1. Eudora Pro's Main window toolbar.

Trash Button

The Trash button transfers the current message or messages to the Trash Mailbox. It works like the **Delete** command in the **Message** menu.

Out Button

The Out button opens your **Out** Mailbox. It works like the Out command in the **Mailbox** menu.

In Button

The In button opens your **In** Mailbox. It works like the In command in the **Mailbox** menu.

Check Mail Button

The Check Mail button examines your POP server to see if you have new mail. It works like the **Check Mail** command in the **File** menu.

New Message Button

The New Message button opens an outgoing message composition window. It works like the **New Message** command in the **Message** menu.

Reply Button

The Reply button generates a reply to the current message or message summaries. It works like the **Reply** command in the **Message** menu.

Forward Button

The Forward button forwards the current message or message summaries. It works like the **Forward** command in the **Message** menu.

Redirect Button

The Redirect button redirects the current message or message summaries. It works like the **Redirect** command in the **Message** menu.

Previous Button

The Previous button opens the previous message in the current mailbox.

Next Button

The Next button opens the next message in the current mailbox.

Attach File Button

The Attach File button displays the Attach File dialog. It works like the **Attach File Redirect** command in the **Message** menu.

Check Spelling Button

The Check Spelling button checks the spelling of the current message composition window, text file, or signature window. It works like the **Check Spelling** command in the **Edit** menu.

Nicknames Button

The Nicknames button displays the Nicknames window. It works like the **Nicknames** command in the **Edit** menu.

Print Button

The Print button prints a current message, text file, signature file, Filter Report window, dialup Navigation Trace window, or Ph window. It works like the **Print** command in the **File** menu.

Help Button

The Help button displays context-sensitive Help, which is described in the On-line Help section later in this chapter.

THE RIGHT MOUSE BUTTON

In addition to toolbar and main menu commands, you may often use the right mouse button. To do so, position the mouse pointer over a Eudora window, click on the right mouse button, and select a command from the ensuing context-sensitive list.

To check for new mail without maximizing the Eudora icon, position the mouse pointer over the icon, click on the right mouse button, and select Check Mail.

MESSAGE COMPOSITION WINDOW

The Eudora Pro message composition window, shown in Figure 9-2, is quite similar to the Eudora Light version. Eudora Pro allows you to create two signatures. The Pro version's Attachment Type Combo box includes an additional kind of attachment, and the Return Receipt icon is new.

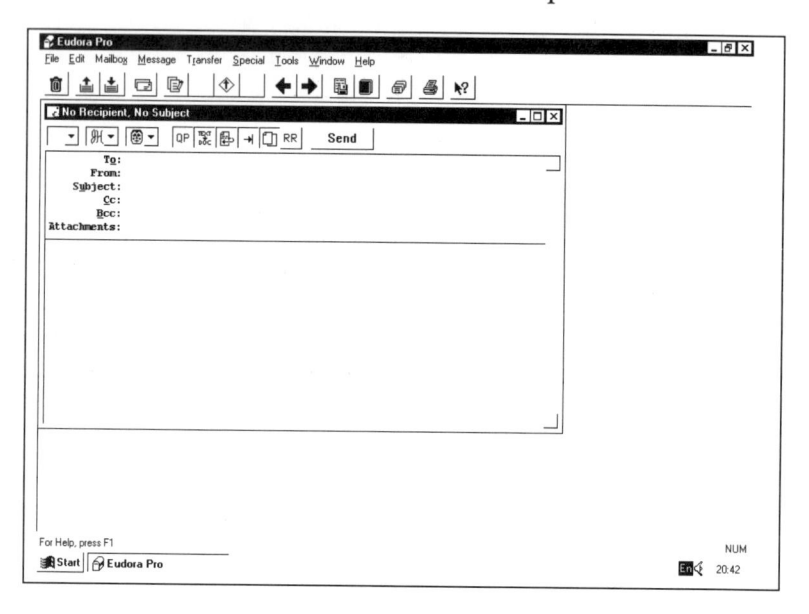

Figure 9-2. Eudora Pro's message composition window.

Signatures

Create an alternate signature by selecting the Alternate Signature command from the Tools menu. You can use the signature for business mail and the alternate signature for personal e-mail, or vice versa.

Attachment Type Combo Box

The Attachment Type Combo Box allows you to select the format of documents attached to outgoing messages. Like Eudora Light, Eudora Pro encodes attachments in the widely used Multipurpose Internet Mail Extensions (MIME) or Bin Hex, which is mostly used with Macintosh-mail programs or with older versions of Eudora. Eudora Pro also offers the Uuencode format, often used when communicating with older PC or UNIX systems.

Return Receipt

Pressing the Return Receipt button requests notification when your outgoing message is delivered.

Warning: Your recipient's e-mail software may not honor return receipt requests.

MESSAGE SUMMARIES

When there are messages in a mailbox, they are listed as individual message summaries. As shown in Figure 9-3, each message is divided into eight columns: Status (S), Priority (P), Attachment (A), Label, Sender (Who), Date, Size (K), and Subject. The Attachment and Label columns are not available in Eudora Light.

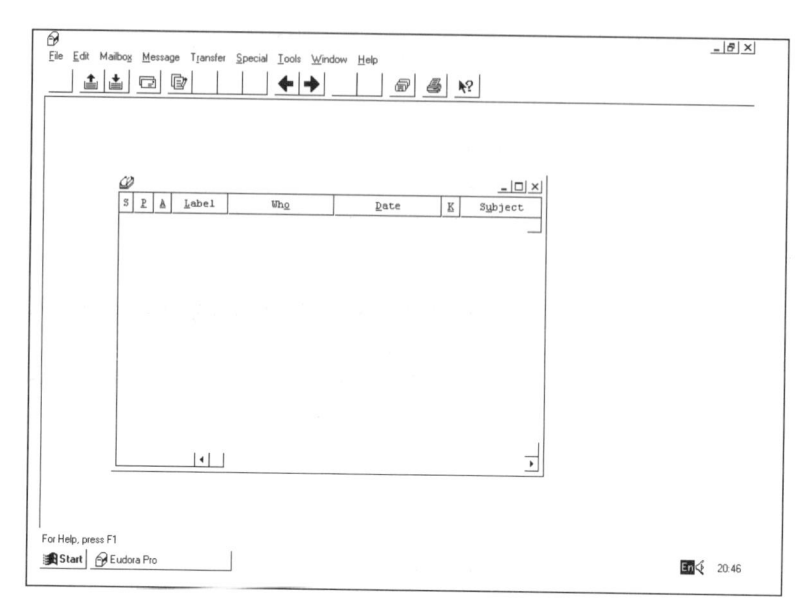

Figure 9-3. Eudora Pro's message summaries box.

The Attachment column displays the attachment icon for messages with attachments. The Label column displays the message label, and the message summary assumes the label color defined in the Labels Option dialog box. The recipient assigns a label to incoming messages, either manually or automatically using a filter as described in the "Message Filtering" section.

You can change the message Status, Priority, and Label directly from the message summary. Position the mouse over any message summary or use the keyboard to highlight several message summaries, then click the right mouse button. Finally, choose from the available selections.

To change the current message summary's status, activate the **Change Status** command in the **Message** menu and then choose the desired message status.

INCOMING MESSAGE WINDOW

Click on a message summary to generate the incoming message as shown in Figure 9-4. Its toolbar contains the following icons: BLAH, BLAH, BLAH, Trash, Fetch, and Priority Popup.

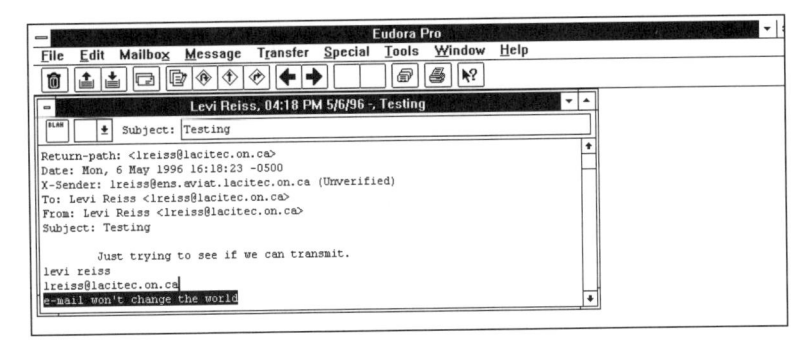

Figure 9-4. Eudora Pro incoming message.

BLAH, BLAH, BLAH icon

Click this interestingly named icon to display complete message headers as shown in Figure 9-5.

Tip: These message headers may help you debug a network problem.

THE EUDORA USER'S GUIDE

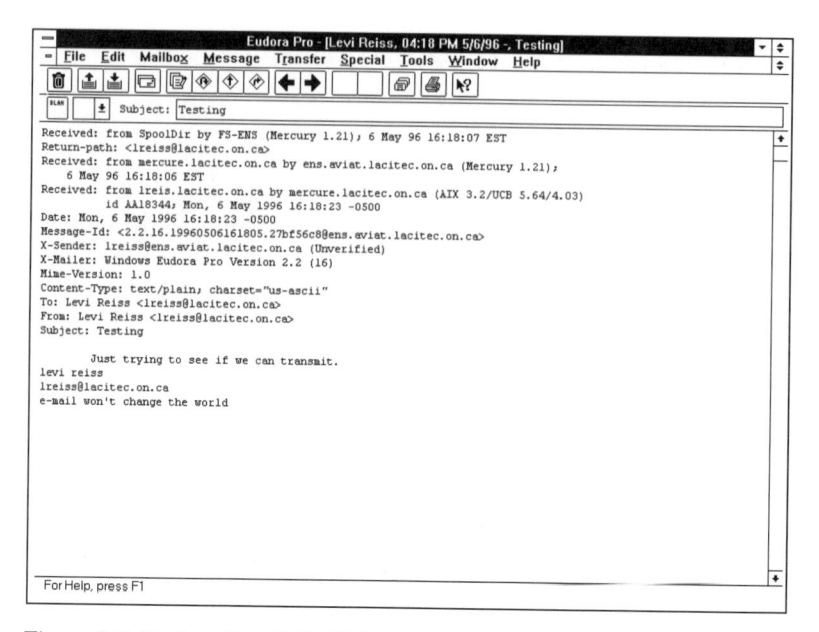

Figure 9-5. Eudora Pro Blah, Blah, Blah icon displays complete message headers.

Trash icon

The Trash icon manually deletes messages from the server. Click on this icon to delete the current message from the server on the next mail check. The Trash icon appears only for messages on the server.

Fetch icon

The Fetch icon downloads skipped messages as defined by the Skip messages over ? K option in the Checking Mail Options. It appears only next to skipped messages that have not been downloaded. To download the skipped message, click on the Fetch icon and check your mail again.

MESSAGE FILTERING

Eudora Pro's message filtering is a major reason that users switch from Eudora Light to Eudora Pro. Message filters provide additional control over incoming and outgoing messages. Filters enable users to assign labels, change message subjects and priorities, and transfer messages to specified mailboxes. Filters can be applied automatically or manually.

Access the Filters window shown in Figure 9-6 from the **Tools** menu. The left side of the Filters window includes the user-defined filter list and four filter editing buttons. The New button creates a new filter; the Remove button deletes an existing filter; and the Up and Down buttons change the order in which filters are activated.

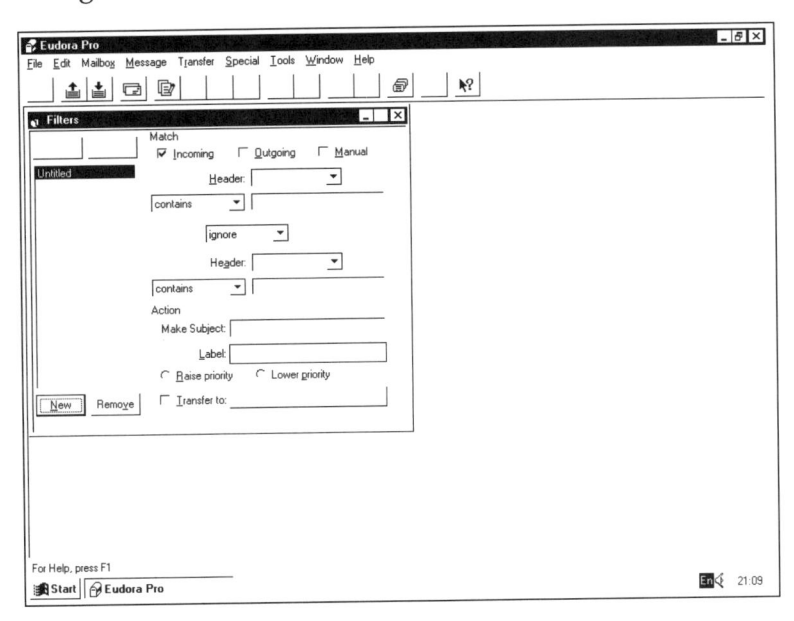

Figure 9-6. Eudora Pro's Filters window.

The right side of the Filters window displays two groups of filter parameters, Match and Action. Match specifies the message filtering parameters. Action specifies the operations performed on messages meeting the Match criteria. Before describing Match and Action in detail, let's see how to create filters.

Click on the New button to create a new filter named "Untitled" at the bottom of the filter list. You will name this filter shortly.

MATCH AREA

The Filters Window Match area specifies message filtering criteria. Its various components are described next.

Incoming, Outgoing, and Manual

The first line of the Match area includes three independent check boxes. A check mark in the Incoming box activates the filter for all incoming messages. A check mark in the Outgoing box activates the filter for all outgoing messages after they are sent. A check mark in the Manual box enables manual filter activation for current messages using the **Filter Messages** command in the **Special** menu.

Filter Terms

Each filter uses one or two "terms" as filtering criteria. The conjunction combo box combines two terms into a single filtering function. Each filtering term contains three fields: the Header field; the Match Type field; and the Matching Text field.

Before examining these three fields in detail, consider a simple example. To select messages whose Subject field contains the word *chocolate*, code *Subject* in the Header field, *contains* in the Match Type field, and *chocolate* in the Matching Text field, as shown in Figure 9-7. The action taken (such as transferring the filtered messages to a given mailbox) is defined in the Action area. Now that you have an idea of how these three fields work, let's examine their use in greater detail.

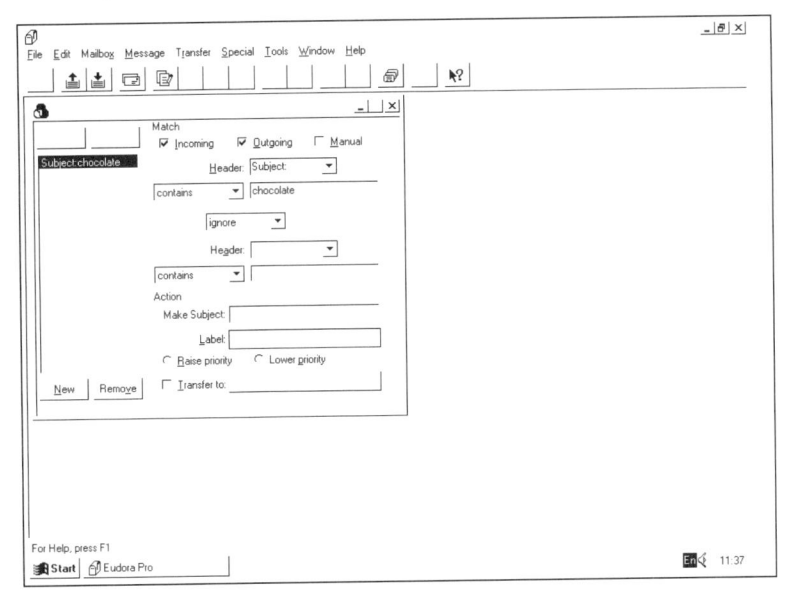

Figure 9-7. Eudora Pro's filtering to select messages whose subject field contains "chocolate."

The Header field specifies the message segment to be searched. You can enter a value manually or choose from the following values that appear in the combo box list:

- To:
- From:
- Cc:
- Reply-To:
- <<Any Header>> (searches all message headers)
- <>Body>> (searches the message body)

The Match Type field specifies what constitutes a successful match. The match options are

- contains/doesn't contain — if the specified message segment contains/doesn't contain the Matching Text field contents, the filter is activated.

- is/is not—if the specified message segment is/is not a total match of the Matching Text field contents, the filter is activated.

- starts with/ends with—if the specified message segment starts with/ends with the Matching Text field contents, the filter is activated.

- appears/doesn't appear—if the specified message header field appears/doesn't appear in the message header, the filter is activated.

Note: The appears/doesn't appear match option uses Header field functions instead of the Matching Text field contents.

The Matching Text field specifies the character string for selecting messages.

Tip: Keep this value as short and specific as possible. If it's too complicated, you may not find messages that match.

Conjunction

The conjunction combo box appears above the second Header field in the Match area of the Filters window. It enables you to link two filter criteria such as "chocolate" in the Subject field or "Sweet Tooth candies" in the To: field. The conjunction options are

- ignore—ignore the second criterion; filter messages according to the first criterion only.

- and—filter messages that meet both criteria.

- or—filter messages that meet either or both criteria.

- unless—filter messages that meet the first criterion but not the second term. For example, you could select messages whose Subject: field contains "chocolate" except those whose To: field contains "Sweet Tooth candies," as shown in Figure 9-8.

THE EUDORA USER'S GUIDE

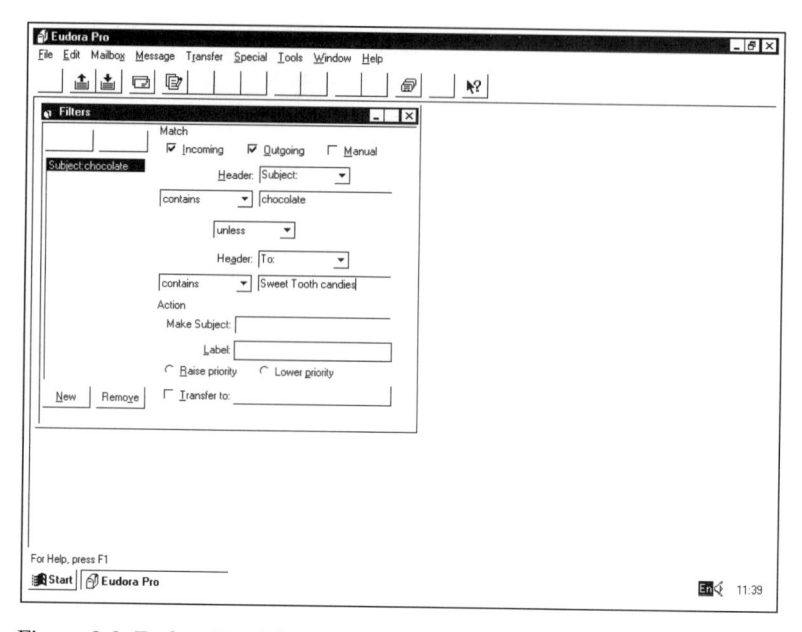

Figure 9-8. Eudora Pro Message filtering illustrating unless (but not).

ACTION AREA

The Filters Window Action area specifies what to do with selected messages. For example, you can modify the subject, create a color-coded label, change the message priority, or transfer the message to a different mailbox, such as shown in Figure 9-9.

CHAPTER 9: EUDORA PRO FOR WINDOWS

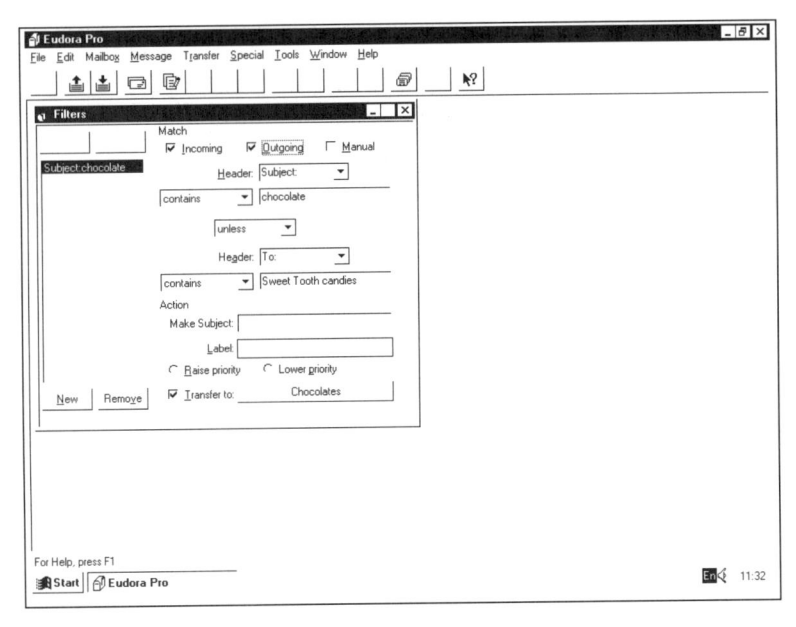

Figure 9-9. Eudora Pro's Filters Window Action area.

Make Subject Field

Change a filtered message's subject by typing the new subject in the Make Subject field. The mailbox window will contain the new subject. The & symbol saves typing by retaining the previous subject. For example, if your original subject was "chocolate" and you type "suppliers of:&" in the Make subject field, the new message subject becomes suppliers of chocolate.

Label Popup

Use the label popup to assign a color-coded label to a message summary. Recall that the Label options dialog box customizes label titles and colors.

Raise/Lower Priority Options

The Raise Priority option increases the priority of selected messages by one level. The Lower Priority option decreases the priority of selected messages by one level.

Transfer To Field

The Transfer To field transfers selected incoming and outgoing messages to a mailbox specified in the **Transfer** menu. Hold down the SHIFT key during mailbox selection to copy messages instead of transferring them.

SAVING FILTER CHANGES

Use the **Save** command in the **File** menu to save filter changes. Eudora warns you if you try to close the Filters window without saving your changes.

ACTIVATING FILTERS

After setting up your filters, you must activate them. Selecting the Incoming or Outgoing options in the Match area automatically activates the filter for all incoming or outgoing messages. Selecting the Manual option requires you to activate the filter manually for current messages. To do so, select the **Filter Messages** command from the **Special** menu.

Filter Activation Order

The filter list at the left side of the Filters window specifies the order in which filters are activated (topmost first). To move a filter up the Filters window list, click on the filter name to highlight it, and then click on the Up button. Use a similar procedure to move a filter down the list.

Warning: Be careful; placing filters in the wrong order can lead to unpleasant surprises.

RECEIVING FILTERED MESSAGES

If the Open mailbox (new mail only) option in the Getting Attention Options dialog box is enabled, all mailboxes receiving unfiltered messages open upon delivery. If this option is disabled, the Filter Report displays those mailboxes that received new messages, as shown in Figure 9-10.

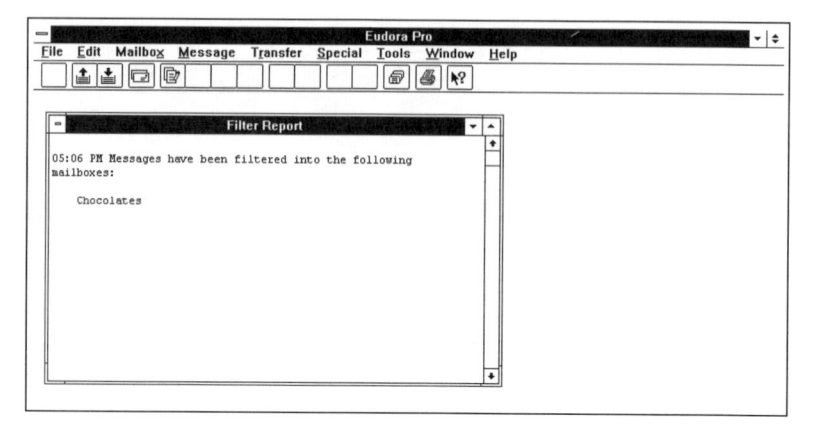

Figure 9-10. The Filter Report displays which mailboxes received new messages.

CHECKING SPELLING

Eudora includes a built-in spelling checker that works with the body of current message composition windows, text files, and signature files. It includes a built-in dictionary and allows you to create a custom dictionary. You can configure it in the Spell Checking Options dialog box or from the Options button in the Check Spelling window as shown in Figure 9-11. To launch the spell checker, click on the **Check Spelling** button in the Main window toolbar or select the Check Spelling command in the **Edit** menu. If it can't find any misspellings, it displays the No misspellings found alert.

CHAPTER 9: EUDORA PRO FOR WINDOWS

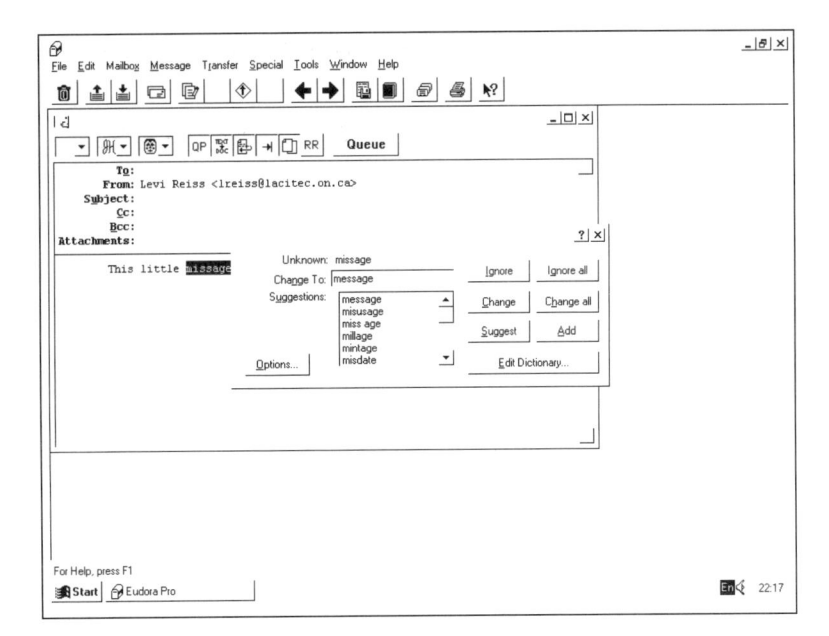

Figure 9-11. Eudora Pro's Check Spelling feature.

Unless a text segment is selected, Eudora Pro checks the entire message body or text file, starting from the beginning. If it finds a misspelled, unknown, or repeated word, the Check Spelling dialog box is displayed with the word listed in the Unknown field.

There are several ways to correct the misspelled word. You may enter the correct spelling word in the Change To field, select it from Suggestions list and click the Change button, or double-click on it in the Suggestions list. After doing so, the spell check continues.

CHECK SPELLING DIALOG BOX

Check Spelling options include ignoring an unknown word, changing the word, suggesting the correct spelling, adding the word to a custom dictionary, editing your dictionary, and changing the spell-checking preferences via the Options button. Each of the fields and buttons is described below.

Unknown Field

An unknown word is one not found in Eudora's built-in dictionary or your own custom dictionary. The Change To Field, Suggestions Field and Ignore, Ignore All, Change, Change All, or Suggest Add buttons, described below, process unknown words.

Change To Field

The Change To field is used with the Change and Change All buttons. It contains the corrected value of the unknown word.

Suggestions Field

This field lists Eudora's suggestions for the correct spelling of the unknown word. If the Always Suggest option is turned on, suggestions automatically appear here. If not, you must click the Suggest button to display Eudora's suggestions.

Ignore Button

Click the Ignore button to skip this occurrence of the unknown word.

Ignore All Button

Click the Ignore All button to skip this occurrence and all subsequent occurrences of the unknown word.

Change Button

This button replaces this occurrence of the unknown word by the contents of the Change To field.

Change All Button

This button replaces this occurrence and all subsequent occurrences of the unknown word by the contents of the Change To field.

Suggest Button

This button displays Eudora's suggestions for the correct spelling of the unknown word in the Suggestions field.

THE EUDORA USER'S GUIDE

Add Button

This button adds the unknown word to your custom user dictionary.

Edit Dictionary Button

This button displays the Edit User Dictionary dialog box shown in Figure 9-12. This dialog box lists in the Dictionary field all words appearing in your user dictionary. Use it to add words to or delete words from your personal user dictionary, and to remove all dictionary entries.

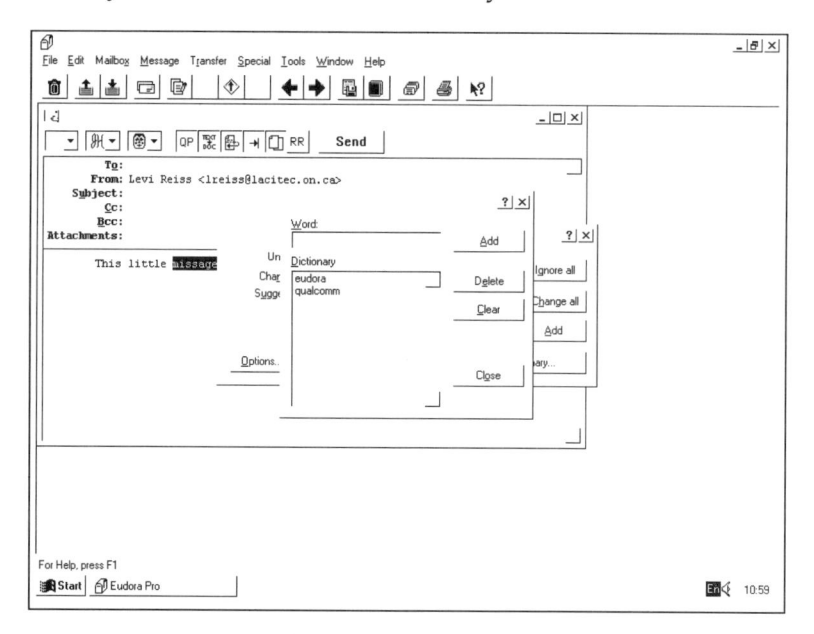

Figure 9-12. Eudora Pro's Edit User Dictionary dialog box.

Note: User dictionary words are stored in lower case only.

To add a word to the user dictionary, type its correct spelling in the Word field and click on the Add button. The word appears in the Dictionary field. To remove a word from the user dictionary, type it in the Word field or locate it in the Dictionary field and click on it to display it in the Word field. Then, click on the Delete button. To delete the entire user dictionary, click on the Clear button and then confirm.

Options Button

The Options button displays the spell-checking Preferences dialog box, which contains six spell-checking options. These options include:

Ignore capitalized words—ignores words starting with capital letters, such as proper nouns.

Ignore words with numbers—ignores words containing numbers.

Ignore words with mixed case—ignores words containing both upper- and lowercase characters.

Report words with mixed case—reports words containing both upper- and lowercase characters and identifies them as mixed case.

Report doubled words—reports words appearing twice in sequence in text and identifies them as doubled words.

Always suggest—displays Eudora's suggestions for the correct spelling of an unknown word in the Suggestions field.

ADDITIONAL NEW FEATURES

Once you get used to these new features, you will wonder how you ever lived without them. They include the Message Application Program Interface (MAPI), using active URLs, dragging and dropping, print preview, additional nicknames processing capabilities, sharing a windows PC with other users, and extensive help facilities. Two new files are shown as well.

MESSAGE APPLICATION PROGRAM INTERFACE (MAPI)

The Message Application Program Interface (MAPI) lets you send e-mail messages from any compatible application; for example, certain word processors, spreadsheets, and graphics applications. MAPI-compatible applications include a **Send** or **Send mail** command in their **File** menu. When selected, the Eudora Pro MAPI server displays a new outgoing message accompanied by the attached current document. Complete the To: field, add information to the message body if so desired, and click on the Send or Queue button.

Use the MAPI Options dialog box to run the Eudora MAPI server. To generate this dialog box, select the **Options...** command from the **Tools** menu and click on the MAPI category. This dialog box includes three options for loading the Eudora MAPI server. The server can always run, it can run only when Eudora Pro is running, or it can never run. These options take place immediately upon selection.

Note: Running the Eudora MAPI server prevents Microsoft Exchange from running.

There are several options for saving or deleting MAPI attachments. When MAPI attaches a file and sends a message, that file is immediately copied into the Attach directory or a user-specified directory. MAPI allows you to save the file, delete it after sending messages, or delete it after the accompanying messages are emptied from the trash.

USING ACTIVE URLS

Eudora Pro recognizes several types of Universal Resource Locators (URLs), including http, finger, ftp, gopher, and ph. Position the mouse over a URL, and its arrow becomes a pointing hand. Double-click to open the URL; for example, to access a given World Wide Web location. Clicking on a ph URL displays the Ph window.

DRAGGING AND DROPPING

Eudora Pro supports a "Drag and Drop" feature for attaching files to messages. To do so, create a new message and then open the Windows Explorer or File Manager. Locate the desired attachment files, select them, and drag their file icons inside the message. You can also drag one or more files onto Eudora's Main window. This opens a new composition window with the files attached. Finally, you can drag a file onto the Eudora icon, which attaches the file to an existing composition window or creates a new composition window if none was previously open.

PRINT PREVIEW

This valuable Eudora Pro feature previews printed output for a current message, a text file, a signature file, the Filter Report window, the dialup Navigation Trace window, or the Ph window. To generate a print preview, make the message or window current and select the **Print Preview** command from the **File** menu. The Print Preview dialog box is then displayed. If you like what you see, click on the Print button. The Print Preview dialog box also displays the Next or Previous page of a multiple-page file, can display Two Pages at a time, and can display a Zoom In and Zoom Out view of each page.

NICKNAMES

Eudora Pro adds a few wrinkles to nickname processing. It supports multiple nicknames files and allows you to access a nicknames file on a server.

MULTIPLE NICKNAMES FILES

Eudora Pro supports multiple nicknames files. Place supplementary nicknames files such as mailing lists in the **Eudora\nickname** directory.

Displaying the Nicknames window displays all nicknames. If the selected nickname is not part of your standard nicknames file, its file name appears in the upper right corner of the nicknames window. When creating a new nickname, you can use the new nickname dialog box to select the nickname's file.

*Warning: Keep the standard Eudora Nicknames file (**nndbase .txt**) in your **Eudora** directory. Do not place it in the newly created Nickname directory.*

Accessing a Nicknames File on a Server

Eudora Pro can access one or more nicknames files from a network server. To do so, add the ExtraNicknameDirs entry to the [Settings] section of the **eudora.ini** file. Code the directory and nicknames file names. When the nicknames files are located in different directories, use a semicolon (;) to separate the directory names.

Note: If the new nickname has the same name as an existing nickname, Eudora Pro asks you if you want to add the selected names to the existing nickname or replace the existing nickname with these new names.

SHARING A WINDOWS 95 PC WITH OTHER USERS

To share a PC with other users, make a separate mail directory and create shortcuts to the Eudora executable file for each user. The mail directories may have any name, and may be placed anywhere, including on floppies or network drives. Specify the directory used in the Target field of your shortcut.

GETTING HELP

Eudora Pro offers extensive context-sensitive help. You won't have to contact your support coordinator or service provider often. Clicking on the Help button generates a window similar to that shown in Figure 9-13. Clicking on the first underlined text (hyperlink) generates a window similar to that shown in Figure 9-14.

Using the Help Topics

Help topics provide information about the current version of the software, instructions on how to do certain tasks with Eudora Pro, and some tips and tricks for using Eudora Pro. To use them, select **Topics** from the **Help** menu and browse through the Help contents.

Depending on the operating system you are running, you can also use the Find or Search options to find information in the Help Topics without browsing through them.

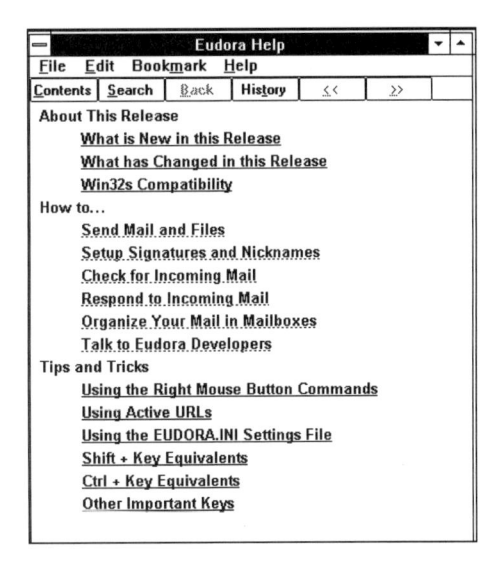

Figure 9-13. Initial Eudora Help display.

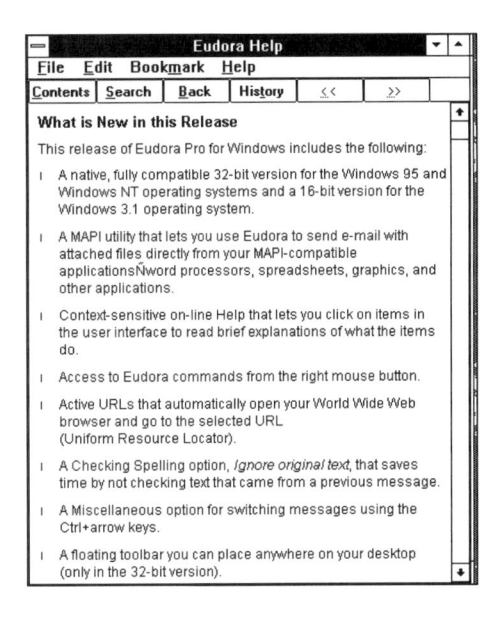

Figure 9-14. Clicking on an underlined topic in the Help window in Figure 9-13 generates topic-specific information.

NEW FILES

Eudora Pro includes two very important new files, the **filters.pce** file and the **signatur.alt** file, described next.

filters.pce

Eudora filter names and extensions are saved in the **filters.pce** file. A sample follows:

```
rule Subject:chocolate

transfer Chocolat.mbx

incoming

outgoing

header Subject:

verb contains

value chocolate

conjunction unless

header To:

verb contains

value Sweet Tooth candies
```

signatur.alt

The alternate signature is kept in the **signatur.alt** file. A sample appears next:

```
Levi Reiss

lreiss@lacitec.on.ca

All the E-mail services fit to transmit
```

OPTIONS

Eudora Pro contains 16 categories of options, accessed from the **Tools** menu. Eudora Light contains 11 categories of settings, accessed from the **Special** menu. There is often a major correspondence between these two sets. In fact, sometimes, the corresponding options and settings are exactly the same. We next examine Eudora Pro's option categories, in the order that they appear on the screen. We focus on the differences with Eudora Light.

GETTING STARTED OPTIONS

The Getting Started options are shown in Figure 9-15. The corresponding Eudora Light settings were discussed in Chapter 8.

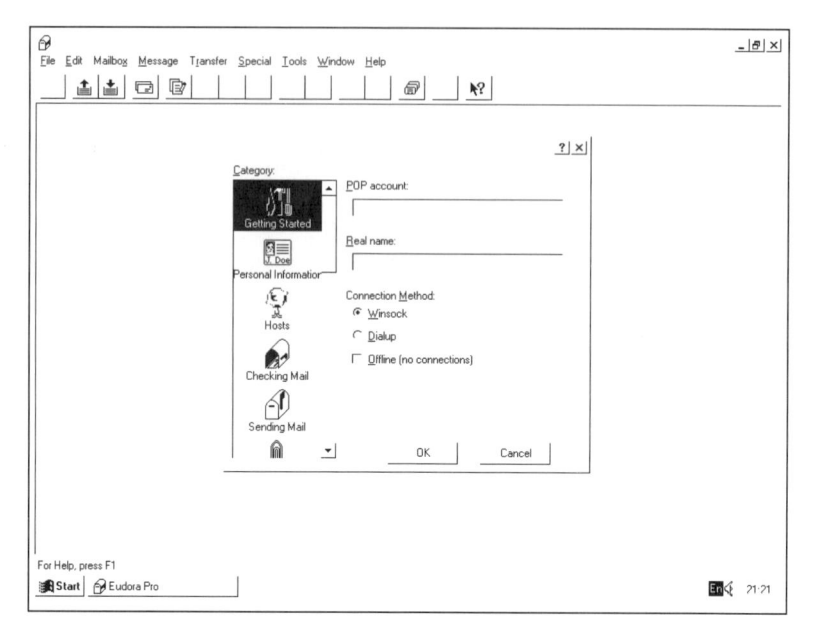

Figure 9-15. Eudora Pro's Getting Started options.

Connection Method: [Winsock]

Eudora Pro offers additional connection methods. TCP/IP software users should select Winsock independent of whether they are using a direct network connection, SLIP, or PPP. Modem users who don't have access to TCP/IP software should select Dialup.

Tip: No matter what hardware and software you are using, select Offline to save connection charges.

PERSONAL INFORMATION OPTIONS

The Personal Information options are shown in Figure 9-16. The corresponding Eudora Light settings were discussed in Chapter 8.

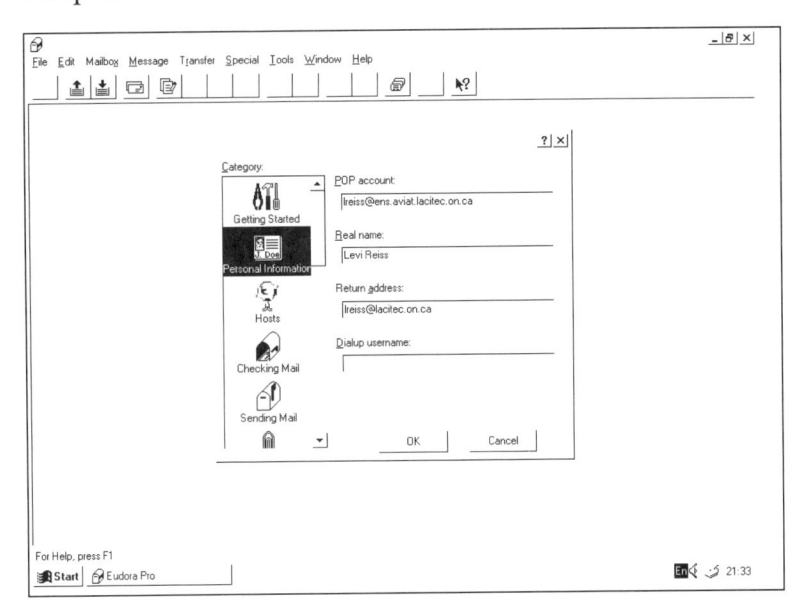

Figure 9-16. Eudora Pro's Personal Information options.

Dialup username: [none]

Dialup users can enter a secondary user name such as their login name to a terminal server. This name is used during the dialup process. See Appendix E of the Eudora Pro manual for more information about this field.

Note: If your dialup user name is identical to your POP account user name, you may leave this field blank.

HOSTS OPTIONS

The Hosts options include POP account, SMTP, Ph, and Finger. They are identical to the Eudora Light Hosts settings discussed in Chapter 8.

CHECKING MAIL OPTIONS

The Checking Mail options are shown in Figure 9-17. The corresponding Eudora Light settings were discussed in Chapter 4.

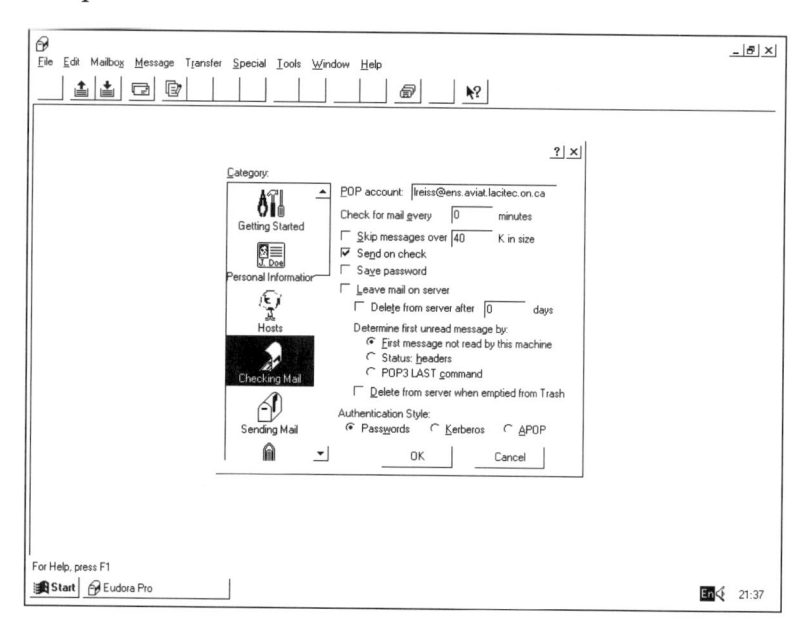

Figure 9-17. Eudora Pro's Checking Mail options.

Skip messages over ? K [off, 40]

Eudora Light provides an option for skipping big (greater than 40 K bytes) messages. You don't wait for the entire message to be downloaded; it transfers the first few lines and lets you decide whether or not to transfer the entire message. Eudora Pro provides the same option with one important difference; you determine what constitutes a big message, 20 K, 40 K, 60 K, etc. To download the complete message, click on the Fetch icon in the incoming message window and check mail again.

Delete from server after ? days [off, 0]

This option includes an enable/disable check box and an edit box for specifying the number of days to keep mail on the server before deleting it.

Warning: Saving messages indefinitely on the server creates mail storage problems.

Determine first unread message by [First message not read by this machine]

Eudora Pro allows you to define what constitutes an unread message. The choices include

First message not read by this machine—any message not that this machine has not yet read is considered unread. This default value is useful when using several PCs to process your mail.

Status: headers—any message whose Status: header is not read is considered unread. Old versions of Eudora used this method exclusively.

POP3 LAST command—any message after the LAST downloaded message is considered unread. This method is more efficient than the Status: headers method when connecting to a POP server that provides the LAST command.

To receive all your messages on multiple PCs:

> for each PC select the "First message not read by this machine" option, and set the "Delete from server after ? days" option to a high enough number of days that you will be able to check for mail on each PC.

To receive all your messages on one PC and read new messages from other machines:

> for each PC select the "First message not read by this machine" option. On the PC chosen to receive all your messages, turn off the "Leave mail on server" option. Turn it on for all the other PCs.

Delete from server when emptied from Trash [off]

This option deletes, at the next mail check, those messages left on the POP server that have been deleted from your Trash Mailbox.

Authentication Style [Passwords]

Eudora Pro supports three different network authentication technologies: Passwords, Kerberos, and APOP. Ask your e-mail administrator which one is being used at your site.

SENDING MAIL OPTIONS

The Sending Mail options are shown in Figure 9-18. The corresponding Eudora Light settings were discussed in Chapter 3.

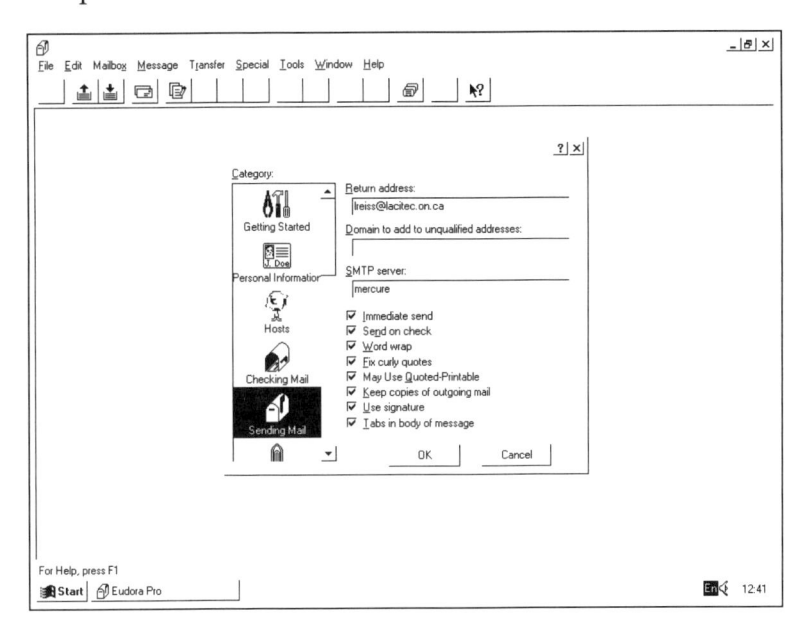

Figure 9-18. Eudora Pro's Sending Mail options.

DOMAIN TO ADD TO UNQUALIFIED NAMES: [NONE]

Recall that a domain name specifies the Internet address in a form legible to people, for example, ibm.com. An unqualified name is one that doesn't contain an @ sign followed by a domain name. The value entered in this text box serves as a default domain name. If you address a message to someone with an unqualified name, Eudora Pro automatically adds this domain. This option saves you typing, especially if you are writing to multiple users in the same domain.

ATTACHMENTS OPTIONS

The Attachments options are shown in Figure 9-19. The corresponding Eudora Light settings were discussed in Chapter 8.

Delete attachments when emptying Trash [off]

This option directs Eudora Pro to delete an attachment when deleting the associated message, provided that the attachment resides in the user-specified Attachments Directory. If you want to delete a message but save its attachment, either turn this option off or move the attachment to another directory before deleting the message.

CHAPTER 9: EUDORA PRO FOR WINDOWS

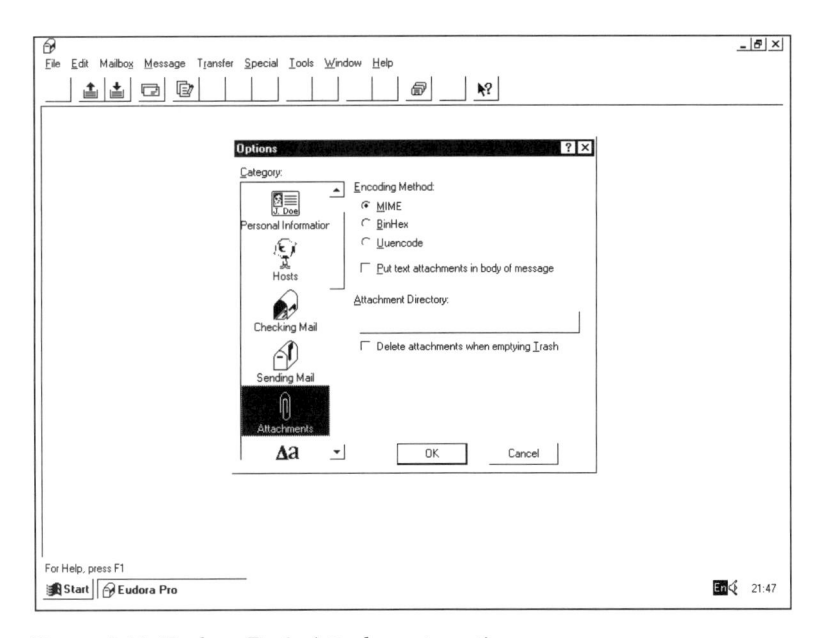

Figure 9-19. Eudora Pro's Attachments options.

FONTS & DISPLAY OPTIONS

The Fonts & Display options include Screen Font, Print Font, Message window width, Message window height, Zoom windows when opening, Show all headers (even the ugly ones), Show toolbar, Show toolbar tips, Show status bar, and Show category icons. They are identical to the Eudora Light Fonts & Display settings discussed in Chapter 8.

LABELS OPTIONS

The Labels options shown in Figure 9-20 define the title and color for the seven labels that categorize messages. Label titles are entered in the text box to the right of the label number. Change a label color by clicking on the label number to display the Color dialog box shown in Figure 9-21. Choose from among the 48 predefined basic colors or create your own custom colors. In the latter case, first click on the Define Custom Colors button to display the custom colors palette shown in Figure 9-22. Then select one of the 16 custom color boxes. Click anywhere on the color palette to select the color hue and saturation. Adjust the color by using the color control bar to the right of the color palette. When you are finished adjusting the color, click on the Add to Custom Colors button. Then select the desired label color and click on OK to confirm.

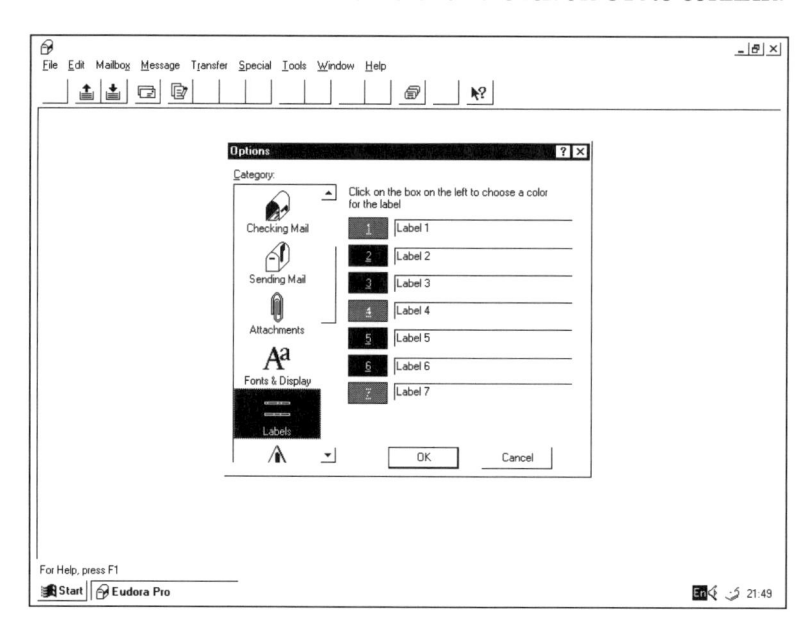

Figure 9-20. Eudora Pro's Labels options.

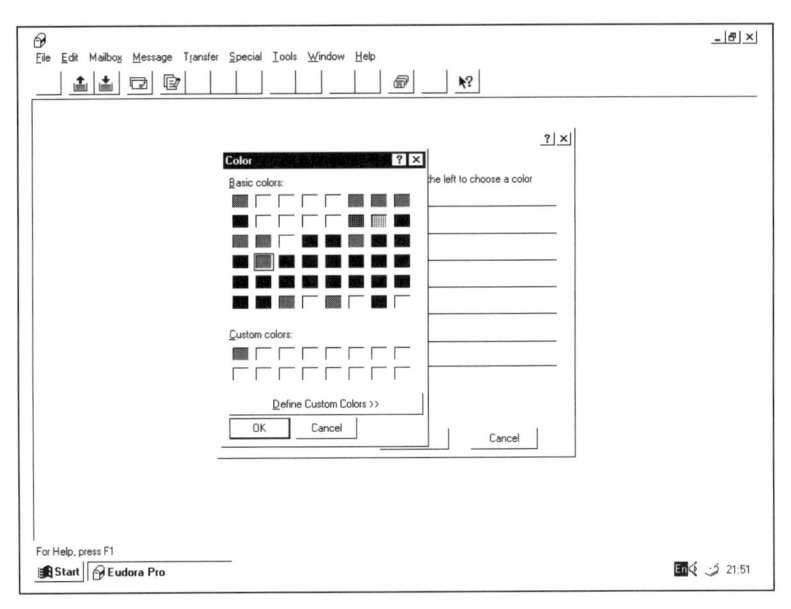

Figure 9-21. Eudora Pro's Color dialog box.

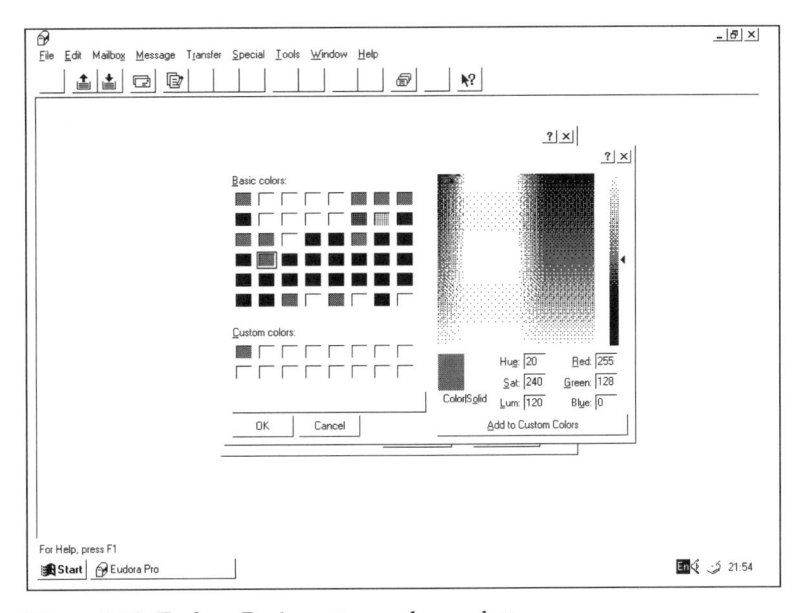

Figure 9-22. Eudora Pro's custom colors palette.

229

GETTING ATTENTION OPTIONS

The Getting Attention options include Use an alert dialog box, Open mailbox, and Play a sound. They are identical to the Eudora Getting Attention settings discussed in Chapter 4.

REPLYING OPTIONS

The Replying options include Reply to all [otherwise when Shift is down], When replying to all, and Copy original's priority to reply. They are identical to the Eudora Light Replying settings discussed in Chapter 5.

DIALUP OPTIONS

The Dialup options shown in Figure 9-23 configure your connection when using a modem. The present version of Eudora Light does not support dialup modem connections.

Warning: Configuring the Dialup options requires technical knowledge. You may have to contact your Eudora support coordinator or service provider to complete this entry.

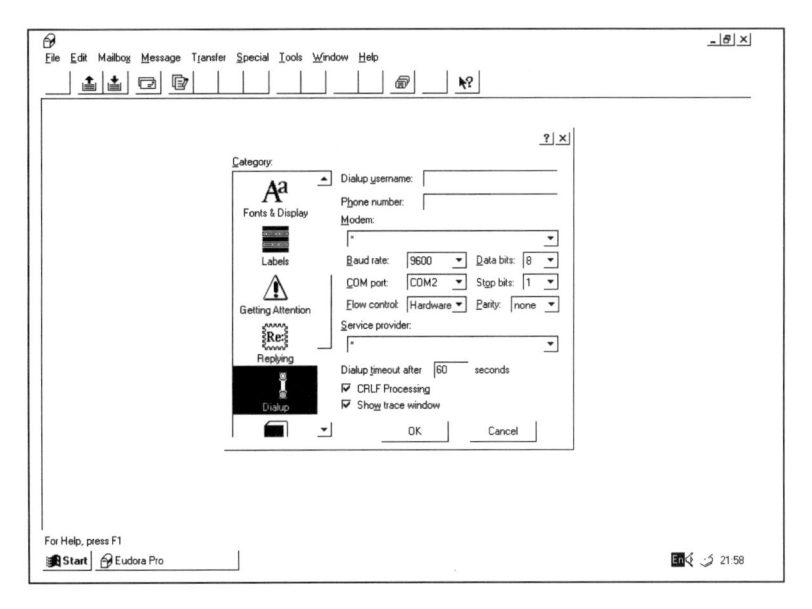

Figure 9-23. Eudora Pro's Dialup options.

Dialup username: [none]

Enter your dialup user name here.

Note: If your dialup user name is the same as your POP account user name, you may leave this field blank.

Phone number: [none]

Enter your terminal server dialin phone number here.

Tip: Include the prefix (such as 8 or 9) needed to access an outside line, if applicable.

Modem: [*Default:Hayes (unreliable transfers)]

This popup field specifies your modem type. Select from the listed modems or choose *Default:Hayes (unreliable transfers).

*Note: The default modem does not always work. If you are experiencing difficulties, try modifying the **serial.mod** dialup file, as described in Appendix E of the Eudora Pro Windows User Manual.*

Baud rate: [9600]

This popup specifies the speed at which your modem communicates with the terminal server. Select the value corresponding to your modem speed.

COM port: [COM2]

This popup specifies the COM port that connects your modem with your PC.

Flow Control: [Hardware]

This popup specifies the modem flow control, which is the ability of a modem and PC to stop data flow before internal buffers overflow. Modems may use either hardware or software flow control. Hardware flow control is preferred and is strongly recommended at baud rates exceeding 9600 baud.

Data bits: [8], Stop bits: [1], Parity: [none]

These popups specify various terminal server settings. The default values are correct for almost all cases. Consult with your local Eudora support coordinator or service provider before changing any of these values.

Service provider: [*Default (must modify)]

This popup specifies the service provider whose terminal server connects to Eudora. Select from service provider list or enter *Default (must modify).

*Note: If you have chosen the default, you must modify the **serial.nav** dialup file to work with your service provider, as described in Appendix E of the Eudora Pro Windows User Manual.*

Dialup timeout after ? seconds [60]

This option specifies the number of seconds before a dialup connection times out, in other words stops trying to make the connection.

CRLF Processing [on]

Correct processing of carriage returns (ENTER key) is necessary when configuring a dialup connection to your terminal server. Because Telnet programs routinely convert carriage returns into carriage return (cr)/linefeed(lf) pairs, by default Eudora reverses this process, converting cr/lf pairs to plain carriage returns. You must turn this option off if your terminal server does not translate carriage returns to cr/lf pairs, or if you are running srialpop to establish an echoless session (as described in Appendix E of the Eudora Pro Windows User Manual).

Show Trace Window [on]

This option opens the Trace Window when a dialup session starts. The window displays the characters that Eudora Pro sends and receives. The Trace Window can help determine dialup errors.

SPELL-CHECKING OPTIONS

As discussed previously in this chapter, spell checking is another important new feature of Eudora Pro. Its options, shown in Figure 9-24, are listed next.

Ignore capitalized words [off]

Ignores words starting with capital letters, such as proper nouns.

Ignore words with numbers [off]

Ignores words containing numbers.

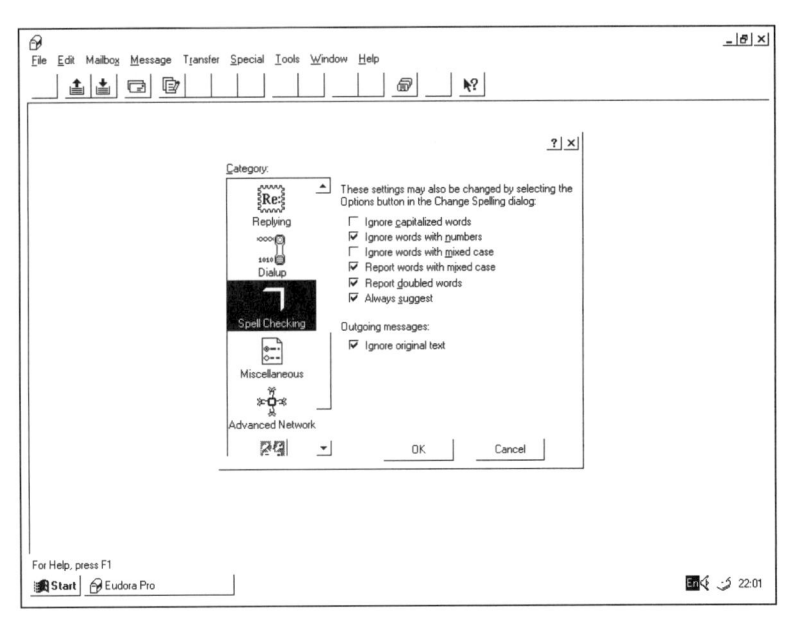

Figure 9-24. Eudora Pro's spell-checking options.

Ignore words with mixed case [off]

Ignores words containing both upper- and lowercase characters and identifies them as mixed case.

Report words with mixed case [on]

Reports words containing both upper- and lowercase characters and identifies them as mixed case.

Report doubled words [on]

Reports words that appear twice in sequence in text and identifies them as doubled words.

Always suggest [on]

Displays Eudora's suggestions for spelling of an unknown word in the Suggestions field by default.

Ignore original text [on]

Ignores all text preceded by a >. Eudora assumes that this text originated in another message, and need not be checked.

MISCELLANEOUS OPTIONS

The Miscellaneous options are shown in Figure 9-25. The corresponding Eudora Light settings were discussed in Chapter 8.

Ctrl+arrow keys [off]

This option enables you to switch messages by holding down the CTRL key and then pressing the arrow keys.

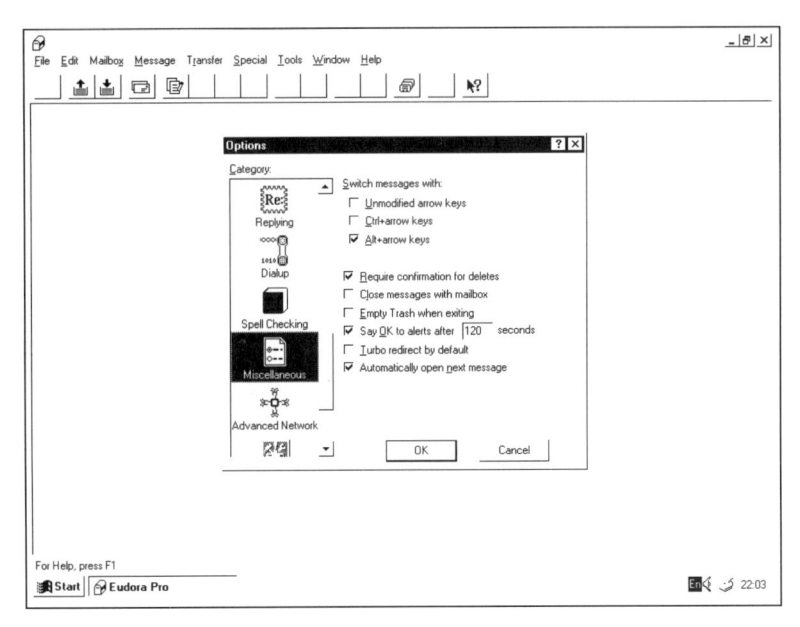

Figure 9-25. Eudora Pro's Miscellaneous options.

Note: The CTRL+arrow keystrokes do not work when on-screen composition windows are open.

Turbo redirect by default [off]

Turbo redirect accelerates message redirecting when using the Quick Recipient list Redirect To command. It redirects the message to the selected recipient, queues the new message, and deletes the original message. This option activates turbo redirect whenever the Redirect To command is used.

Note: If Turbo redirect is the default, holding down the SHIFT key during a Redirect To operation disables Turbo redirect. If Turbo redirect is not the default, holding down the SHIFT key during a Redirect To operation enables Turbo redirect.

MAPI OPTIONS

These options, shown in Figure 9-26, control the Eudora MAPI Server discussed previously in this chapter.

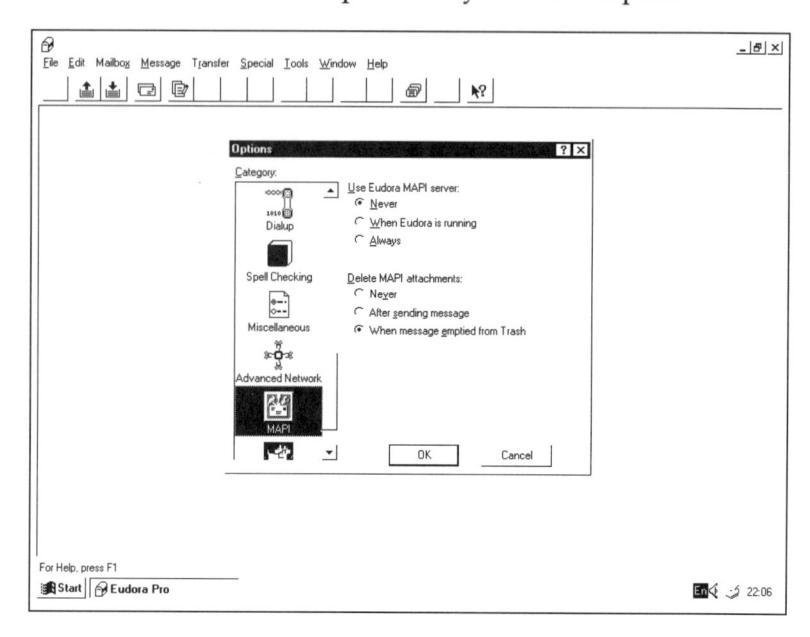

Figure 9-26. Eudora Pro's MAPI options.

Use the Eudora MAPI server:

Never [default]

This option prevents the Eudora MAPI server from being loaded automatically.

When Eudora is running

This option loads the Eudora MAPI server when Eudora is running.

Always

This option always loads the Eudora MAPI server on startup.

Delete MAPI attachments:

Never

This option prevents MAPI attachments from being deleted from the attachment directory.

After sending message

This option deletes MAPI attachments from the attachment directory when their corresponding messages are sent.

When message emptied from Trash [default]

This option deletes MAPI attachments from the attachment directory when their corresponding messages are emptied from the trash.

KERBEROS OPTIONS

These options, shown in Figure 9-27, control the Kerberos authentication system. If your network uses Kerberos for authentication, consult your Eudora support coordinator or service provider to obtain the correct values.

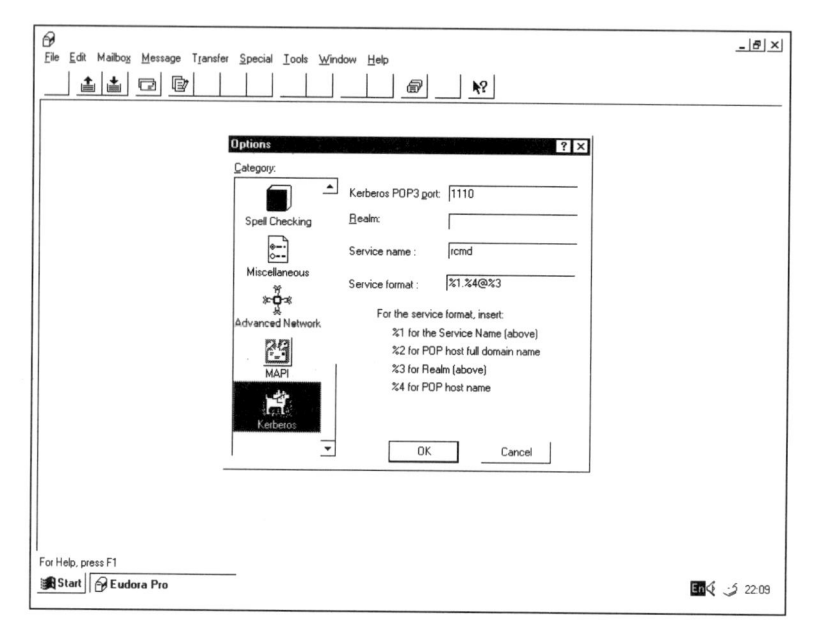

Figure 9-27. Eudora Pro's Kerberos options.

Note: Eudora Light does not support the Kerberos authentication system.

Kerberos POP3 port: [1110]

This value specifies the port on which the Kerberos POP system is listening.

Realm: [none]

This option specifies the network realm in which the Kerberos server resides.

Service name: [rcmd]

This option specifies the type of service that you're requesting.

Service format: [%1.%4@%3]

This option specifies the name of the ticket that Eudora requests from the Kerberos server.

APPENDIX A

EUDORA LIGHT MENU COMMANDS AND INSTALLATION NOTES

This appendix describes the options associated with the Eudora Light (PC version) menu commands. It includes installation notes to help you get the program up and running.

Menu Commands The PC version of Eudora Light includes eight menu commands. Reading from left to right they are: File, Edit, Mailbox, Message, Transfer, Special, Window, and Help.

FILE

The **File** menu shown in Figure A-1 includes basic file and mail program functions.

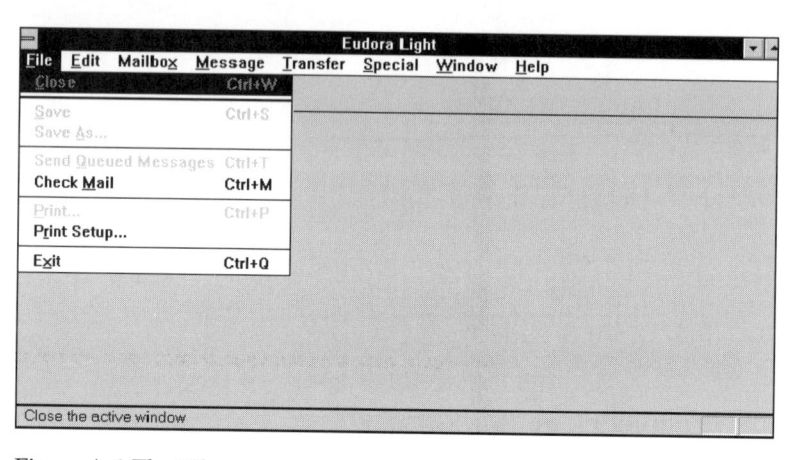

Figure A-1. The **File** menu.

Close   Closes the current window.

Save   Saves changes made to active window, which may be a message composition window, a signature window, or a Nicknames window.

Save As...   Saves the selected message or messages to a plain text (ASCII) file.

Send Queued Messages Sends all messages presently queued for delivery.

Check Mail   Transfers new mail from the POP server. The time in parentheses (if displayed) indicates when Eudora will next check for mail.

APPENDIX A

Print...   Prints the selected message(s), Ph window, or Signature.

Print Setup...   Configures your printer.

Exit   Quits Eudora.

EDIT

The **Edit** menu shown in Figure A-2 includes options for editing text, finding character strings, and editing and sorting message summaries.

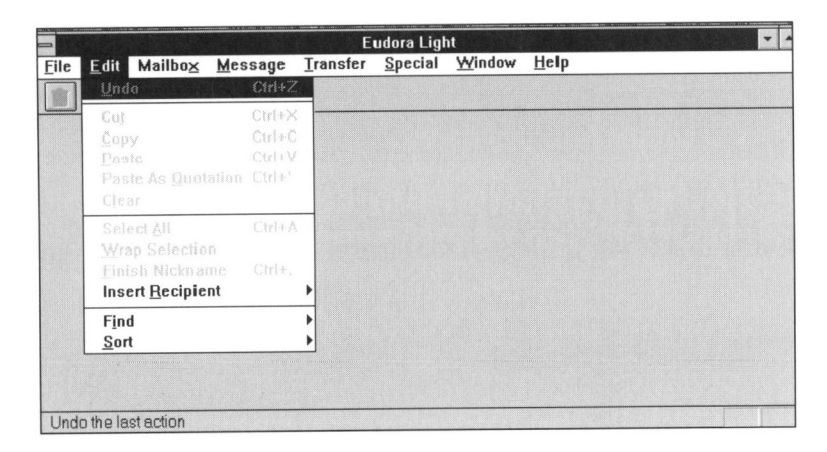

Figure A-2. Eudora's **Edit** menu.

Undo   Rolls back the most recent edit operation.

Cut   Deletes selected text and places it on clipboard.

245

Copy	Copies selected text to the clipboard.
Paste	Places the clipboard contents at the insertion point.
Paste As Quotation	Places the clipboard contents at the insertion point, prefacing each line with a > to signify that the text is quoted.
Clear	Deletes selected text.
Select All	Selects the entire contents of a message or mailbox.
Wrap Selection	Inserts an ENTER keystroke at the end of each selected line selected of the message. Use the SHIFT key to unwrap text.
Finish Nickname	Completes the nickname entered into a message header.
Insert Recipient	At the insertion point, insert the chosen nickname or address from the Quick Recipient list.
Find	Searches for the designated character string within one or more messages.
Sort	Sorts message summaries in a mailbox. To reverse the sort order, press the SHIFT key.

MAILBOX

The **Mailbox** menu shown in Figure A-3 opens a mailbox or activates an open mailbox.

In The In Mailbox stores incoming messages until they are deleted or transferred to another mailbox.

APPENDIX A

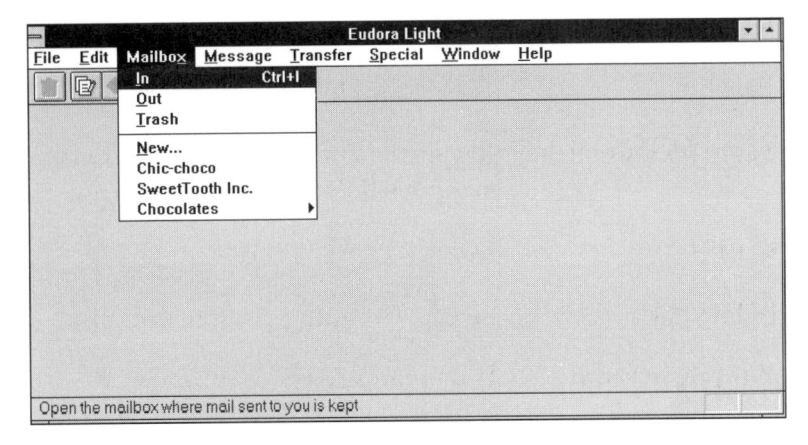

Figure A-3. Eudora's **Mailbox** menu.

Out The Out Mailbox stores messages you wrote, including queued messages (at least until sent) and copies of sent messages.

Trash The Trash Mailbox stores deleted messages.

New... Displays the New Mailbox dialog box, which creates a new mailbox.

[Your Mailboxes] Your individual mailboxes appear in this menu.

MESSAGE

The **Message** menu shown in Figure A-4 creates and deletes messages.

New Message Opens the new message composition window.

Reply Replies to the sender of the current message.

247

THE EUDORA USER'S GUIDE

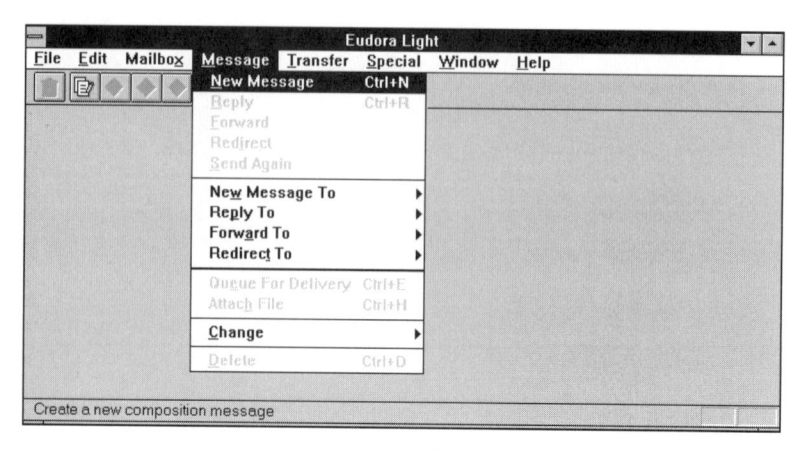

Figure A-4. Eudora's **Message** menu.

Forward   Forwards the current message to one or more other correspondents.

Redirect   Forwards the current message to one or more other correspondents, with the return address of the individual who sent the original message.

Send Again   Resends a message that didn't reach the intended correspondent.

New Message To   Sends a message to one or more people on the Quick Recipient list.

Reply To   Sends a reply to the current message to one or more people on the Quick Recipient list.

Forward To   Forwards the current message to one or more people on the Quick Recipient list.

Redirect To   Redirects the current message to one or more people on the Quick Recipient list.

APPENDIX A

Queue For Delivery/ Send Immediately Depending on the selection made in the Immediate Send option of the Sending Messages setting, this menu item either saves the message in the Out Mailbox (queuing it for future delivery) or sends it immediately.

Attach File... Attaches one or more files to the current message.

Change Modifies queueing and priority options.

Delete In general, transfers the selected message(s) to the Trash Mailbox. If you are in the Trash mailbox, this menu item permanently deletes selected message(s).

TRANSFER

The **Transfer** menu shown in Figure A-5 transfers the selected message(s) to the active mailbox.

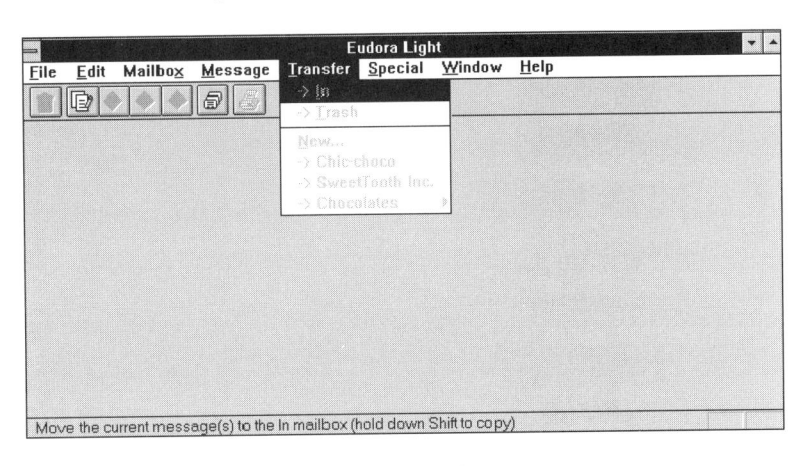

Figure A-5. Eudora's **Transfer** menu.

249

THE EUDORA USER'S GUIDE

In Transfers the selected message(s) to the In Mailbox.

Trash Transfers the selected message(s) to the Trash Mailbox.

New... Displays the New Mailbox dialog box, which creates a new mailbox. You may transfer the selected message(s) to this mailbox.

[Your Mailboxes] Transfers the selected message(s) to your active, custom mailbox.

SPECIAL

The **Special** menu shown in Figure A-6 includes miscellaneous but important Eudora functions, such as those associated with nicknames and the Quick Recipient list.

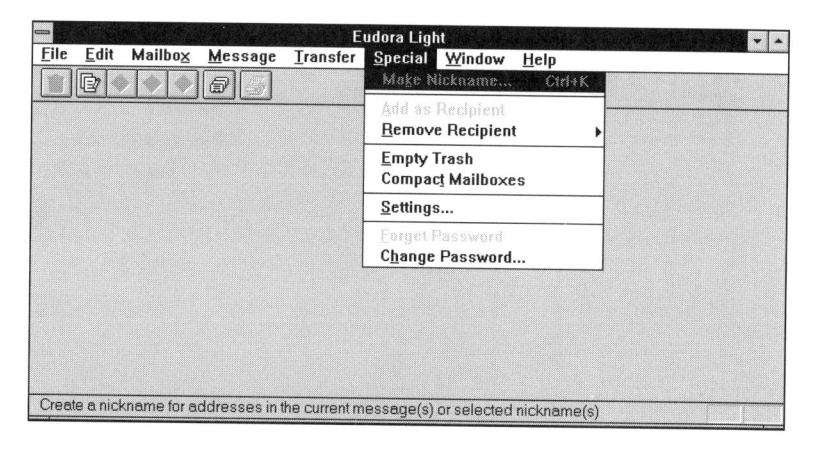

Figure A-6. Eudora's **Special** menu.

APPENDIX A

Make Nickname...	Creates aliases for e-mail addresses appearing in the current message.
Add as Recipient	Adds selected text to the Quick Recipient list.
Remove Recipient	Removes one or more selected recipients from the Quick Recipient list.
Empty Trash	Deletes all messages from the Trash Mailbox.
Compact Mailboxes	Recovers unused space in all mailboxes.
Settings...	Displays the Settings dialog box.
Forget Password	Instructs Eudora to request your password at the next mail check.
Change Password	Changes your password on the POP server computer. This requires a special server.

WINDOW

The **Window** menu shown in Figure A-7 includes Eudora window management options. Many of these options are standard MS-Windows options.

Cascade	Cascades open windows.
Tile Horizontal	Horizontally tiles open windows.
Tile Vertical	Vertically tiles open windows.
Arrange Icons	Neatly arranges all icons at the bottom of the Main window.

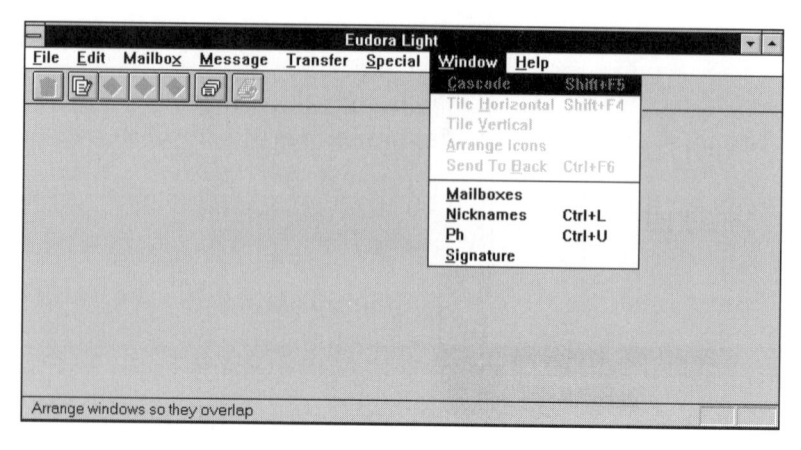

Figure A-7. Eudora's **Window** menu.

Send To Back   Places the current topmost window behind all displayed windows.

Mailboxes   Displays the Mailboxes window.

Nicknames   Displays the Nicknames window.

Ph   Displays the Ph window.

Signature   Displays the Signature window.

HELP

The **Help** menu shown in Figure A-8 includes the Help options menu and the About Eudora screen.

Contents   Displays on-line help contents.

Search for Help on... Displays a list of search topics.

APPENDIX A

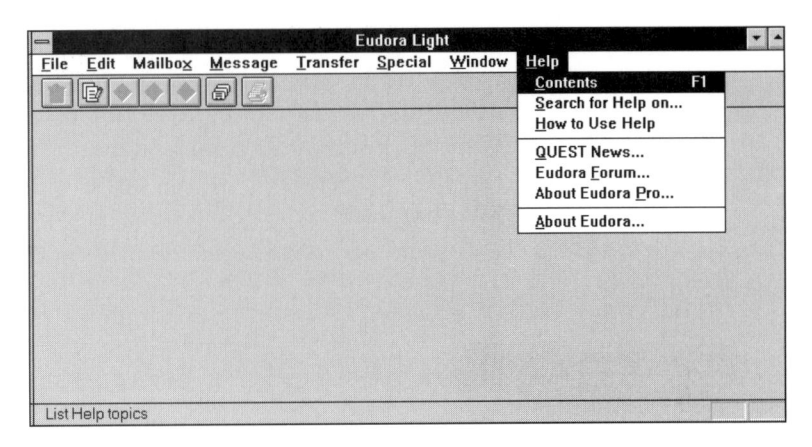

Figure A-8. Eudora's **Help** menu.

How to Use Help Displays the Microsoft Windows How to Use Help window.

QUEST News... Displays a dialog box to subscribe to the QUEST News mailing list.

Eudora Forum... Display a dialog box to subscribe to the Windows Eudora Forum mailing list.

About Eudora Pro... Displays the About Eudora Pro screen.

About Eudora... Displays the About Eudora screen.

INSTALLATION NOTES

Assuming that your computer system meets the minimum requirements, listed in Chapter 2, to get Eudora up and running, you must do three things: First, download the software; second, install the software, and third, make some initial settings. This appendix describes these three activities for the freeware version of Eudora (PC only). Chapter 9 tells you how to get started with Eudora Pro for the PC. Appendix B tells you how to get started with the Mac versions.

DOWNLOADING EUDORA LIGHT

You can get the latest version (1.5.4) of Eudora Light from Qualcomm's FTP site (accessible from the World Wide Web).

FTP Site:	ftp.qualcomm.com
Directory:	/quest/windows/eudora/1.5/
Program:	eudor154.exe (2012Kb)
Documentation:	52word.exe (377Kb, Word for Windows format)

Tip: Make sure to read the README file, available in the same directory.

If you have access to another e-mail account, you can download the software by sending a message to majordomo@qualcomm.com with the following message body:

`get freeware Win/Eudora.hqx`

This file must be decoded using the BinHex program.

APPENDIX A

You can download the software and documentation by sending a message to majordomo@qualcomm.com with the following message body:

`get freeware Win/Eudora.uu`

`get freeware Win/doc.uu`

These two files must be decoded using the uuencode program.

Warning: No matter how you obtain them, the program and documentation are large files; be patient and have your wallet ready if you pay by the minute.

INSTALLING EUDORA LIGHT

Use the following steps to install Eudora:

1. Exit all current applications.

2. Access Windows Explorer (Win95) or File Manager (Win3.1), and double-click on Setup.exe.

3. Read the Welcome screen, then click Next.

4. Specify a directory to install Eudora, and click Next.

5. Specify the version of Eudora to install (16 bit or 32 bit for Win95, 16 bit for Win3.1), then click Next. The Setup program will recommend which version to install.

6. Verify the displayed settings, then click Next or Back to make corrections.

7. Click Yes to view the README file.

Tip: Store the executable file and the Help file in the same directory.

8. Make sure that your **autoexec.bat** file contains the following line:

`set temp=dirname`

where dirname specifies the directory (such as c:\temp) used to store all temporary files.

Tip: If you are using Win3.1 create a new program group that enables you to run Eudora by double-clicking on an icon.

CONFIGURATION

Chapter 2 showed you the minimum necessary configuration steps; namely, completing the Getting Started settings with your POP account, Real Name, and connection method. If your return address is not the same as your POP account, you will have to enter it in the Sending Mail Settings (see Chapter 3.) You should also complete the Getting Attention Settings (see Chapter 4.)

Tip: Don't be shy; contact your Eudora support coordinator to get the correct values, if necessary.

APPENDIX B

INSTALLING EUDORA MAC VERSIONS

This appendix tells you what you need to have and to know to get either version of Eudora up and running on your Macintosh.

INSTALLATION NOTES

Assuming that your computer system meets the minimum requirements (listed below), you must do three things: first, obtain the software; second, install the software; and third, make some initial settings. This appendix describes these three activities for both the Light and Pro versions of Eudora for the Mac.

REQUIREMENTS

The following minimum requirements are necessary to run either version of Eudora for the Mac:

- Macintosh Plus or later model

- 340 K or more RAM

- Mac System 7 or later (Eudora Light version 1.3.1 works with System 6.0.x)

- Connection to Post Office Protocol version 3 (POP3) server to receive incoming messages

- Connection to Simple Mail Transfer Protocol (SMTP) server to transmit outgoing messages

- Direct connection: MacTCP 2.0.6 or later or Open Transport 1.1 or later and Ethernet card or DDP/IP gateway

- Remote connection: (e.g., SLIP, PPP, or ARA) MacTCP 2.0.6 or later or Open Transport 1.1 or later and a modem and connection software

- Serial dialup connection A modem and Apple Modem Tool 1.5.1 or later

DOWNLOADING EUDORA LIGHT

You can get the latest version (1.5.4) of Eudora Light from Qualcomm's FTP site (accessible from the World Wide Web).

FTP Site:	ftp.qualcomm.com
Directory:	/quest/mac/eudora/1.5/
Program:	eudora154.hqx (333 K) or eudora154fat.hqx (642Kb, accelerated for Power PC)
Documentation:	man151-word.sea.hqx (487 K, Word for Windows format) or man151.pdf.hqx (1,479 K, Word for Windows format)

Tip: Make sure to read the README files, available in the same directory.

To install Eudora Light, simply copy it to your hard drive and decompress.

Tip: Add Eudora to your Apple Menu, or create an alias for it to keep it on your Desktop.

INSTALLING EUDORA PRO

It's fairly simple to install Eudora Pro: for starters, instead of downloading software from the Interet, you start by opening shrink-wrapped diskettes. Then, do the following:

1. Restart your Macintosh while holding down the SHIFT key. This disables the Macintosh extensions.

2. Insert Eudora Pro diskette 1 (of 2) into the diskette drive.

3. Double-click on the Eudora Pro Installer icon to start the installation program. After the system displays the Eudora Pro splash screen, click on Continue to display the Eudora README window.

4. After reading the contents of the README window, click on Continue to display the User Code dialog box. Enter the five-digit user code printed on the inside cover of the Eudora Pro Macintosh Installation Guide, or supplied by your on-site Eudora support coordinator, and click Continue. If you don't know your user code, you may leave this field blank. The system displays the Eudora Install dialog box, which allows you to make a selective installation. Click on an item to display its description.

5. For a complete installation, select Eudora Pro full installation and click on Install. To select individual items, click on them (hold down the COMMAND key to select multiple items).

Warning: Installing the Portal software will overwrite the current MacTCP configuration settings as supplied by your Internet Service Provider. In this case you must reconfigure these settings to continue with your current service provider. Remember, you are not obliged to select Portal or MacTCP and MacSLIP. Your current service provider may be able to help you install MacTCP and MacSLIP.

6. When you are ready, click on Install. The Restart dialog box appears if you are doing a full installation, or

you are installing either MacTCP and MacSLIP or Portal. Click on Yes to consent to restarting the Macintosh at the end of the installation. Then, in response to the Eudora Version Selection dialog box, select the version to install from the following:

680x0 — This is the smallest version. It runs on all Macintoshes, including Power Macs, but is slower on Power Macs than the other two versions.

PowerPC — This version runs only on Power Macs.

Universal (or Fat) — This version requires the most disk space. It runs on any Macintosh and runs as fast as the PowerPC version on a Power Mac.

7. After selecting the version, select the destination for the Eudora Pro folder and click on Install. If MacTCP is already installed on your Macintosh and you are installing the full version or Portal, the system warns you that your MacTCP Prep file will be overwritten for use with Portal, as mentioned in step 5. Click on Overwrite or Cancel, which restarts the installation without installing Portal.

8. When prompted, insert Eudora Pro diskette (2 of 2) into the diskette drive.

9. As discussed in step 6, you may be prompted to restart your Macintosh once the installation is complete. Click on Restart.

10. Even if you are not prompted, restart the computer to enable the Macintosh extensions.

CONFIGURATION

Chapter 2 showed you the minimum necessary configuration steps; namely, completing the Getting Started Settings with your POP account, Real Name, and connection method. If your return address is not the same as your POP account, you will have to enter it in the Sending Mail Setting (see Chapter 3). If your SMTP account is not the same as your POP account, you will have to enter it in the Sending Mail Settings (see Chapter 3.) You should also complete the Getting Attention Settings (see Chapter 4).

Tip: Don't be shy; contact your Eudora support coordinator to get the correct values, if necessary.

APPENDIX C

EUDORA AND EUDORA PRO FOR THE MAC

This appendix introduces the changes between the Mac and PC versions of Eudora. Recall that Appendix B tells you how to install the Mac versions of Eudora Light and Eudora Pro. For simplicity we have divided this appendix into a general section and sections related to individual chapters such as Chapter 2, Getting Started with Eudora.

GENERAL INFORMATION

We have not included obvious changes, such as using the **Quit** command of the **File** menu to leave the Mac version, instead of the **Exit** command of the **File Menu** to leave the PC version. Such changes should be obvious to those with even a bit of Macintosh experience.

WINDOWS AND ICONS

While many windows such as the message composition window are quite similar between the corresponding versions of Eudora, some are not. For example, the No new mail alert differs between the Mac and PC versions, as does the New mail alert window. The Mac versions do not include a toolbar or a Main window icon resembling a rural mailbox that notifies you of new mail and queued messages. On the other hand, double-clicking on a Mac title bar opens the mailbox in which the message resides.

SETTINGS DIALOG BOX

The Eudora Light for the Mac Settings dialog box contains the following categories: Getting Started, Personal Information, Hosts, Checking Mail, Sending Mail, Attachments, Fonts & Display, Getting Attention, Replying, and Miscellaneous. The Eudora Pro for the Mac Settings dialog box contains the following categories:

APPENDIX C

Getting Started, Personal Information, Hosts, Checking Mail, Sending Mail, Attachments, Fonts & Display, Getting Attention, Replying, SLIP Cooperation, and Miscellaneous.

GETTING STARTED WITH EUDORA (CHAPTER 2)

Getting started with Eudora on the Mac involves differences in message summaries, the composition window, and the icon bar.

Message Summary

A Mac version message summary includes the following fields: status, priority, and label of the message; the name or address of the sender or intended recipient; the time and date the message was sent or scheduled to be sent, its size in K; and the contents of its Subject: field. It does not include an attachment indicator field. To change the priority of the current message(s), hold down the COMMAND key and press a number key from 1 (highest) to 5 (lowest). Use the Macintosh Label control panel to assign label colors and titles.

Select one summary, hold down the SHIFT key, and select another summary to select both summaries and all included summaries. Hold down the COMMAND key to select several summaries that are not in order.

Note: To drag one or more current message summaries from one open mailbox to another, place the cursor over the Who, Date, K,

265

or Subject message summary column and hold down the mouse button. This changes the cross pointer to an arrow. Move the highlighted message into any open mailbox window and release the mouse button.

Composition Window

The composition window title is enclosed in brackets, << >>.

ICON BAR

The Mac icon bar of the message composition window includes three popup menus—Priority Popup, Signature Popup, and Attachment Type Popup—and six icons—Quoted-Printable Encoding, Include Macintosh Information, Word Wrap, Tabs in Body, Keep Copy, and Return Receipt—and the Send or Queue button. The PC icon bar includes three combo boxes—Priority Combo Box, Signature Combo Box, and Attachment Type Combo Box—and seven buttons—Quoted-Printable Encoding, Text As Document, Word Wrap, Tabs in Body, Keep Copy, Return Receipt (Pro Version only), and the Send or Queue. Only the differences appear in this appendix.

Attachment Type Popup

The Attachment Type popup selects the encoding format of documents accompanying outgoing messages, namely: AppleDouble, AppleSingle, BinHex, or Uuencode Data Fork. Specify Apple Double for recipients that use MIME;

specify Apple Single when sending Macintosh applications or files; specify BinHex for old Macintosh mailers and previous versions of Eudora; and specify Uuencode Data Fork for older PC or UNIX systems.

Include Macintosh Information

Clicking on this icon includes Macintosh resources and types in basic MIME attachments.

Tip: Omit this information when sending attachments to non-Macintosh users.

Word Wrap

Recall that selecting Word Wrap causes Eudora to continue text on succeeding lines with line breaks at about 76 characters. Sending the message "wraps" the text, inserting a carriage return at the end of each line.

Note: To "unwrap" incoming message text before copying it into a file, hold down the OPTION key while copying text from the message.

Tabs in Body

Recall that selecting Tabs in Body replaces a TAB key press by enough spaces to move the insertion point to a multiple of 8 characters from the start of the line.

Note: This icon also controls processing tabs in text pasted into the message window and in plain text attachments sent without Macintosh header information.

Password Protection

The Mac Eudora password is case-sensitive, while the PC Eudora password may be case-sensitive, depending on the POP server.

Stopping a Mail Check

To stop a mail check in the middle, hold down the COMMAND key and type a period.

SENDING E-MAIL (CHAPTER 3)

The Mac version of the Sending Mail Settings does not include the Tabs in Body of Message option, provided with the PC version. Other differences appear when using nicknames.

NICKNAMES

Nicknames are similar in the Mac and PC versions. However, the keystrokes are often different. In the Mac version, you can highlight multiple nicknames in the Nicknames window by pressing the SHIFT key (sequential nicknames) or the COMMAND key (disjoint nicknames). In either case, select **Make Nickname...** from the **Special** menu. When addressing mail from the Nicknames window, press the SHIFT key and the To:, Cc:, or Bcc: buttons to keep the Nicknames window current. Press the OPTION key and the To:, Cc:, or Bcc: buttons to insert the full nickname expansion into the appropriate message field.

RECEIVING E-MAIL (CHAPTER 4)

Several differences occur when receiving e-mail. These differences include the **Other...** command in the **Mailbox** menu, Checking Mail Settings, the Icon Bar, Attachments, Searching, a new feature called stationery messages, and Getting Attention Settings.

Other... Mailboxes

It is possible to locate a mailbox outside the Eudora Folder; for example, in a different folder or on a different network volume. To open such a mailbox, select the **Other...** command from the **Mailbox** menu. This displays a standard file dialog for selecting the mailbox.

Open mailboxes remain on the **Mailbox** and **Transfer** menus only while Eudora is active. In contrast, open mailboxes within a folder or subfolder remain on these menus until removed.

Note: Eudora warns you when you attempt to open a text file other than a mailbox.

CHECKING MAIL SETTINGS

The Checking Mail Settings control how Eudora checks for and receives your incoming mail messages. The Mac version includes the Don't Check When Using Battery option, discussed next.

Don't Check When Using Battery [off]

This option prevents Eudora from checking for mail whenever your Macintosh is running on battery power. Use it if your battery power is low.

ICON BAR

The Mac icon bar of the incoming message window includes the priority popup; the BLAH, BLAH, BLAH icon; the message Subject field; the Fetch icon; the Trash icon; and the Tow Truck icon. The PC icon bar includes the BLAH, BLAH, BLAH icon; the Trash icon; the Fetch icon; the priority popup; and the Subject field. Only the differences from the MS-Windows version appear below.

Tow Truck

Use the Tow Truck icon to transfer a current message into any other mailbox displayed on the desktop. The process is the usual drag and drop.

Message Summary Date Column

The Date column displays the date and time the message was sent or is scheduled to be sent. Eudora for the Mac includes the Age-Sensitive and Fixed methods for displaying date information in mailbox windows. The Age-Sensitive option time-stamps today's mail, stamps with the day of the week mail that arrived within the last six calendar days, and date-stamps mail that arrived before the previous week. The Fixed option date-and-time stamps all mail messages using the current short date and time format.

ATTACHMENTS

There are several differences in the way the Mac and PC versions handle attachments. These include receiving attachments, specifying an attachment folder, automatically opening attachments, and sending attachments to non-Eudora users. You won't have to consult the PC material; the full details of Mac attachment handling follow.

Receiving an Attachment

If you have not specified an Attachment Folder as described next, when you first receive an attachment Eudora creates an Attachments Folder located in the Eudora Folder. This folder automatically receives all incoming attachments.

Specifying an Attachment Folder

To specify the folder destined to receive incoming attachments, select the **Settings...** command from the **Special** menu. Then, select the **Attachments** settings and click on the large button beneath the Attachment Folder prompt. Double-click on the folder name and click on the Use Folder button. The selected folder name appears in the Attachment Folder button. To change the folder, click on the Attachment Folder button and repeat the process.

Eudora decodes attachments automatically and saves them in the selected folder. The attachments name is recorded in the accompanying message. Multiple attachments with the same name are distinguished by a number appended to the end of the attachment's name.

Note: If Eudora cannot find a given folder, it alerts you and creates an Attachments Folder in the Eudora folder to receive attachments until you designate a new Attachment Folder.

Automatically Opening Attachments

To open an incoming message's attachment automatically, highlight the attachment name or double-click on the attachment title and select the **Open Selection** command from the **Edit** menu. The application launches and the attachment opens.

Sending Attachments to Non-Eudora Users

If you send an attachment to someone using an e-mail package other than Eudora, the attached file is appended to

APPENDIX C

the message in the chosen attachment format (BinHex, AppleDouble, AppleSingle, or Uuencode). Specify AppleDouble if the message recipient does not use a Macintosh. If the recipient does have a Macintosh, BinHex is the best format, but BinHex must be decoded before use with mailers other than Eudora.

Note: Stuffit is one popular application for decoding BinHex attachments.

STATIONERY MESSAGES

Eudora lets you create a "stationery" message file from any outgoing message. This process creates templates of commonly used messages and save them as files.

Send a stationery message by double-clicking on the stationery message icon. This displays a composition window that includes the stationery message header and text. You can add or change this information and queue or send the message. Sending the message closes the composition window. Repeat the process as often as you like.

Using a Stationery Message for All Outgoing Messages

A stationery message can be a template for all outgoing messages. Eudora will use this template whenever you send, reply to, or forward a message.

To create this message template, first create an outgoing message that contains only the text to appear in the new composition window of all outgoing messages. Select the

Save As command from the **File** menu to display the Save As dialog box. In response to the prompts, name the file Stationery and place it in the Eudora Folder. Finally, select the **Stationery** option and click on the Save button in the dialog box. You can use the template for all outgoing messages except those sent via the **Redirect** and **Send Again** commands. If you no longer wish to use the stationery file for all messages, remove it from the Eudora Folder. To change the stationery file, create a new one that replaces the old one.

Note: Before sending a message, you can remove or edit whatever information you want.

Getting Attention Settings

The Getting Attention Settings control how Eudora gets your attention to announce new mail or for other reasons (Mac only). The Mac version includes the "Flash an icon in the menu bar" option. While the PC version lets you select a single sound, the Mac lets you select two sounds, one for new mail and another for other announcements.

Flash an icon in the menu bar [on]

Select this option and Eudora will flash an icon in the menu bar when it needs you. Eudora uses two different icons— a Mail flag for new mail and an envelope containing an exclamation point for other announcements.

APPENDIX C

Open mailbox (new mail only)

Select this option to open a mailbox when new mail arrives. Eudora places the new mail in the mailbox, scrolls to the end of the mailbox, and selects the first unread message in the last unread batch of messages.

Playing a sound [on]

If you choose this option, Eudora audibly gets your attention. Use a popup menu to select the desired New Mail sound and the Attention sound (accompanying other announcements).

ADDITIONAL DIFFERENCES

Additional differences appear when searching for text in a message and sorting messages in mailboxes.

Unsuccessful Search Box

If the find is unsuccessful, Eudora displays the not found alert.

Stopping a Find

To abort a search in the middle, press the COMMAND key and type a period (.).

Sorting Messages Within Mailboxes

Unlike the PC version, Eudora for the Mac cannot sort message summaries by Attachment.

ANSWERING E-MAIL (CHAPTER 5)

The differences associated with answering e-mail include transferring messages, the Mailboxes window, and Replying Settings. The reply window does not display the time and date of the original message.

Transferring Messages

You can transfer messages between any two mailboxes. While this process is quite similar for Mac and PC versions of Eudora, there are some differences. Press the OPTION key while transferring a message to copy it into the new mailbox instead of transferring it.

Note: To undo mailbox transfers, use the **Undo** *command of the* **Edit** *menu. (This option is not available in the PC version.)*

Mailboxes Window

The Mac version calls the topmost folder the "Eudora Folder", whereas the PC version calls it the "Top Level". The Mac version does not include a folder icon to the left of folders listed in the Mailboxes window. Use the COMMAND key instead of the CTRL key to select multiple mailboxes or folders simultaneously. The Mac version lets you move a mailbox or folder from one folder to another. In contrast, the PC version allows you to move only a mailbox (but not a folder) from one folder to another.

Quote selection only

When replying to a message you may wish to quote only part of it. To do so, highlight the desired text and press the SHIFT key when selecting the **Reply** command from the **Message** menu.

REPLYING SETTINGS

The Replying Settings control how Eudora processes your replies to incoming messages. The Mac and PC versions are very similar. In both cases the default is to reply to all, but you can check a box to reply only to the original sender. The Mac version reverses the selection (all or not) when you press the OPTION key. The PC version reverses the selection (all or not) when you press the SHIFT key.

BECOMING AN E-MAIL PRO (CHAPTER 8)

As you might guess, there are many differences between becoming an e-mail pro for the Mac and for the PC versions of Eudora. Once you master one version, you may be asked to master the other.

GETTING STARTED SETTINGS

The Connection Method differences in the Getting Started Settings include MacTCP instead of Winsock and Communications Toolbox instead of Dialup.

Connection Method: [MacTCP]

Select MacTCP to use Eudora via a network connection; select Communications Toolbox to use Eudora via a modem; and select Offline to disable any communications.

PERSONAL INFORMATION SETTINGS

The Personal Information Settings differ in the Dialup Username.

Dialup Username: [none]

If you are using Eudora with the Communications Toolbox and have a secondary user name for the dialup process, such as your login name to a terminal server, enter it here.

APPENDIX C

HOSTS SETTINGS

The Hosts Settings describe your servers to Eudora. The Mac version includes the DNS Load Balancing option, discussed next.

DNS Load Balancing: [off]

The DNS (Domain Name System) Load Balancing option allows you to divide the workload of a group of Eudora users over multiple host computers. Your network administrator will tell if you should check this box.

Note to Network Administrators: DNS Load Balancing directs Eudora to choose a random address from the list of addresses returned by the DNS (otherwise, Eudora would always choose the first address from the list). If you have several machines able to provide the same services, list all their IP addresses under one domain name and tell your users to use that domain name and to check the DNS Load Balancing check box.

ATTACHMENTS SETTINGS

The Attachments Settings control how Eudora sends and receives attachments. The appendix section in (Chapter 4, Receiving E-mail) describes Eudora version differences in the Encoding method and Attachment folder. The Mac version's "Trash attachments with messages" option is equivalent to the PC version's Delete attachments in body of message option. The Mac version's "TEXT files belong to" option follows.

TEXT files belong to [TeachText]

Selecting the **Save As...** command from the **File** menu instructs Eudora to create a Macintosh document to be opened with the named application such as a word processing program. Change the setting by single-clicking on the application name button (the default is TeachText) and completing the displayed dialog.

FONTS & DISPLAY SETTINGS

The Fonts & Display Settings control how Eudora displays messages. Unlike the PC version, the Mac version does not include the following check boxes: Show all headers (even the ugly ones), Show toolbar, Show toolbar tips, Show status bar, and Show category icons. In contrast, it includes Date formats: and Display dates using: settings, described next.

Date formats: [Age-sensitive]

Eudora uses two methods of displaying date information in mailbox windows, Age-sensitive and Fixed. The "Age-Sensitive" option time-stamps today's mail, stamps with the day of the week mail that arrived within the last six calendar days, and date-stamps mail that arrived before the previous week. The "Fixed" option date-and time-stamps all mail messages using the current short date and time format.

Display dates using: [Sender's timezone]

Eudora displays incoming message summary time and date information using either the "Local timezone" option to use your time and date or the "Sender's timezone" option to use the sender's time and date.

SLIP COOPERATION

The SLIP Cooperation Setting of Eudora Pro controls the Eudora connection to your service provider using MacSLIP and MacTCP. Normally, when Eudora or another application requests a connection, MacSLIP automatically dials your provider to establish a PPP connection. This connection remains open until you close it or a timeout period occurs. The settings below modify this behavior.

Warning: These settings work ONLY with MacSLIP from Hyde Park Software.

Don't make automatic checks when SLIP is down [off]

Selecting this option directs Eudora to ignore the "Check for mail every ? minutes" option in the Checking Mail Settings unless your MacSLIP connection is active. Doing so reduces unnecessary connections to your service provider.

Disconnect SLIP if Eudora connected it [on]

If this option is on, MacSLIP disconnects after a mail check if connected by Eudora but does not disconnect if connected by another application. If this option is off, MacSLIP does not disconnect automatically at the end of a mail check. This option minimizes connection time to your service provider.

MISCELLANEOUS SETTINGS

These settings control miscellaneous, but often important, functions.

Command-Arrow keys [on]

This option works like the "ALT+ arrow keys" option on the PC version. When selected, switch messages by holding down the COMMAND key and then pressing the arrow keys.

Note: COMMAND–*arrow keystrokes work whether or not the composition windows are open.*

Say OK to alerts after 2 minutes

The Mac "Say OK to alerts after 2 minutes (default off)" option replaces the more flexible PC option Say OK to alerts after ? seconds (default on, 120).

Note: Enabling this option may cause some Communications Toolbox connection tools to provide less progress information.

Turbo Redirect by default

The "Turbo Redirect by default" option may be reversed by pressing the OPTION key.

Automatically open next message [on]

Unlike the PC version, in the Mac version the default value of this option is on.

LABELS SETTING

Unlike the Eudora Pro for PC version, the Mac versions do not include a labels setting. Use the Macintosh label control panel to assign label colors and titles.

MAIL STORAGE

When you first start Eudora, it creates a Eudora Folder within your System Folder. Under normal circumstances, you need not access the Eudora Folder, whose contents appear next.

Eudora Settings

The Eudora Settings file contains individual Settings information, the Quick Recipient list, and the list of open windows.

Eudora Nicknames

The Eudora Nicknames file contains your nicknames. Recall that Eudora Pro allows you to have multiple nicknames files.

Note: This file is a plain TEXT file in UNIX ".mailrc" format.

In, Out, and Trash

There is one mailbox file, in UNIX mail format, for each of your mailboxes. To open any mailbox (and launch Eudora if it is not already running), double-click on its file.

In.toc, Out.toc, and Trash.toc

These files are the table of contents associated with your mailboxes file. They may help Eudora access your mailboxes more rapidly.

Eudora Log, Old Log

Eudora keeps records of all mail transfers in the Eudora Log and Old Log files. When the Eudora Log file reaches its maximum size (approximately 100 K), Eudora creates a new Eudora Log file, overwriting the Old Log file.

Eudora Filters

The Eudora Filters file contains the Eudora filter names and extensions.

Signatures

The Signature and Alternate (Pro version only) files in the Eudora Signatures folder contain the primary and alternate signatures.

System 7 Aliases

Eudora allows aliases for mailbox and .toc files that you moved outside the Eudora Folder. You can open these mailboxes from within Eudora by putting these aliases in the Eudora Folder or a subfolder within the Eudora folder.

*Note: Opening a mailbox with the **Other...** command of the **Mailbox** menu automatically creates a mailbox alias and places it in the Eudora Folder. Eudora deletes this alias upon exiting. If you use this command to open the mailbox from within a mail folder or subfolder, Eudora does not delete the alias upon exiting.*

"DRAG AND DROP" EUDORA

You can use the Macintosh System "drag and drop" feature with Eudora; for example, to start Eudora, open plain text files, open stationery files and mailboxes, and attach files to messages. To drag and drop, first select it and drag its icon until the mouse pointer is directly over the Eudora application icon and the Eudora icon highlights. Release the mouse button to launch the operation. The "dragged" file remains unchanged in the initial location.

Note: If you hold down the COMMAND key while performing a drag and drop operation, Eudora processes the files as attachments.

Dragging and dropping launches Eudora if it is not already running. By default, Eudora applies the Settings file in the Eudora Folder. To apply a different Settings file, drag the appropriate Eudora Settings file onto the Eudora icon. Multiple settings files are useful when several users with different settings and mailbox files share the same Macintosh.

CHECKING SPELLING

Eudora includes the Spellswell 7 Spelling Checker, a Word Services Suite application, developed by Working Software. This section describes the spelling checker's basic functions when used with Eudora. The Spellswell 7 User Manual, located in the Documentation folder within the Eudora Pro folder, contains more information on Spellswell 7, including additional specialized dictionaries and how it functions with other applications.

The spelling checker includes a customizable word dictionary with more than 90,000 entries. It can check for spelling mistakes and typographical errors in message composition windows, text files, and signature files. Besides misspellings, the spelling checker also can find multiple errors, including uncapitalized proper nouns, sentences that start with uncapitalized words, hyphenation errors, missing spaces and apostrophes, extra spaces between words, incorrect abbreviations, and repeated words.

Sharing a Macintosh with Other Users

When sharing a Macintosh with other users, make a copy of the Eudora Folder for each user. Give the copies any names you want, and place them anywhere, including on floppies or network volumes. Launch Eudora by double-clicking on the Eudora Settings file for the given folder.

EUDORA PRO (CHAPTER 9)

The differences between Eudora Pro for the Mac and for the PC include the folder, message filtering, and nicknames. These differences are described next.

Eudora Pro Folder

During the installation, the Eudora Pro Folder is installed on your hard drive in the location you specify. This folder contains the Eudora Pro icon, a Documentation icon, a Spellswell (spelling checker) icon, and several other icons.

Message Filtering

Mac filters are in the **Window** menu, whereas PC filters are in the **Tools** menu.

Filter Terms

Recall that the Match Type popup field controls the type of match made by the Eudora filter. Besides the contains/does not contain, is/is not, starts with/ends with, and appears/does not appear match options, which are also available on the Eudora Pro for the PC, Eudora Pro for the Mac includes the intersects nickname field, which works as follows:

If you specify a message header field and an e-mail address in the Matching Text field included in a nickname, the filter is invoked accordingly. Use this option when a nickname represents a mailing list from which you want to filter one or more addresses.

MAPI

(Message Application Program Interface) is not available in the Mac versions of Eudora.

Multiple Nicknames Files

Place the Nicknames files in a new folder within the Eudora Folder located in your System Folder and call it Nicknames Folder.

Warning: Do not place the standard Eudora Nicknames file in the Nicknames Folder. Keep it in your Eudora Folder.

INDEX

A

Abbreviations, 134-135

Accessing Internet services, 137-152

Activating Eudora, 72

Adding a nickname to Quick Reception list, 60

Adding an e-mail address to Quick Reception list, 60

Addressing mail via the Nicknames window, 58

Advanced Network Settings, 154, 170-172

Advanced Network Settings dialog box, 171

Advantages of e-mail, 3-6

Alias, 54

Alternate signatures (Eudora Pro), 192

Answering e-mail, 99-118

AppleDouble format, 16

ASCII file, 14, 53, 161

Attach File window, 52

Attachment Settings window, 53

Attachment Type combo box, 36, 53

Attachments, 11, 14, 52-53

Attachments Settings, 154, 160-161

Attachments Settings dialog box, 160

Attachments: field, 53

Attachments: message header field, 39, 52

Automatic mail checking, 40-41, 70-72

B

Bcc: message header field, 39, 54, 58, 61
Bin Hex, 14, 53, 193
Binary file, 14, 16
BITNET, 145
Blind carbon copies, 11
Browsers, 2

C

Canned messages, 116-117
Cc: message header field, 39, 54, 58, 61
Censorship and mailing lists, 139, 140
Change Queueing window, 47-48
Changing and removing nicknames, 56-57
Checking for mail, 23-24, 70-74
Checking Mail Settings, 93-95
Checking Mail Settings window, 93
Closing a message box, 26
Coding standards, 14
Compacting mailboxes, 84-85
Composing a message, 19-21
Composition window, 19
Computer ethics, Ten Commandments for, 136
Creating a mailbox, 76
Creating a mailbox during transfer, 100
Creating a mailbox folder during transfer, 101
Creating a new mailbox or folder, 104-105
Creating a signature, 64-65
Creating an outgoing message, 34-40
Creating and using nicknames, 54-59

Creating mail folders, 77
Cyberrodents, 7

D

Deferred send, 46
Detaching a file, 53
Digital signature, 13
Disadvantages of e-mail, 6-8
Dorner, Steve, 9

E

E-mail etiquette, 125-131
    when receiving messages, 129-131
    when sending messages, 126-128
E-mail program features, 9-13
    advanced, 13
    basic, 10-11
    intermediate, 11-12
E-mail versus telephone cost, 4
E-mail versus voice mail, 5
E-mail
    advantages of, 3-6
    and organizational hierarchy, 122-123
    anonymity, 6
    answering, 99-118
    attachments, 6, 14-16
    becoming a pro, 153-182
    checking for, 23-24, 70-74
    disadvantages of, 6-8
    likelihood of misunderstanding, 125

permanence of, 7, 121-122, 139

safety rule, 122

security, 13

size limitation of, 8

special nature of , 120-125

speed of, 7

Editing queued messages, 50

Electronic mail, 2-3 (see also e-mail)

Email (see e-mail)

Emoticons, 131-134

Encryption, 14

Enter Password dialog box, 23

Eudora Light, 9

    for Macintosh, 18

    for Windows, 18

Eudora Pro, 9, 126, 139

    activating message filters, 205

    advanced installation of, 186-187

    Attachment colum in message summaries, 194

    Attachment Type combo box, 193

    Attachments options, 226-227

    BLAH, BLAH, BLAH icon in incoming message window, 195-196

    check spelling dialog box, 208-211

    check spelling options button, 211

    Checking Mail options, 222-225

    checking spelling, 206-211

    conjunction combo box, 201

    Dialup options, 230-234

    dragging and dropping, 213

    Edit User Dictionary dialog box, 210-211

    Fetch icon in incoming message window, 196

    files, 218-219

    filter terms, 199-201

    Filters window, 197

    Fonts & Display options, 227

    for Macintosh, 18

    for Windows, 18, 183-241

    Getting Attention options, 230

    getting help, 218

    Getting Started options, 219-220

    incoming message window, 195-196

    Kerberos options, 240-241

    Label column in message summaries, 194

    Labels options, 228-229

    Main window toolbar, 187-191

    MAPI options, 238-239

    Message Application Program Interface (MAPI), 212

    message composition window, 192-193

    message filtering, 197-206

    message filtering action area, 202-204

    message filtering match area, 198-201

    message summaries, 193-194

    Miscellaneous options, 236-237

    nicknames, 214-215

    Personal Information options, 221

    print preview, 214

receiving filtered messages, 205-206

Replying options, 230

return receipt, 193

saving message filter changes, 204

Sending Mail options, 225-226

sharing a Windows 95 PC, 216

signatures, 192

Spell-checking options, 234-236

standard installation of, 184-185

Trash icon in incoming message window, 196

uninstalling, 185

using active URLs, 213

Eudora

activating, 72

commercial version, 15

error message, 73

getting started, 17-42

product information, 180

quitting, 42

Eudora, system requirements, 18-19

Exiting Eudora, 42

Expansion (nickname), 54, 58, 59

F

File compression, 16

Find dialog box, 86, 88

Finding text within messages, 85-90

Finger server, 159

Finish Nickname option, 58

Folders, creating, 77

Font dialog box, 162, 163

Fonts & Display Settings, 154, 161-165

Fonts & Display Settings dialog box, 162

Forward button, 33

Forwarding messages, 112-114

Frequently Asked Questions (FAQ), 151

From: message header field, 20, 27, 38, 113, 156

G

Getting Attention Settings, 95-96

Getting Attention Settings window, 95

Getting Started Settings, 154-157

Getting Started Settings dialog box, 155

Getting started with Eudora, 17-42

H

Host Settings dialog box, 158

Hosts Settings, 154, 158-159

I

Icon bar, 35-37

Immediate send, 45

In Mailbox, 71, 72, 78, 110, 175

In Mailbox window, 25-26

changing to an icon, 26

columns, 25

opening, 42, 72

pull-down menu, 27

Incoming Message icon bar, 82

INDEX

Priority Popup combo box, 82
Subject text box, 82
Incoming Message title bar, 82
Incoming Message window, 81-82
Insertion point, 20, 61
Installing Eudora Pro, 183-187
Internet, 1-2, 136, 137, 138, 140, 150
Internet services, accessing, 137-152
Internet service provider, 144, 147, 149, 151
Internet, Net-Happenings list, 146

K

Keep Copy button, 37, 51

L

Leave Mail on Server Option, 73-74
Leaving Eudora, 42
LISTSERV, 141, 142, 143
Locating a mailbox or folder, 104

M

Macintosh, 15,16
Mail storage files, 172-177
Mail transport agents, 62
Mail transport servers, 178-181
    incoming mail, 179-180
    outgoing mail, 179
Mailbox
    creating, 76
    creating during transfer, 100, 101, 104-105

menu, 77
name list, 102
Mailboxes and Folders, 75
    compacting, 84-85
Mailboxes window, 78, 100, 103-109
Mailing lists, 4, 137, 138-139, 146
    accessing, 141-143
    and censorship, 139, 140
    canceling subscriptions to, 143
    categories, 140-141
        closed, 141
        moderated, 141
        unmoderated, 141
    command confirmation request, 143
    list of, 145
    finding, 144-146
    launching, 144
    new list, 146
    sending messages to, 142
Main Window Icon, 31
Main Window Toolbar, 32-34
Majordomo, 141
Make Nickname command, 57
Manual mail checking, 41, 72
Message attachments, deleting, 39
Message body, 40
    composing, 19-21
    creating an outgoing message, 34-40
    deferral options, 47
    deletion , 83-85

filtering, 123, 139
Header, 20, 37-39
indentification, 5
priorities, 12, 63-64, 118
proliferation, 124
redirection and signatures, 116
summaries, 25-26, 42, 50, 51, 72, 79-81
summary fields
    priority, 80
    date, 81
    sender, 80
    size, 81
    status, 79-80
    subject, 81
when forwarding, 113, 114
when redirecting, 115, 116
when replying, 110
Message, opening, 42
MIME (Multipurpose Internet Mail Extensions), 11, 15-16, 53, 68, 193
Miscellaneous Settings, 154, 166-170
Miscellaneous Settings dialog box, 167
Moving mailboxes, 106-107
Multipurpose Internet Mail Extensions, see MIME

N

Naming a new mailbox, 105
Netiquette, 7, 120, 136
Netscape (Navigator), 2
New button, 54
New Mail dialog box, 71, 76, 100, 101

New Mail! alert, 25
New Mailbox window, 77
New Message button, 33
New Nickname window, 54-55
Newbies, 3, 127
News, reading, 150
Newsgroup categories, 147-148
Newsgroups, starting, 149-150
Newsreaders, 139
Nicknames, 54, 61-62
    and the Quick Reception list, 61-62
    button, 34
    changing and removing, 56-57
    creating and using, 54-59
    expansion, 54, 58, 59
Nicknames window, 54,55, 56, 57, 60, 61
    Address(es) field:, 54, 56
    buttons, 58
    Nickname field:, 54, 56
    Notes field:, 54
    Sample Notes field:, 54

O

Opening a message, 42, 72
Opening an attachment, 82
Opening the In Mailbox, 42, 72
Out Mailbox, 29, 37, 46, 50, 67, 68, 79, 80, 168

P

Password change server, 181
Personal Information Settings, 154, 156-157
Ph name server, 159
Ph server, 181
Plain text file, 14, 53, 161
POP (Post Office Protocol) account, 155, 157, 158
POP server, 40, 41, 66, 67, 70, 72, 73-74, 93, 94, 178, 179
    obtaining a, 180-181
    password, 23, 24, 72
POP3, 18, 19
POP3 server account address, 20
Postal Service, 3, 4
Post Office Protocol, see POP and POP3
Pretty Good Privacy, 13
Print button, 34
Priorities, 12
Priority combo box, 35, 64
Processing incoming messages, 109-112
Progress window, 22, 41, 46

Q

Qualcomm (Incorporated), 9, 18, 141, 180
Queue button, 37, 46, 47, 67
Queued message, 46-50
Quick Recipient list, 56, 57, 59-62
Quitting Eudora, 42
Quotation marks, 67
Quoted-Printable Encoding button, 36

R

Receiving attachments, 97-98
Receiving attachments, non-Eudora users, 98
Receiving e-mail, 25-26, 42, 69-98
Redirect button, 33
Redirecting a message, 114-117
Removing a mailbox or folder, 107-108
Removing a Quick Recipient from the list, 61
Renaming a mailbox or folder, 108-109
Reply button, 33
Reply command options, 111-112
Replying Settings, 117-118
Replying Settings dialog box, 117
Replying to a message, 27-28, 110-112
Resending rejected messages, 62
Returned messages, 63
Right mouse button (Eudora Pro), 191
Rinaldi, Arlene, 136
ROT-13, 151

S

Sample newsgroup message, 149
Save As window, 92
Saving messages in files, 91-92
Saving multiple messages, 92
Saving outgoing messages, 29-30, 51
Scheduling message transmission, 47
Select a directory dialog box, 97
Select Sound file dialog box, 96
Selecting multiple messages, 78-79

Send button, 37, 45, 67
Sending e-mail, 22, 43-68
Sending Mail settings, 65-68
Sending Mail Settings window, 44-45, 46, 49, 65-66
Sending queued messages, 49-50
Sending scheduled messages, 50,51
Sharing a PC, 178
Shouting, 127
Signature, 36, 64, 68, 126, 192
    combo box, 36
    creating, 64-65
    icon, 65
Simple Mail Transfer Protocol, see SMTP
Skip Big Messages Option, 74
Smilies, 131-134
SMTP (Simple Mail Transfer Protocol), 19
SMTP server, 66, 67, 159, 178, 179
Snail mail, 3, 14, 75,112
Sorting messages within mailboxes, 90-91
Stopping a search, 90
Subject: message header field, 20, 38-39
Subscribing to mailing lists, 141-142

T

Tabs in Body button, 37
TCP/IP, 171, 220
Telephone tag, 4
Test message, 21
Text as Document button, 36,53

Title bar, 34-35
To: message header field, 21, 27, 38, 54, 58, 61
Toolbar tip, 32
Transferring a message to a different mailbox, 100
Trash button, 33
Trash Mailbox, 51,68, 83, 169

U

UNIX, 180-181, 193
USENET newsgroups, 137-138, 139, 144, 146-152
USENET newsgroups, list of , 152
Using the Quick Recipient list, 60-61
Uuencode format, 193
Uuencoded files, 15

W

Winsock, 171, 220
Word Wrap button, 36, 40
Word wrapping, 67